MW01633573

Integrated Operational Risk Management

Integrated Operational Risk Management

Tools, Techniques and Meeting Regulatory Expectations

JIMI HINCHLIFFE AND
ANDREW SHEEN

WILEY

This edition first published 2025

Registered Offices
John Wiley & Sons, Inc., 111 River Street, Hoboken, NJ 07030, USA
John Wiley & Sons Ltd, New Era House, 8 Oldlands Way, Bognor Regis, West Sussex, PO22 9NQ, UK

For details of our global editorial offices, customer services, and more information about Wiley products visit us at www.wiley.com.

The manufacturer's authorized representative according to the EU General Product Safety Regulation is Wiley-VCH GmbH, Boschstr. 12, 69469 Weinheim, Germany, e-mail: Product_Safety@wiley.com.

Wiley also publishes its books in a variety of electronic formats and by print-on-demand. Some content that appears in standard print versions of this book may not be available in other formats.

Library of Congress Cataloging-in-Publication Data is Available:

ISBN 9781394303816 (Cloth)
ISBN 9781394303823 (ePub)
ISBN 9781394303830 (ePDF)

Cover Design: Jon Boylan
Cover Image: © itchaznong/stock.adobe.com

Set in 10/12pts, SabonLTStd by Straive, Chennai, India.

SKY10105134_050725

Contents

About the Authors

Dr Jimi M.V. Hinchliffe has over 25 years of experience in operational risk management and regulation. In almost a decade at the UK regulator – the UK FSA – Jimi held several roles, including operational risk policy SME, Basel 2 Technical Specialist, acting manager of the Basel 2 Implementation team, and in four years as a supervisor, managed relationships with large Japanese and US GSIFI banks and investment firms. Jimi was then Director and then Executive Director at the largest Japanese mega-bank, MUFG, with roles including Head of EMEA Regulatory Affairs and Head of Compliance Policy, Risk and Regulatory Affairs Department. Since 2016, he has been a consultant, supporting various clients, including banks, investment firms and a large pension fund, regarding operational risk management, resilience, TPRM and regulatory affairs. Jimi is a former director of the Institute of Operational Risk (IOR), and between May 2017 and March 2021 was Chairman of the IOR in England & Wales. Jimi was made a Fellow of the IOR in 2016. Jimi is also a member of the CISI and is on the CeFPro Non-Financial Risk Advisory Board.

Andrew Sheen has been actively involved in operational risk management since the late 1990s when the Basel Committee on Banking Supervision's (BCBS) focus on this topic saw it emerge as a distinct risk discipline. Having worked as the Head of Operational Risk at an international bank and also a UK investment bank, Andrew joined the UK Financial Services Authority (UK FSA) where he led the Operational Risk Policy team and then the Risk Frameworks team, charged with reviewing operational risk and governance frameworks in firms of all types and sizes. When the UK FSA split into two, Andrew moved into the Prudential Regulation Authority. During his time with the regulators, Andrew is proudest of his participation in the BCBS Operational Risk Working Group. When the time came to take the difficult decision to leave the regulatory world, Andrew had the pleasure of working at HSBC and then Credit Suisse, up until his retirement.

Andrew subsequently added being retired to the list of things he is not very good at and established a consultancy to provide Operational Risk and Resilience advisory services and training.

Looking back over 50 years in risk management, Andrew is surprised at how many of the firms he worked for no longer exist for one reason or another, but stresses he can take no credit for their demise and was no longer with them when they ceased to exist (although he would say that, wouldn't he). Drafting his contributions to this book also caused Andrew to reflect on the many friendships he has made during his career and he would like to thank everyone who has helped shape his knowledge and experience.

Preface

Operational risk management (ORM) has always been a cornerstone of effective organisational management. However, managing these risks has become more challenging in today's complex business environment, especially in financial services and banking, where interdependencies between technology, systems, processes and people are growing exponentially. The ever-greater utilisation of third parties to deliver services also presents unique challenges for firms, especially in relation to managing threats to resilience. These myriad challenges are particularly pronounced in the UK, a global financial hub with a dynamic regulatory landscape that continuously evolves to address emerging risks and systemic vulnerabilities.

This book explores the critical importance of adopting an integrated approach to ORM that aligns risk management practices with strategic objectives while remaining responsive to increasing regulatory expectations. With the rise of operational resilience as a regulatory priority, organisations in the UK, and elsewhere, face increasing pressure to demonstrate their ability to prevent, adapt to, recover from and learn from operational disruptions and utilise ORM tools to deliver more demanding resilience outcomes. This book outlines the foundational principles of ORM and provides a practical roadmap for a successful and integrated approach.

This book combines the regulatory insights of two former regulators, real-world examples and actionable strategies to equip practitioners with the tools they need to navigate the complexities of ORM robustly and sustainably. Drawing on the latest guidance from the international standard setter, the BCBS, and focusing on UK regulators, including the Financial Conduct Authority (FCA), Prudential Regulation Authority (PRA) and Bank of England, we delve into the synergies between compliance and proactive risk management.

Whether you are a risk professional, compliance officer, NED, senior manager or someone looking to deepen their understanding of ORM, this book aims to provide you with the knowledge and confidence to enhance your organisation's operational resilience through an integrated approach to ORM. As operational risk continues to evolve, so must our approaches to managing it. By fostering a culture of integration, collaboration, forward-thinking and always learning from errors, we can not only meet regulatory requirements but also unlock the strategic value of risk management as a driver of organisational success.

We hope this book serves as a valuable resource and sparks meaningful conversations about the future of ORM in the UK and beyond.

CHAPTER 1

Introduction

A ship is safe in harbor, but that's not what ships are built for.
—John A. Shedd

Over the following 19 chapters, we will explore a topic that has become, over the last 25 years, a topic of growing importance. From a risk type that, as we shall see in Chapter 1, didn't even have a name, **Operational Risk Management** (ORM) has burgeoned into a topic at least on parity with the more traditional risk types of credit and market risk. The number of articles and books written, the large community of ORM professionals, the fervent interest in ORM conferences (such as Risk.net's 'Op Risk Europe' and 'Op Risk America' and CefPro's 'New Generational Operational Risk' events) and the attention given to it by regulators – both national and supranational – is testament to the importance of this once-maligned subject.

Two decades ago, the **Basel Committee on Banking Supervision's** (BCBS) Basel 2 introduced operational risk into the capital regime for internationally active banks (which in the EU was then also applied to domestic banks and investment firms). A series of high-profile scandals, most notably the collapse of **Barings Bank** due to the rogue trading of Nick Leeson, alerted regulators to the importance of the risks arising from *people*, *processes*, *systems* and *external events*. Unlike credit and market risks – which had previously been the primary focus of regulators and risk managers – operational risk had the potential to be **catastrophic** – as in the case of Barings. Basel 2 not only required firms to assign capital for operational risk but also crucially introduced 'sound practices' for its management.

In the years that followed, firms busily created **operational risk functions,** introduced new tools, including **Risk Control Self-Assessment** (RCSA) and **scenario analysis,** started collecting **operational risk loss data** and using **external loss data** (including from external loss databases including the old

British Banking Association's (BBA's) 'GOLD' and ORX) and created new operational risk **governance committees** to provide governance and oversight. The most ambitious firms (and those mandated by their regulators such as in the USA) pursued the Holy Grail of ORM, **'The Advanced Measurement Approach'** (AMA), which was the most sophisticated of the three options available under the Basel 2 regime and required not only highly sophisticated capital modelling but also advanced management of operational risk.

By the late 2000s, most regulated firms in the UK employed operational risk managers and had established **operational risk frameworks.** This contrasted with the early 2000s, at which time when the UK Financial Services Authority (UK FSA) wanted to engage with the industry on the nascent Basel 2 and CRD regime, it had to engage with staff from compliance, finance and regulatory reporting functions within firms – operational risk functions simply didn't exist!

Many predicted that the controversial decision by the Basel Committee to kill off the AMA in 2015, a signal to many practitioners of the diminished status of operational risk, might be a final nail in the coffin for ORM as a distinct function altogether! Especially so, given the trend post-GFC of **fragmentation,** whereby firms created new functions (often with separate risk frameworks) to consider hot topics like **cyber conduct, vendor management, market conduct, fraud, financial crime** and so forth. ORM as a distinct function or even as an **umbrella** seemed to be redundant!

To paraphrase the great Mark Twain, the report of operational risk's death was grossly exaggerated!

Lyndon Nelson, formerly a senior regulator at UK FSA and then PRA, in an excellent speech in June 2018 on operational resilience at OpRisk Europe ('Resilience and continuity in an interconnected and changing world', 13 June 2018), recounted how he had addressed a group of new operational risk managers and he had explained that they would be 'pioneers'. Lyndon explained that operational resilience will establish itself on par with financial resilience and be a key part of the firm's risk profile. As regulators have made clear, operational resilience is an **outcome** and it is delivered through the **management of operational risk.**

WHY ANOTHER BOOK ON ORM

So readers may well ask, **'Why *another* book on Operational Risk Management?'** After all, there are a plethora of excellent practitioner books out there. Our riposte is there are compelling reasons why we believe our book is worthwhile.

First, as highlighted above, operational risk as a discipline, including due to the regulatory focus on operational resilience as the outcome of effective operational risk management, is **growing in importance and profile.** By focusing on resilience **outcomes** rather than the process of managing ORM, regulators have reignited interest in ORM and the tools of ORM. As such, it is timely to re-examine the tools of ORM in light of the outcomes now expected by boards and regulators.

Second, the inexorable progress of **technology**, including greater automation of processes, use of GenAI, LLM, NLP and the application of innovative new technology to the managing of risk, adds a new dimension to the operational risk landscape, both in terms of the nature of risk and how it is managed. **Cyber risk** is a perennial feature in the annual 'Top Ten Risks' carried out by various organisations, including Risk.net, where they survey ORM professionals to get a sense of the risks *keeping risk professionals awake at night* and digital resilience is a top focus of regulators.

Third, the inexorable rise in **outsourcing** by firms and the consequent focus by regulators on managing third and nth party risk make non-financial risk management ever more important. The regulatory focus on operational resilience and managing vulnerabilities arising from third parties and sub-outsourcing has again elevated the importance of this dimension to non-financial risk management.

Finally, there are some excellent books by practitioners, most notably the books by Ariane Chapelle, Elena Pykhova, Michael Grimwade, Cathy Hampson, Tony Blundon and John Thirlwell, but none of these excellent books bring out the critical importance of operational resilience and none are written with a specific focus on the **regulatory context, history** and **expectations.** One of the key concerns and expectations of regulators, and a key theme of our book, is the need for an integrated approach to ORM that seeks to break down the silos in non-financial risk management (i.e. between the different types of operational risk), avoid duplication, improve efficiency and add value. We will also argue that ORM should also have a legitimate role in seeking to address silos in the overall Enterprise Risk Management (ERM) framework given that these silos are a potential source of operational risk.

OUR APPROACH

In the 19 chapters that follow, we will explain ORM's place within the broader **ERM universe** (Chapter 2) and explore the **origins and evolution** of ORM as a discipline (Chapter 3), including the roles of the **BCBS, UK FSA** and the **Institute of Operational Risk** (IOR). In Chapter 4, we will delve into the **different approaches** taken by regulators to operational risk management, including in the UK, the USA, the EU and Asia.

In Chapters 5–7, we will explore **ORM Tools** and **Frameworks,** setting out *best practices* on the **building blocks** (including governance, risk appetite and taxonomy), **risk identification** and **assessment** (including best practices for RCSA and scenario testing) and how to **assess and manage controls,** including how to achieve the optimum balance of control.

In Chapter 8, we will discuss **operational resilience**, including its **origins** and **evolution**, the **relationships to** Business Continuity Management (**BCM**) **and ORM,** the **BCBS principles** and national approaches. We will also consider the EU's **Digital Operational Resilience Act** (DORA) and the relationship between **concepts of harm** in operational resilience and consumer regulations. Chapter 9 will review **risk incidents**, including how to get to the **root causes** using the bow tie. Chapter 10 will explain how **Third Party Risk Management** (TPRM) is the *elephant in the room* for ORM and resilience.

We will then consider **monitoring** and **reporting** of operational risk and the *Holy Grail* of **predictive** Key Risk Indicators (**KRIs**) in Chapter 11, before explaining how to **mitigate and manage risks** (Chapter 12) and **risk reporting** (Chapter 13). We will conclude by exploring hot topics and the future, including **the art of regulatory relations** (Chapter 14), **the rise and fall of AMA** (Chapter 15) and how to select and get the best use out of a Governance, Risk and Compliance (**GRC**) **system** (Chapter 16). We will then explore the potential use of **GenAI** and other **innovative new technologies** (Chapter 17), the **importance of** Environment, Social and Governance (**ESG**) and its interaction with ORM (Chapter 18) and future challenges, including the future **role for ORM professionals** (Chapter 19).

PART

One

Background and Regulatory Context

As ex-regulators, Jimi and I are surprised and disappointed at the number of times we talk to risk professionals who have no understanding of the objectives of the regulators with whom they interact or the context within which they themselves operate. This is perhaps best illustrated by a conversation I once witnessed with a senior banker who simply had no understanding of the role of the Financial Conduct Authority, despite being able to see their building from his window.

This part of our book seeks to establish a common understanding of the role of the risk function, board and senior management in the management of risk. We also explore the origins and evolution of operational risk and their role in the creation of the Basel 2 framework that saw regulators recognise operational risk as a distinct discipline requiring a capital allocation, for the first time. The origins of operational risk discuss at some length the collapse of Barings Bank. Those unfamiliar with this key event might want to watch the 1999 film *Rogue Trader*, where Ewan McGregor takes the part of Nick Leeson. We conclude this part by considering the roles of a number of regulatory authorities and the international regulatory framework. It is interesting to note that, at the time of writing, there is some discussion of creating a single UK financial regulator. Perhaps we will see a return of the Financial Services Authority (2001–2013) to replace the Prudential Regulation Authority and the Financial Conduct Authority.

CHAPTER 2

Enterprise Risk Management

While banks and other financial institutions have been managing operational risk since their inception, and arguably earlier when bank's founders began to consider establishing an institution, operational risk only emerged as a distinct discipline in the late 1990s as the Basel Committee on Banking Supervision (BCBS) began to consult on the introduction of Basel 2 with its 'new' capital charge for operational risk. This process resulted in the BCBS capital framework definition of operational risk as:

> the risk of loss resulting from inadequate or failed internal processes, people and systems or from external events. This definition includes legal risk, but excludes strategic and reputational risk.

While this definition has understandably been widely adopted, some firms have nuanced their firmwide definition to reflect their operational risk management framework (ORMF) (rather than operational risk capital measurement) and in recognition of the evolution of operational risk management over the last 25 years. For example, some firms have adapted their definition to read:

> Operational risk management is the risk of loss or impact on strategic objectives and business plans as a result of inadequate or failed processes, people and systems or from external events. This definition includes legal risk, strategic risk and reputational risk.

This revised definition recognises that not all operational risk events result in a loss and that strategic risk and reputational risk are key components of operational risk.

This definition also recognises that not all operational risk events result in a loss, and some may even result in a gain. I am aware of a firm that failed to transfer its dollar earnings into sterling at the end of each month in accordance with the bank's policy. When this error was identified and the dollar earnings were transferred into sterling, the bank discovered that the resultant sterling impact was greater than would have been experienced if the policy had been followed. This was clearly an operational risk event but did not result in a loss, in this instance, as the dollar had depreciated. Of course, a dollar appreciation would have generated a loss.

The BCBS also identified the seven loss event types, and firms are required to be able to map their losses to these categories:

1. Internal fraud;
2. External fraud;
3. Employment practices and workplace safety;
4. Clients, products and business practices;
5. Damage to physical assets;
6. Business disruption and system failure;
7. Execution, delivery and process management.

Once again operational risk categories in many firms have evolved over time and we will discuss taxonomies in greater detail in Chapter 5, Operational Risk Management Building Blocks.

Operational risk is best viewed as a combination of risks rather than, as in some firms, operations risk. While I do not propose to provide a complete list here, the risks identified in 'Figure 2.1' go beyond a firm's operations and would be included in the firm's risk universe. I use operational risk as an umbrella term to capture all these risks, which accounts for the umbrella in Figure 2.1 and the umbrellas on the front cover! A large number of firms manage their risks in these distinct silos, often using different GRC software and causing angst in the front line as each silo undertakes its version of a Risk and Control Self-Assessment (perhaps in the form of a Compliance Self-Assessment (CSA), Financial Crime Self-Assessment (FCSA) and People Risk Self-Assessment (PRSA), etc.). The sad reality is that these firms find themselves comparing apples with pears and fail to provide the various risk committees with a coherent holistic assessment of the risks faced by the firm. In my experience, the only function in a position to unite these risk silos is operational risk and where I have seen this unification achieved successfully it is clearly a tribute to the Head of Operational Risk and the heads of the other risk silos.

Recognition of the need to establish a unified approach to operational risk management has led to the emergence of non-financial risk, rather than the operational risk umbrella, as a term and discipline. I am using the term non-financial risk management to capture all of the risks which are not covered by traditional financial risk management. As a result, I am taking

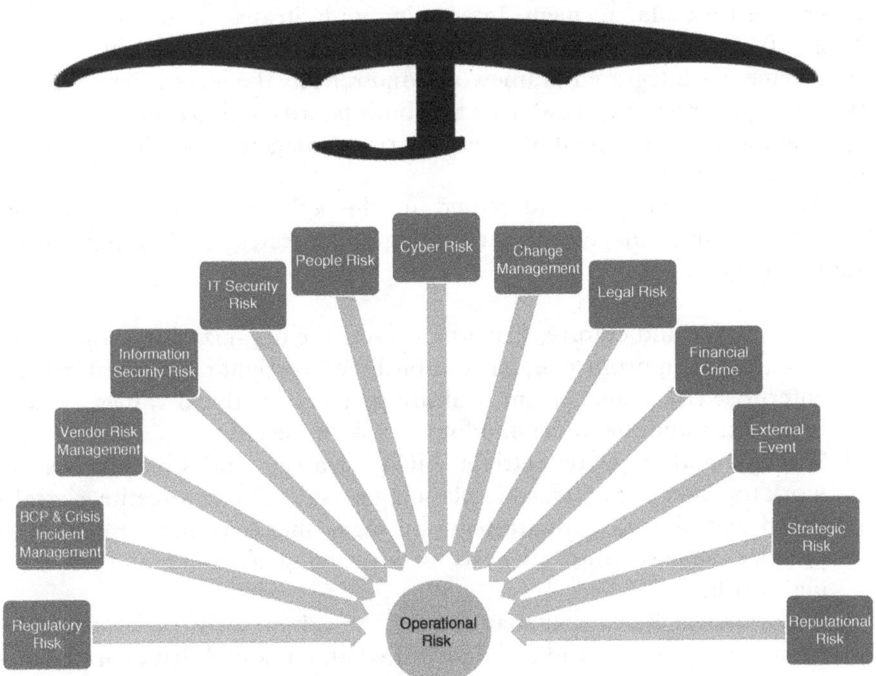

FIGURE 2.1 Operational Risks

non-financial risk to capture all risks except liquidity, capital, credit and market risk. I realise that in many ways, the term non-financial risk can be confusing, after all the BCBS defines operational risk 'as the risk of loss resulting from inadequate or failed internal processes, people and systems or from external events'. Losses certainly have a financial impact. I guess in the end this positive definition is better than the alternative negative definition of everything except liquidity, capital, credit and market risk. I imagine we would all rather have a business card that announces we are the 'Head of Non-Financial Risk' than one that says 'Responsible for everything except liquidity, capital, credit and market risk'.

For many firms, the move from risk silos to non-financial risk and financial risk creates a pathway to Enterprise Risk Management (ERM). This is a holistic systemic risk approach that requires a high degree of communication and coordination within the organisation to identify and manage risks across the firm. The five components of an ERM framework are identified by the Committee of Sponsoring Organizations of the Treadway Commission (COSO) in their publicly available executive summary

'Enterprise Risk Management, Integrating with Strategy and Performance' (June 2017). This is an update to COSO's '2004 Enterprise Risk Management – Integrated Framework' and reflects the increasing complexity of risk, emergence of new risks and both boards and executives increasing awareness and oversight of enterprise risk management while demanding improved risk reporting.

The five components identified in the COSO executive summary 'Enterprise Risk Management, Integrating with Strategy and Performance'[1] (June 2017) are:

1. **Governance and culture:** Governance sets the organization's tone, reinforcing the importance of, and establishing oversight responsibilities for, enterprise risk management. Culture pertains to ethical values, desired behaviours and the understanding of risk in the entity.
2. **Strategy and objective-setting:** ERM, strategy and objective-setting work together in the strategic-planning process. A risk appetite is established and aligned with strategy; business objectives put strategy into practice while serving as a basis for identifying, assessing and responding to risk.
3. **Performance:** Risks that may impact the achievement of strategy and business objectives need to be identified and assessed. Risks are prioritised by severity in the context of risk appetite. The organisation then selects risk responses and takes a portfolio view of the amount of risk it has assumed. The results of this process are reported to key risk stakeholders.
4. **Review and revision:** By reviewing entity performance, an organisation can consider how well the enterprise risk management components are functioning over time and in light of substantial changes, and what revisions are needed.
5. **Information, communication and reporting:** ERM requires a continual process of obtaining and sharing necessary information, from both internal and external sources, which flows up, down and across the organization.

As we should expect, many regulators define the role of the Board in general terms, probably requiring the Board to ensure the safety and soundness of the firm and to act prudently. Specific expectations around the Board's role in operational risk are often not articulated. Therefore, to understand the regulator's expectation we should reference the BSBS Revisions to the Principles for the Sound Management of Operational Risk[2] published in March 2021 and many regulators simply require their firms to comply with these principles. I must declare an interest here, having had the great pleasure of representing the Financial Services Authority and Prudential Regulation Authority on the BCBS Operational Risk Working Group and having been involved in the drafting of the June 2011 Principles for the Sound Management of Operational Risk,[3] in what was one of the most enjoyable periods of my working life. As a great admirer of the BCBS operational risk documents I am always surprised at the number of operational risk professionals who are either unaware of these 'Sound Management Principles' or their content. In my chapters, endnotes are provided directing readers to the relevant BCBS documents that are available free from their website. If you have not recently, or ever, visited the BCBS website[4] I would encourage you to do so.

The Revisions to the Principles for the Sound Management of Operational Risk document provides a mechanism for firms to assess the robustness and effectiveness of their ORMFs. When reading these principles, it is important to take a full account of the principles and also the supporting paragraphs. The BCBS has devoted the first four principles to the roles and responsibilities of the Board; these are:

Principle 1: The board of directors should take the lead in establishing a strong risk management culture, implemented by senior management. The board of directors and senior management should establish a corporate culture guided by strong risk management, set standards and incentives for professional and responsible behaviour, and ensure that staff receives appropriate risk management and ethics training.

Principle 2: Banks should develop, implement and maintain an ORMF that is fully integrated into the bank's overall risk management processes. The ORMF adopted by an individual bank will depend on a range of factors, including the bank's nature, size, complexity and risk profile.

Principle 3: The board of directors should approve and periodically review the ORMF, and ensure that senior management implements the policies, processes and systems of the ORMF effectively at all decision levels.

Principle 4: The board of directors should approve and periodically review a risk appetite and tolerance statement for operational risk that articulates the nature, types and levels of operational risk the bank is willing to assume.

In the case of the principles impacting Boards, the supporting paragraphs include references to: establishing a code of conduct along with supporting training; integrating the ORMF into the overall risk management process and the specific expectations of the Board regarding the operational risk management process. One interesting change included in the revisions is the amendment to principle 1 to specify that the senior management should implement the risk management culture. The revisions to the principles also detail the expectations of the senior management who play a crucial role in implementing the ORMF:

Principle 5: Senior management should develop for approval by the board of directors a clear, effective and robust governance structure with well-defined, transparent and consistent lines of responsibility. Senior management is responsible for consistently implementing and maintaining throughout the organisation policies, processes and systems for managing operational risk in all of the bank's material products, activities, processes and systems consistent with the bank's risk appetite and tolerance statement.

Principle 6: Senior management should ensure the comprehensive identification and assessment of the operational risk inherent in all material products, activities, processes and systems to make sure the inherent risks and incentives are well understood.

Principle 7: Senior management should ensure that the bank's change management process is comprehensive, appropriately resourced and adequately articulated between the relevant lines of defence.

Principle 8: Senior management should implement a process to regularly monitor operational risk profiles and material operational exposures. Appropriate reporting mechanisms should be in place at the board of directors, senior management and business unit levels to support proactive management of operational risk.

In the case of the principles impacting Senior Management, the supporting paragraphs include references to: the senior management translating the ORMF into specific policies and procedures that can be implemented and verified; some of the tools that can be used to identify and assess operational risk (see Chapter 6, Risk Identification and Assessment); the need for policies and procedures for the review of new products, activities, processes and systems; and the need for banks to continuously improve the quality of operational risk reporting.

I would urge readers to benchmark their ORMF against the 'Revisions to the Principles for the Sound Management of Operational Risk' and ensure that any gaps are identified and remediated. Best to identify and remedy them yourself before an incident exposes the deficiency or perhaps worse, an internal audit or the regulator comes to town.

While some readers may feel that the focus of the BCBS's attention is on Globally Systemically Important Financial Institutions (G-SIFIs) and these principles should not therefore apply to them, the mandate of the BCBS is to 'strengthen the regulation, supervision and practices of banks worldwide with the purpose of enhancing financial stability'. In addition, these principles are equally relevant to non-bank financial institutions and indeed some non-financial institutions use these principles to help shape their operational risk frameworks.

Regulators would expect firms to have an independent operational risk function and for this function to report to a Chief Risk Officer (CRO). In the UK, this role is considered to be a key senior management function and is one of the roles (SMF 4) designated under the UK Senior Manager and Certification Regime. The CRO is a member of the senior management team responsible for the identification, assessment and management of the firm's risks, both financial and non-financial. The role of the second line operational risk function is usually described as 'oversight and challenge' although unfortunately for me this generic term creates a picture of the second line leaning back in their chairs, with their feet on the desk, a cigar in one hand and a strong drink in the other. This definition is not therefore necessarily very useful, so let us explore in more detail what this activity might involve. I would expect the role of the CRO to include ensuring that the second line operational risk team:

- Continues to maintain its independence;
- Develops the ORMF policies, procedures and guidelines;
- Develops and maintains a taxonomy covering causes, events and impacts;
- Provides ongoing Operational Risk training;
- Undertakes oversight of the first lines implementation of the ORMF;
- Challenges
  - The operational risk identification and assessment processes undertaken throughout the firm, including but not limited to: the risk and control self-assessments; scenario analysis and the recording of risk events;
  - Control testing and assessments;
  - The reports and information provided by the second line;
- Monitors first line compliance with the firm's operational risk appetite.

The manner in which the 'challenge' is undertaken can be an important determinant of the operational risk team's relationship with the rest of the organisation. Clearly, an effective operational risk team needs to establish and maintain good working relationships throughout the firm, and I have found that a partnership model works best as long as it does not undermine the independence of the team. There will always be a concern that the risk function will be seen as a blocker rather than a partner and in April 2024 Lloyds Bank announced plans to reduce risk management roles as part of a restructure.

As part of some of the consultancy assignments we have undertaken, Dr. Jimi Hinchliffe and I have worked with some firms that are required by the UK FCA to comply with the Financial Reporting Council's 'UK Corporate Governance Code' published in July 2018.[5] It would therefore be remiss of me not to briefly describe the code here. The Code contains five components:

1. Board leadership and company purposes;
2. Division of responsibilities;
3. Composition, succession and evaluation;
4. Audit, risk and internal control;
5. Remuneration.

The section dealing with audit, risk and internal control requires the board to 'establish and maintain an effective risk management and internal control framework, and determine the nature and extent of the principal risks the company is willing to take in order to achieve its long-term strategic objectives'. In addition, 'the Board should monitor the company's risk management and internal control framework and, at least annually, carry out a review of its effectiveness. The monitoring and review should cover all material controls, including financial, operational, reporting and compliance controls'.

We can expect the importance of ERM to continue to increase in the next few years in the face of a number of increasing challenges, including: global political events; climate change; cyber-crime; AI (friend or foe); crypto assets; and increasing unknown unknowns. Firms can strengthen their ERM frameworks by:

- Ensuring they have a robust and effective risk and governance framework – firms must benchmark and maturity assess themselves against international standards, remediating any gaps or weaknesses;
- Ensuring they can always quickly identify risks and challenges;

- Ensuring they have a robust scenario testing programme;
- Understanding why things go wrong;
- Managing risk and not data – many firms use Word and Excel to manage their risks but in reality are managing data and not risk, rather than utilising a GRC system that enables them to manage risk;
- Ensuring they have clear roles and responsibilities.

CHAPTER 3

The Origins and Evolution of ORM

In this chapter, we explore the origins and evolution of operational risk management (ORM), starting with scandals, particularly the collapse of Barings Bank in 1995 due to Nick Leeson's rogue trading. We will consider how international regulators, through the Basel Committee on Banking Supervision (BCBS), responded through Basel 2 and then examine the role of the UK Financial Services Authority (FSA). Finally, we review the role of the Institute of Operational Risk (IOR) in the origins and evolution of ORM.

SCANDALS AND MORE SCANDALS!

Scandals have plagued the UK financial services sector, and scandals played an important role in the regulatory focus on operational risk. In the following section, we will explore the collapse of Barings in 1995 and the influence of rogue trader Nick Leeson on the evolution of ORM. We will then touch on how misselling scandals in the UK in the 1990s affected ORM's development.

Nick Leeson contributed more than anyone to developing ORM as a new, distinct and vital discipline! For it was the rogue trading scandal in which Leeson brought about the collapse of Barings Brothers Bank in 1995 (Barings was one of the oldest and most blue-blooded of the City's merchant banks) and the subsequent high-profile nature of the scandal (in part due to the book by Leeson, and the accompanying movie titled 'Rogue Trader' released in 1999 starring Ewan McGregor) that awoke international regulators to this new risk type, and propelled the management of operational risk to the top of the regulatory agenda.

Leeson's infamy contributed significantly to the profile of this new risk type, called, at the time by regulators for want of a better term, 'other risks'.

In other words, risks other than the traditional credit and market risks. Indeed, the EU Commission Working Group, which read across the operational risk-related elements of the Basel 2 regime to what would later become the EU Capital Requirements Directive (CRD), was called 'The Working Group on **Other Risks**'.

Barings Bank was a UK-based merchant bank that failed after a trader named Nick Leeson engaged in a series of unauthorised trades that went sour catastrophically in 1995. Having lost over one billion dollars (more than twice its available capital), Barings went bankrupt due to activity in the far-off Singapore operation. The bank's assets were subsequently acquired by the Dutch ING Group, forming ING Barings, for £1. Following the rogue trading debacle, Leeson wrote his aptly titled 'Rogue Trader' book while serving time in a Singapore prison.

Leeson began heading up the bank's new Singapore trading operation in 1992 at the young age of 25 and focused on directional trading on the Nikkei exchange using futures contracts. The trading strategy was to arbitrage slight differences in prices between the Osaka Securities Exchange (OSE) in Japan and the Singapore International Monetary Exchange (SIMEX). This strategy, known as index arbitrage, involved no directional or unhedged positions and was supposed to be low risk. Leeson initially made a lot of money; for instance, in 1994, he received a bonus of £450,000 for reporting profits of £28 million – an astonishing 60% of the bank's total earnings for the year! However, one of Leeson's team made a large error (old-style pit trading was prone to significant operational risks, and mistakes were not uncommon) and to house the error temporarily, Leeson created the now infamous '5 × 8 error account'. Rather than address the errors or recognise the losses, the account was used increasingly to conceal his losses that grew to £100s of millions.

Initially, Leeson tried to trade his way out of the losses. At one point, he accumulated a staggering £7 billion notional position on the Nikkei using futures contracts (many multiples of the group's total capital reserves)! Leeson was also feverously selling options to generate income to help fund the enormous daily margin payments on his futures positions. As Leeson became increasingly desperate to conceal the scale of his losses, he succumbed to blatant fraud, including forgery of documents to senior management and the auditors to hide losses, exaggerate profits and conceal mounting risks. Disaster eventually struck Leeson when the Kobe Earthquake on 17 January 1995 sent the Nikkei into freefall, losing over 10% of its value in less than a week. After briefly trying to prop up the market – an indication of the hubris of the star trader – Leeson fled to Frankfurt, where he was arrested and returned to jail in Singapore.

The collapse of Barings due to Leeson's rogue trading quickly became a case study in both rogue trading and how *not* to manage operational risk, as just about everything in the case of Barings was done wrong:

- Lack of preventative **segregation controls** between the front and back office. Leeson was in charge of the derivatives trading desk and clearing, settlement and accounting. ACA Compliance Chief Services Officer Carlo di Florio, a former senior executive at both FINRA (Financial Industry Regulatory Authority) and the US Securities and Exchange Commission (SEC), said this convergence of duties was tantamount to having 'the fox guarding the hen house'.[1] As Leeson states in *Rogue Trader:* 'The lack of proper controls and supervision in both Singapore and London allowed me to take ever-greater risks without anyone pulling me back'.[2]
- Failure to identify and manage **conflicts of interest**, especially concerning the lack of segregation between the front and back office. As Leeson noted, 'I was effectively both the front office and the back office, placing the trades and settling them. That is a recipe for disaster'.[3]
- Lack of **detective controls**, for example, trade surveillance. Leeson could commit his fraudulent activity for a prolonged period without detection due to the absence of detective controls. Where controls that would otherwise have helped detect the fraud (e.g. reconciliation controls) did exist, Leeson was able to manipulate them due to his role spanning the front and back office.
- Lack of **oversight** and **challenge** from the second line risk and compliance functions. Risk and compliance functions were weak and ineffective so Leeson could effectively run rings around them.
- Lack of **effective governance** to oversee the Singapore operation – both locally within the Singapore office and at the group level in London. The board and senior management appeared happy to recognise the profits without questioning the risks taken or checking whether anything was untoward. Leeson recollects that 'they [London] didn't ask questions because they were making so much money. Everyone was happy, and no one wanted to spoil the party' (Leeson and Whitley 1996, p. 62).
- Failures of **day-to-day line management**. Line management oversight is one of the most potent preventative and detective controls for internal fraud. Leeson reported day-to-day to Simon Jones, who oversaw the trading business at Barings Investment Bank, to Ron Baker, Head of Barings Futures Division, and to Peter Norris, the CEO of

Baring's Investment Bank. This matrix reporting led to confusion and a lack of proper accountability for supervising him, which resulted in Leeson being effectively unsupervised locally in Singapore and at the group level.

- **Remuneration** included large profit-driven bonuses, which undoubtedly drove excessive risk-taking. Although remuneration didn't become a big regulatory focus until the Global Financial Crisis, the Barings crisis illustrated the enormous power of huge profit-driven bonuses to incentivise excessive risk-taking.
- Failure of the **Internal Audit Function** to properly review Leeson's activities and to identify the fundamental gaps in controls and blatant conflicts of interest.

The Bank of England, responsible for regulating Barings, produced a detailed report on the Barings crisis and highlighted the significant failings in internal controls and risk management. The report, titled **'Report of the Board of Banking Supervision Inquiry into the Circumstances of the Collapse of Barings'**,[4] was published in **July 1995** and highlighted:

- **Operational risk:** The bank's failure to appreciate and manage operational risks effectively.
- **Excessive risk by a single trader:** Nick Leeson's unauthorised trading activities and the excessive risks he undertook without proper supervision.
- **Lack of oversight and internal controls:** Deficiencies in the bank's internal control mechanisms, particularly in Barings Futures Singapore, allowed Leeson's activities to go unchecked.

They concluded that there was a failure to recognise the importance of operational risk and to control the excessive risks a single trader takes. The lack of oversight and basic internal controls in Barings Futures Singapore allowed this to happen.

The **Barings crisis** highlighted the importance of managing operational risks – such as internal fraud – and the importance of robust internal oversight and controls, which were largely overlooked by regulators up to this point. The collapse of Barings Bank and significant rogue trading scandals at Sumitomo (1995) and Daiwa Bank (1996) were important factors in including **operational risk** as a separate risk category in the **Basel 2 capital regime**. Finalised in **2004**, Basel 2 introduced an explicit framework for managing and holding capital against **operational risk**.

MISSELLING OF RETAIL INVESTMENT PRODUCTS IN THE UK: ENDOWMENT MORTGAGES AND PERSONAL PENSIONS

In addition to the rogue trading scandal at Barings, the 1990s also witnessed a series of egregious misselling scandals in the UK, including those involving endowment mortgages and personal pensions.[5] Misselling scandals were a key priority for the newly created UK FSA in 1997 and inevitably influenced thinking on the new Basel 2 capital accord, on which the UK had a significant influence.

Personal pensions were especially prone to misselling, particularly where individuals in generous state 'defined benefit' occupational pensions were persuaded by commission-driven salesmen to 'opt-out' often into far less generous 'defined contribution' pension schemes. The Parliamentary Review that was set up to investigate the pensions misselling scandal noted 1.6 million cases of personal pensions being inappropriately sold between 1987 and 1994. Compensation for misselling eventually amounted to £11.5 billion, with another estimated £2 billion in administration costs.[6]

In the case of endowment mortgages, evidence of misselling was rampant in the 1980s and 1990s, where commission-hungry armies of salesmen were unleashed on often unsophisticated customers without appropriate oversight. In some circumstances, endowment mortgages may be appropriate, where the interest is paid on the mortgage and an investment product bought that will, in theory, pay off the mortgage loan (hopefully with some surplus) at maturity. However, evidence emerged (which was widely covered in the press) of egregious sales practices. One example of sharp practice was the so-called 'Carpets and Curtains' policy, where salesmen would target people who were moving home and persuade them to cash in their existing endowment policy and use the termination value of the policy to buy 'carpets and curtains'. A new policy would then be sold (generating commission to the salesman). Another example was the so-called 'Television Policy', where customers would be persuaded to terminate their existing policy to pay for a TV and video recorder and start a new policy. Of course, consumers suffered immensely from this sales strategy of churning policies, as the commission paid to salespeople was up front.[7]

The consequence of the misselling scandals, the negative publicity and the criticism of regulators and compensation paid was again to reiterate the importance of managing operational risks – in this case both people risks and third-party risks from sales-staff who were not directly employed – and the need for more robust internal controls. The misselling scandals also reiterated the impact of remuneration as a driver of behaviour (and misconduct). Combined with the rogue trader scandals, the failure of financial firms to manage their sales forces added weight to the rationale for introducing more regulation on ORM.

BCBS, BASEL 2, CRD AND THE RESPONSES TO SCANDALS

The collapse of Barings Bank led to a significant regulatory response aimed at strengthening the global financial system and preventing the recurrence of the scandal. The failure of Barings exposed weaknesses in **internal controls, risk management** and **regulatory oversight**, prompting the international regulatory community (under the remit of BCBS but very much driven by the UK and the USA) to take the following actions to strengthen standards in banking:

Strengthening internal controls and risk management in banks: The international regulatory community, through BCBS, emphasised the need for banks and financial institutions to have stronger internal controls and more robust risk management practices. The collapse highlighted the dangers of insufficient oversight of traders and the failure to segregate duties. Institutions were also required to enhance their risk management frameworks, particularly around monitoring and controlling trading activities. This included clearer reporting lines and independent oversight of risk-taking functions – obvious lessons from the Barings debacle.

Regulatory reforms and introduction of new standards: The BCBS responded by revising its guidelines (Basel 1) to address weaknesses in risk management and internal controls. The collapse of Barings Bank was one of the key events that led to the inclusion of operational risk in the Basel 2 capital framework, which required banks to hold capital against operational risks and to place much greater emphasis on the management of risk arising from people, processes, systems and external events. The Basel 2 framework introduced a structured approach to managing and measuring operational risk.

First, it established the industry standard definition of operational risk: **'the risk of loss resulting from inadequate or failed internal processes, people, systems, or external events'**.

Second, Basel 2 introduced an **operational risk event taxonomy** that classifies operational risks into specific categories to help banks better identify, assess and manage them. Basel 2 identified seven major **event types** (or risk categories) that could lead to operational risk losses: internal fraud; external fraud; employment practices and workplace safety; clients, products and business practices; damage to physical assets; business disruption and system failures; execution, delivery and process management (see Chapter 2). The Basel 2 taxonomy is a foundation for reporting operational risk losses to regulators and helps ensure that firms hold sufficient capital to cover potential losses arising from these risks (see Chapter 5 for more on taxonomies).

Third, Basel 2 provided banks with three main methods to calculate operational risk capital requirements, each with increasing complexity and risk sensitivity. The idea was that as firms became more sophisticated in their management of operational risk, they would progress to the more refined and risk-sensitive methodologies and that this would be incentivised by – other things being equal – a lower capital charge[8]: the so-called evolutionary framework:

- **Basic Indicator Approach (BIA):** This most straightforward approach required banks to hold capital equal to a fixed percentage (15%) of their average annual gross income over the past three years. This was the most straightforward and least risk-sensitive approach to calculating operational risk capital.
- **Standardised Approach (TSA):** In this approach, banks were required to divide their activities into different business lines (such as retail banking, commercial banking, trading, etc.) and apply specified percentages (ranging from 12% to 18%) to the gross income of each line to calculate operational risk capital. This method was more risk-sensitive than BIA as the percentages were based on a BCBS quantitative impact study (QIS) on the relative riskiness of different lines of business, but was still calculated based on historical income data (so it didn't even reference loss experience in the firm) so was ultimately backward-looking.
- The **Alternative Standardised Approach (ASA)** in **Basel 2** for operational risk was a variation of the TSA, designed for banks with specific types of business models, such as retail or commercial banking. It aimed to provide a more risk-sensitive method for calculating operational risk capital than the TSA. In the ASA, operational risk capital requirements were still calculated based on business lines, but the process for determining the income proxy differed for some lines. Specifically for **retail** and **commercial banking,** instead of using gross income as the indicator, the ASA allowed banks to use the sum of outstanding loans and advances as a proxy. This aimed to better align capital charges with actual operational risks associated with the volume of lending activity.
- **Advanced Measurement Approach (AMA):** The most sophisticated method allowed banks to develop internal models to estimate operational risk capital based on their own loss experience, risk controls and risk exposure. Under AMA, banks could use statistical

techniques and internal data to calculate operational risk capital requirements, provided their models meet regulatory standards and are approved by regulators. The idea – especially in the UK – was to 'let 100 flowers bloom' and allow a nascent area of modelling to flourish, relatively free (or as free as regulators ever allow!) from regulatory prescription.

Fourth, the Basel 2 framework emphasised the importance of **sound ORM practices** alongside capital adequacy (under the 'Use Test', banks should integrate their approach to calculating regulatory capital with how they manage operational risk), encouraging banks to integrate ORM into their overall governance structure. It also promoted using **internal risk assessments, loss data collection** and **risk mitigation techniques** to manage operational risks.

One of the key parts of this was the publication of the **Sound Practices for the Management and Supervision of Operational Risk,** published by the **BCBS** in 2003. This seminal document (subsequently updated several times), influenced very heavily by policy experts at the UK FSA who held the pen, provided high-level principles with supporting guidance for **managing** and – for regulators – supervising **operational risk.** These sound practices were designed to guide banks in developing robust ORM practices and help supervisors assess the adequacy of those practices. 'The Sound Practice Paper', as it quickly became known in the industry, was structured around the eight sections (much more on the Sound Practices in Chapter 4) and quickly became a high-level blueprint for an ORM framework.

Although the reforms by BCBS to the international capital accord were focused on and applicable to internationally active banks (so-called 'Basel Banks'), the rules were typically applied more broadly through domestic regulations, including in the EU, under the **level-playing-field principle,** to all banks and investment firms (even tiny ones).

Emphasis on the role of supervisory authorities: Regulators (and central banks), particularly in the UK, where Barings was headquartered, re-evaluated their approach to supervision. In the aftermath of the Barings scandal, the Bank of England and other regulators were roundly – and rightly – criticised for failing to detect the excessive risks being taken by Leeson or to ensure the firm had robust systems and controls in place to be able to manage such risks. The fragmented approach to regulation was also subject to criticism, concerning supervision in the UK (the UK system of supervision was split between multiple regulatory authorities) and internationally for groups.[9] In 1997, the New Labour Government of Tony Blair transferred bank supervision from the Bank of England to a new regulatory agency, the UK FSA. The UK FSA was consolidated from multiple regulatory agencies covering banking, investment business and insurance.

Increased focus on transparency and reporting: Regulators introduced more stringent reporting requirements concerning banks' trading activities. This aimed to ensure that senior management and boards of directors were fully informed about the risks their institutions took. The need for greater transparency in financial reporting was also emphasised, with regulators pushing for clearer and more accurate disclosures about financial positions and exposures.

Cultural reforms: The collapse of Barings also led to a greater emphasis on ethical standards and a big focus on **culture** within financial institutions. Regulators started to explicitly focus on developing a culture that promotes greater accountability and responsibility at all levels of the organisation, including countering excessive risk-taking and engendering a customer-centric approach to business. Regulators emphasised the importance of robust recruitment practices and the incentives created by remuneration, especially profit-driven bonuses.

Global cooperation and Basel colleges of international supervisors: The collapse of Barings also led to increased international cooperation among regulators. Efforts were made to harmonise regulatory standards across different jurisdictions to prevent similar collapses. As part of the efforts to improve coordination between regulators, the **International Basel College System** was established to steer the implementation of the new Accord. National regulators began to host meetings where host regulators for their banks were invited. The college meetings were used to discuss progress on implementation, with specific sessions held on the individual banks where home and host supervisors could pose questions on progress. In our experience, the Basel colleges were highly effective and valuable for supervisory authorities and global banks, which benefited from a less fragmented approach from regulators.

Changes in regulatory structure – UK FSA: The collapse of Barings, along with widespread criticism of the regulators for failing to prevent the misselling scandals during the 1990s, contributed to the eventual demise of the structure put in place only a decade earlier under the Financial Services Act 1986, and to the creation of the UK FSA in 1997. The new integrated regulator, the UK FSA, assumed responsibility for supervising banks, building societies, insurance and financial markets in the UK. The UK FSA was intended to provide a more integrated approach to financial regulation and supervision and was one of the first actions of the Blair New Labour government. Ex-CBI boss and deputy governor of the Bank of England, Sir Howard Davies, was selected as the first Chairman/CEO of the UK FSA and served from 1997 to 2003.

THE UK FSA AND ITS ROLE IN BASEL 2/CRD

The UK FSA, which was the main regulator for financial services in the UK before it was replaced by the UK FCA and the PRA in 2013, played a significant role in the development and implementation of the **Basel 2 Accord** and its European equivalent, the **CRD.** Basel 2 was a global regulatory framework established by the BCBS to improve regulation, supervision and risk management within the banking sector.

The UK FSA was a key player in policy development within the BCBS. Oliver Page CBE (UK FSA director of MFGD) was a member of the influential Risk Management Group and had perhaps the most significant influence in the development of Basel 2 within the BCBS. Oliver Page was supported by an army of high-calibre technical experts, including Dr Jeremy Quick and Helmut Bauer, who led the technical work on operational risk policy at the BCBS and EU levels, respectively.

In parallel with the development of Basel 2, the EU also began work on how this would be applied within the EU. The very active involvement of the UK FSA and their significant influence within the BCBS and the myriad of technical working groups put the UK in a position to take a leading role in implementing Basel 2 into EU law. The UK FSA played a key role in developing the EU CRD, which implemented Basel 2 within the European Union. The UK was highly effective in ensuring that the CRD met the needs of the UK financial services industry. An example of this tailoring included addressing the unusual structure of the UK market compared to other EU markets, with a large number of small investment firms that would be wiped out by applying the capital requirements in Basel 2. UK FSA staffed EU Commission working groups – including the Working Group on Other Risks (WGOR) for operational risk – and helped develop the detailed directive text underneath the more principles-based Basel 2.

The UK FSA was responsible for directly supervising UK-based financial institutions and ensuring their compliance with new Basel 2's requirements.

POLICY DEVELOPMENT AND SUPERVISORY APPROACH OF THE UK FSA

The UK FSA's policy development under Basel 2 was focused on ensuring that the framework promoted sound risk management while being flexible enough to adapt to different business models. One of the core elements of Basel 2 was the **Three Pillar** approach, comprising:

- **Pillar 1:** Minimum capital requirements – credit, market and operational risks.

- **Pillar 2:** Supervisory review process – Individual Capital Adequacy Assessment Process (ICAAP) and the Supervisory Review Evaluation Process (SREP).
- **Pillar 3:** Market discipline – or disclosures.

The UK FSA embedded this approach into its supervisory approach, mainly through the **ICAAP**, a key part of Basel 2's Pillar 2. This process requires firms to assess their capital needs based on their risk profile, considering severe but plausible scenarios that could impact their base case business plan and consider management actions that could be credibly adopted to combat the risks. The UK FSA would then review and challenge these assessments. This risk-based approach allowed the UK FSA to focus supervision on a discussion of risks and to prioritise resources towards institutions and areas posing higher risks to its objectives, including financial stability.

The UK FSA also supported the adoption of so-called *advanced internal model-based approaches*, such as the Internal Ratings-Based (IRB) approach for credit risk and AMA for **operational risk**, as part of its Basel 2 implementation.

The UK FSA saw these advanced methods as more sophisticated and better aligned with the actual risks faced by institutions compared to standardised approaches. The UK FSA considered, but stopped short of, mandating the advanced approaches for the largest, most systemic firms. Other G8 regulators, including the USA and Japan, mandated that their largest financial institutions use the model-based approaches. The UK FSA eventually decided to adopt a so-called 'no prohibition, no compulsion' approach in line with its 'ARROW'[10] methodology, whereby firms were free to choose their approach to Pillar 1 methodologies, but their approach would be reflected in the ARROW assessment and actions.

ORSG AND COLLABORATION WITH PRACTITIONERS ON POLICY

To flesh out its approach to ORM, the UK FSA fostered collaboration with industry practitioners through the **Operational Risk Standing Group** (**ORSG**). Established in the mid 2000s as Basel 2 implementation was in full flow, this group was pivotal in shaping the UK FSA's policies on ORM under Basel 2. The ORSG included members from financial institutions, industry experts and regulators, providing a platform for dialogue and exchange of best practices.

The ORSG was responsible for advising on developing policies related to operational risk, particularly around using the **AMA**, which allowed firms to use their internal models to assess operational risk exposure. This collaboration enabled the UK FSA to stay attuned to practical challenges faced by firms and to incorporate industry feedback into its supervisory framework.

By working closely with practitioners (a number were also active in the ORRF – see below), the UK FSA sought to ensure that the regulatory framework was practical and pragmatic, allowing firms to manage operational risks in a way that aligned with their business realities. This partnership played a key role in establishing the UK's leadership in ORM within the global banking system.

Well before the ORSG was established, the UK FSA established the Investment Banks Roundtable Group, which comprised the big US investment banks (Goldman, Morgan Stanley and Lehmans) and Cazenove & Co., a British investment bank (before its later acquisition by JP Morgan). The group was established to consider the impacts of the CRD on investment banks, focusing on operational risk capital requirements amid concerns that the CRD would result in dramatic increases in the capital requirements for these important and powerful firms.

The UK FSA's collaborative and consultative approach under Basel 2 demonstrated its commitment to fostering a robust yet flexible regulatory environment for ORM.

THE INSTITUTE OF OPERATIONAL RISK

In April 1999, Professor Brendon Young established the **Operational Risk Research Forum** (ORRF). Brendon had recognised, earlier than most, the need for a greater focus on ORM within banking and financial services. Brendon also recognised the critical importance of gaining insights from practitioners from various backgrounds in developing regulatory policy. Perhaps the most significant contribution of the ORRF and later the IOR was holding a series of workshops involving practitioners, including from Tier 1 banks, academics and regulators.

One of the striking features of the ORRF was that it reached far beyond banking and financial services and into industry, including hosting speakers from areas as diverse as healthcare, construction, manufacturing and aviation. In these early days in the evolution of thinking on ORM, obtaining insights from industries with a more extended history of considering operational risks, including those related to health and safety, was extremely powerful.

The ORRF fostered good relations with regulators, who often attended ORRF workshops to update the group on the progress on Basel 2 and to get feedback from the forum on their thinking and practices. ORRF held events on leading-edge issues, including in collaboration with the Bank of England, the UK FSA, BaFin, the OCC and the New York State Banking Department in the USA, the Dutch National Bank and professional bodies such as the British Bankers' Association, ISDA, the Institute of Actuaries and the Securities & Investments Institute.

In 2004, Brendon Young established the IOR. Brendon was the first Chairman of the IOR and was succeeded in that role by Philip Martin, Ed Sankey, Dr Simon Ashby and finally George Clark. At its peak, the IOR had approximately 1,000 members (mostly associate and professional members) plus several high-profile corporate members, including the UK regulator, the Financial Conduct Authority.

The IOR was organised around a central Council or Board of Directors that was responsible for the strategy and governance of the IOR and regional chapters that were responsible for delivering the strategy, primarily through putting on events – the IOR had a Chapter for England and Wales, Scotland, Ireland, Germany, Nigeria, South Africa and later established chapters in Hong Kong, Thailand and Japan. By far, the most active in terms of events was the England and Wales Chapter, which also had the majority of the members.

The IOR undoubtedly made an important contribution to ORM's evolution, especially in the UK. It did this across key areas:

- **Thought leadership:** A significant contribution of the IOR was the production of Sound Practice Guidance (SPGs), guidance notes on approximately 10 key topics on operational risk, including governance, risk culture, RCSA, scenario analysis and risk appetite. The SPGs were written by practitioner members of the IOR and articulated best practices across the key aspects of ORM. Access to the library of SPGs on the IOR website was a key benefit of membership.
- **Events:** The IOR was committed to facilitating conversations on ORM, and a key part of this was to organise events and networking opportunities for members. Events were primarily delivered through the IOR chapters, and the IOR committed to running at least four events every year. The IOR held numerous events, including those hosted by banks, consultants, GRC vendors and regulators. The IOR also ran one-day masterclasses at the CefPro New Generation Operational Risk Conference in both 2019 and 2020.
- **Professional qualifications:** The Certificate in Operational Risk (CORM). One of the most significant contributions of the IOR was the development of a certified qualification for operational risk practitioners. Developed over several years to a soft launch in 2017, the CORM is an ATHE Level 4 Qualification, providing an entry-level certification for operational risk professionals.

Despite occasionally being beset by internal politics, the IOR has a proud legacy of promoting the discipline of ORM and, through events and the SPGs in particular, undoubtedly contributed to the development of ORM.

THE RISE AND FALL...AND RISE OF ORM?

Soon after Basel 2 was implemented on 1 January 2007, the early rumblings of what became the Global Financial Crisis were heard in the US subprime mortgage market. Only a year after the implementation of Basel 2, the GFC reached its apex, with the collapse of US investment bank **Bear Stearns** in March 2008 (which was acquired by JP Morgan in a fire sale backed by the US Federal Reserve) and **Lehman Brothers** in September 2008, an even larger investment bank, which filed for bankruptcy on 15 September 2008.

In the UK, **Northern Rock** faced a liquidity crisis in 2007, having relied heavily on short-term wholesale funding, which froze during the crisis, leading to a bank run – the first in the UK in over 150 years. The government had to nationalise the bank to prevent broader contagion. **RBS's** acquisition of ABN AMRO was poorly timed and significantly weakened its balance sheet. Excessive leverage and risky investments led to RBS's near-collapse, requiring a £45.5 billion government bailout in 2008, the largest in UK history. **HBOS** suffered from poor risk management and overreliance on wholesale funding. It was merged with Lloyds Banking Group in a government-brokered rescue, with taxpayer support. The UK government spent well over £100 billion on bank bailouts and over £1 trillion in guarantees.

The GFC exposed some fundamental weaknesses in the regulatory framework and led to a tsunami of reforms, including Basel 2.5 and Basel 3 and similar reforms in the EU. We explore the response to the GFC in more detail in Chapter 8, including how it eventually led to a focus on operational resilience. It would be unfair to blame Basel 2 for the GFC. Not least, it was implemented far too late to have been in any way responsible for the GFC, which had its roots in the US government policy, the subprime mortgage market and the failure of banks to understand the risks in securitised subprime assets (with weaknesses in credit rating agencies, who were inherently conflicted when assigning their ratings to subprime assets, and a failure to manage liquidity, as contributory factors). However, ORM, as a discipline, suffered significant challenges post-GFC, including:

- **Fragmentation:** There was a big focus post-GFC on 'conduct' – not least in the UK, where one of the new regulatory agencies was named the Financial **Conduct** Authority. Banks created new 'conduct' functions, often completely separate from the operational risk framework, with new 'Heads of Conduct' rivalling or surpassing ORM in status within firms. ORM functions, frequently struggling with limited resources, were confronted not only with rivalry from new conduct functions but also an increasingly fragmented landscape with cyber fraud, financial crime, vendor management, regulatory change and so forth, all becoming increasingly specialist functions. ORM missed the opportunity, for the most part, to provide an overarching 'umbrella' across the many silos of ORM.

- **Marginalisation:** ORM's failure to provide an umbrella across the different strands of operational risk, combined with regulators' understandable focus – and therefore firms' – on addressing financial (i.e. more capital and liquidity) and strategic resilience, led to ORM becoming increasingly marginalised in the 2010s. The unhealthy state of ORM was personified by the fate of the IOR, which had suffered from the usual challenges of not-for-profit organisations, including reliance on volunteers. By 2018, it was clear that the IOR was financially unsustainable, and in 2019, the IOR voted reluctantly at its AGM[11] to join the Institute of Risk Management. Perhaps inevitably, as a commercial organisation, the IRM focused on the revenue-generating CORM and the events and thought leadership, which had been the mainstay of the IOR, gradually dropped away.
- **More art than science:** A long-standing criticism of ORM has been its subjectivity and lack of the robustness of more mature risk disciplines, such as market and credit risk. Given the relative youth of ORM as a discipline, this is understandable. Still, the failure of ORM and OR professionals to establish state-of-the-art tools, techniques and approaches has contributed to the sense of immaturity.

It wasn't until recently, when regulators began focusing on operational resilience as an outcome of robust ORM, that we saw a resurgence of interest in ORM. In Chapter 8, we will explore that trend and the challenges and opportunities for ORM and operational risk professionals.

CHAPTER 4

Regulatory Approaches and Expectations

Often when we talk to firms, it soon becomes apparent that they lack a clear understanding of the roles and responsibilities of their regulator, or regulators, and therefore of their regulatory risk exposure. Even in the UK, over 11 years after the Prudential Regulatory Authority and Financial Conduct Authority were established on 1 April 2013, UK-regulated firms often struggle to articulate the statutory objectives of their regulator. This coupled with a lack of understanding of the function of the Basel Committee on Banking Supervision and the European Banking Authority places firms at a significant disadvantage. If you don't know why your regulator exists, then you are likely to struggle to establish a relationship with your regulator and unlikely to be adequately prepared when they come calling. Certainly, one of our objectives in writing this book is to improve readers' understanding of the regulatory framework in which they operate, a topic not generally covered in operational risk publications.

In my view, doing something because your regulator demands it may well be one of the worst reasons in the world for doing anything. Firms should always look to strengthen their operational risk management framework and process, and so satisfying the regulator should be seen as a consequence of enhancing the operational risk framework. While working at the Financial Services Authority and then the Prudential Regulation Authority, I was often approached by firms proposing that a specific rule be introduced that would assist them in enhancing their operational risk framework. Firms should improve their framework because they want to improve their operational risk management and strengthen their safety and soundness. Unfortunately, I do have experience working for a firm where the CEO saw little benefit in operational risk management and recognise that while a regulatory requirement might be one of the worst reasons for doing something, it is one of the best reasons for securing the necessary budget allocation and senior management engagement.

A key consideration when discussing international and local regulators is understanding whether their regulations are principles based, rules based or a combination of both:

- Principles-based regulation sets out the core principles that regulated entities should comply with – Principle-based regulations are usually set at a higher level with less detail on how the regulated entity can achieve the principles. This type of regulation is more flexible and less prescriptive and should encourage firms to consider how they can comply with the principle but also demonstrate that they are doing so. Unfortunately, this flexibility is also the Achilles heel of principles-based regulations as it can leave firms unclear or confused on how they can comply with the principle;
- Rules-based regulation is usually carefully crafted and details the actions firms may or may not undertake – Rules-based regulation is generally stricter than principles-based regulation and is inflexible. The rules allow the regulated firm to understand exactly what they can and cannot do and therefore make it easier to understand how firms can comply with the rules and also demonstrate they are doing so. Unfortunately, risk-based regulation can become mechanistic with a 'tick box' approach coupled with the danger that firms will simply follow the rules without consideration of the wider context. One clear advantage of rules-based regulation is that enforcement is usually simpler, as it is easier to demonstrate whether a firm has or has not complied with the rule.

In reality, most regulators adopt a hybrid approach, setting out key principles that firms should follow, which are then supported by rules that help firms comply with the principles. A further complication for firms is that some regulators' rule books contain rules and guidance and it is extremely important to understand whether your activity is covered by rules or guidance, or both:

- Rules apply to all regulated firms;
- Guidance is generally flexible and sets out the regulator's expectations.

Of course, every rule does not apply to every firm and many regulators have different rules for different types of firms. Clearly, some of the rules that apply to investment firms will be different from those that apply to banks or building societies, for example. It is therefore crucial that firms understand the sections of their regulator's rulebook that apply to them, although this is not always easy.

Regulatory risk poses an important operational risk for regulated entities and is one of the risks identified in Figure 2.1. Regulatory risk is the risk that a change in the laws or regulations made by the government or regulatory body could cause losses to a firm, impact its strategy or business plan or result in regulatory sanction. One example might be the introduction of Consumer Duty in the UK. On 31 July 2023, the Financial Conduct Authority introduced a new principle (12) that required regulated firms to 'deliver good outcomes for retail customers'. For those firms and activities captured, this new principle replaced:

- **Principle 6:** A firm must pay due regard to the interests of its customers and treat them fairly;
- **Principle 7:** A firm must pay due regard to the information needs of its clients and communicate information to them in a way that is clear, fair and not misleading.

The new principle and associated rules significantly increased the requirements on those firms and activities captured, and firms subsequently undertook a variety of steps to ensure compliance with the new requirements and manage their exposure to regulatory risk. Firms that fail to mitigate their exposure to regulatory risk face the possibility of supervisory action or enforcement. In the UK this could, for example, take the form of: requiring firms to obtain a (often financially expensive and resource intensive) skilled persons report, financial penalties, capital add-ons and sanctions against individuals under the Senior Managers and Certification Regime (SM&CR).

It is therefore important that firms undertake a gap analysis against regulatory rules and expectations. This approach is regularly used by firms facing new regulatory requirements like Consumer Duty and enables firms to identify areas where they fail to meet regulatory expectations and to take action to remediate the situation. Having worked in a firm that undertook a comprehensive gap analysis against all its regulatory requirements covering risk, I am surprised more firms do not undertake a similar process. This activity is much simplified by the use of a system to facilitate the process. A key ingredient in any gap analysis is an effective and robust independent challenge. All too often there is a tendency for firms to self-assess their compliance through 'rose-tinted' glasses.

The obvious starting point for a section that seeks to help readers understand the international regulatory framework must be the Basel Committee on Banking Supervision (BCBS).[1] The BCBS is 'the primary global standard setter for the prudential regulation of banks'. The institutions represented on the Basel Committee on Banking Supervision comprise 45 central banks and bank supervisors from 28 jurisdictions,[2] with an additional eight observers. The Group of Governors and Heads of Supervision (GHOS) is the oversight body for the BCBS, which reports to the GHOS and seeks its endorsement for major decisions. The internal organisation comprises: the Committee; Groups, working groups, virtual networks and task forces; the Chair and the Secretariat. I had the great pleasure of sitting on two working groups during my time at the UK FSA/PRA and this would be an appropriate time to thank all those I worked with at that time for their help and friendship.

The BCBS sets standards for the prudential regulation and supervision of banks and the expectation is that members will implement these standards, along with their international active banks. The BCBS also publishes guidelines that expand on the standards and provide additional guidance for the implementation of the standards. The Committee also publishes papers on sound practices that generally describe actual observed practices. In drafting this book, readers will see that I have frequently referred to the 'Revisions to the Principles for the Sound Management of Operational Risk',[3] published in March 2021. In my view, this is one of the most significant operational risk publications. The principles were first published in February 2003 (bcbs96), were subsequently updated in June 2011 (bcbs195) and a review was published in October 2014 (bcbs292). All these versions can be found free of charge on the BIS website. Other important publications include the 'Principles for Operational Resilience'[4] (d516). It is frustrating how many firms and operational risk professionals have never taken the time to visit the BCBS website and discover the range of information available. If you are in this category, I would urge you to take the time to review the website and read those documents that are relevant to you.

Many readers will have noted that the BCBS expects members to implement the published standards, along with their internationally active banks and some will cite this as the reason they feel the standards do not apply to them. When talking about both the 'Revisions to the Principles for the Sound Management of Operational Risk' and the 'Principles for Operational Resilience' this is clearly an erroneous argument. The principles can be applied to institutions of all sizes, scales and complexities and I have met non-financial institutions that have leveraged the operational risk principles. I often wonder if those advancing this theory have even read the principles.

The European Union has two BCBS members (the European Central Bank and the European Central Bank Single Supervision Mechanism) and two observers (the European Banking Authority [EBA] and the European Commission). The Single Supervision Mechanism is the system of banking supervision in Europe (comprising the European Central Bank [ECB] and the national supervisory authorities) and was established in 2014 in response to the global financial crisis (GFC). The ECB[5] has a Governing Council that takes monetary policy decisions and a separate independent Supervisory Board. The ECB works with supervisory teams from national competent authorities to supervise significant institutions while national competent authorities exercise oversight over less significant institutions. The European Banking Authority (EBA)[6] is part of the European System of Financial Supervisors, which was established in 2010 following the GFC. This system establishes a layer of micro and macro prudential authorities and includes: the European Systemic Risk Board; the three European supervisory authorities (ESAs) (the European Banking Authority, the European Securities and Markets Authority and the European Insurance and Occupational Pensions Authority) and the national competent authorities (NCAs). The EBA seeks to contribute to enhancing supervisory convergence and building consistent supervisory practices in the EU.

Any consideration of national supervisors by a UK author must of course start in that country. In 1997, and following a number of banking scandals, including the collapse of Barings Bank, the UK's newly elected Labour Government decided to transfer responsibility for the prudential supervision of commercial banks from the Bank of England to a new body, the Financial Services Authority, which was governed by a Board appointed by HM Treasury and combined multiple regulators including the Bank of England Supervision Department and the Securities and Investments Board. Unfortunately, the UK FSA was heavily criticised for its performance in the GFC and the then conservative government began to consider alternative approaches to financial supervision. In the end, the UK adopted the 'twin peaks' model already in existence in Australia and two regulators were established:

- The Prudential Regulation Authority (PRA)[7]
- The Financial Conduct Authority (FCA)[8]

As the name suggests the PRA is a prudential regulator and sits within the Bank of England. The authority supervises a variety of firms by publishing the rules and regulations they must follow and overseeing their activities. The authority supervises about 1,500 financial institutions including banks, major investment firms, insurers, building societies and credit unions. The PRA's website shows that the authority has four objectives:

- Two primary objectives:
  - A general objective to promote the safety and soundness of PRA-authorised firms;
  - An objective solely for insurance firms for the protection of policyholders.

- Two secondary objectives:
  - A competition objective focused on facilitating effective competition in the markets for services provided by PRA-authorised persons carrying on regulated activities;
  - A competitiveness and growth objective focused on facilitating, subject to alignment with relevant international standards: (a) the international competitiveness of the economy of the UK (including in particular the financial services sector through the contribution of PRA-authorised persons) and (b) its growth in the medium to long term.

The focus of the UK FCA is naturally on the conduct of firms to ensure that financial markets are honest, competitive and fair so consumers get a fair deal. In all, the UK FCA currently supervises about 45,000 businesses in the UK, of which it also prudentially supervises about 44,000. The authority has three operational objectives:

- Protect consumers from bad conduct;
- Protect the integrity of the UK financial system;
- Promote effective competition in the interests of consumers.

Most firms providing financial services need to be authorised or registered by the UK FCA.

The difference in focus between the two UK regulatory authorities can be illustrated by reference to the UK's operational resilience requirements and consumer conduct. As part of the operational resilience requirements firms are required to set impact tolerances for the important business services.

As is discussed elsewhere both the PRA and UK FCA have published operational resilience requirements[9] and the differences in regulatory emphasis are evident:

- The UK FCA requires firms to establish impact tolerances at the point at which any further disruption would:
  - Cause intolerable harm to consumers;
  - Pose a risk to market integrity.
- The PRA requires firms to establish impact tolerances at the point at which any further disruption would:
  - Pose a risk to the safety and soundness of the firm;
  - In the case of insurers, pose a risk to policyholder protection;
  - In the case of some firms, pose a risk to the financial stability of the UK.

We have seen that the UK FCA's objectives include protecting consumers from bad conduct and it can be of no surprise that while the UK FCA has published a new consumer duty,[10] the PRA has not.

The USA has more BCBS institutional representatives than any other country and is often the subject of supervisory envy, both given the regulatory sanctions they sometimes impose and also the fines and deferred prosecution agreements imposed by the Department of Justice (DoJ). The DoJ court can appoint a monitor whose role is to oversee the bank's operations as part of the deferred prosecution agreement and, having witnessed this in operation, I can confirm it is an extremely powerful tool. The four US BCBS institutional representatives are:

- The Board of Governors of the Federal Reserve System[11] – The Board of Governors is the governing body of the Federal Reserve System and is run by seven governors who are nominated by the US president and confirmed by the Senate. The term for a governor is 14 years. The Board guides the operation of the Federal Reserve System and oversees the reserve banks, sharing with them responsibility for supervising and regulating certain financial institutions;
- The Federal Reserve Bank of New York[12] – One of 12 Reserve Banks (which have 24 branches). The Reserve Banks are the operating arms of the Federal Reserve System operating within a specific area or district. While they are overseen by the Board they carry out a number of functions including supervising and examining banks and other financial institutions;
- The Office of the Comptroller of the Currency (OCC)[13] – An independent bureau of the US Treasury, the OCC charters, regulates and supervises all national banks, federal savings associations and federal branches and agencies of foreign banks. They ensure that the banks they supervise operate safely and soundly, provide fair access to financial services, treat customers fairly and comply with laws and regulations;
- The Federal Deposit Insurance Corporation (FDIC)[14] – The FDIC was created by Congress to maintain stability and public confidence in the US financial system. The FDIC lists its activities as: insuring deposits; examining and supervising financial institutions for safety and soundness and consumer protection; making large and complex financial institutions resolvable and managing receiverships.

Anyone who has dealt directly with banks in the USA will be aware that supervision of financial institutions does not end with these four BCBS representatives. Many years ago, I visited a US bank in New York and found representatives of the state regulator in the building. Other regulatory bodies therefore include: State Regulators; the National Credit Union Administration (NCUA); the Consumer Financial Protection Bureau (CFPB); the Securities and Exchange Commission (SEC); the Financial Industry Regulation Authority (FINRA) and the Federal Insurance Office (FIO). Obviously, a comprehensive review of the US regulatory structure is beyond the scope of this book.

Given the number of institutions represented on the BCBS, it is of course impossible to cover them all here. Nevertheless, there are some bodies that I feel I should mention, not least because they played a key role in the development of the Principles for the Sound Management of Operational Risk:

- The Japanese Financial Services Authority[15] – Responsible for ensuring the stability of Japan's financial system, protection of depositors, insurance policyholders and securities investors, financial system planning and policymaking; inspection and supervision of private sector financial institutions and surveillance of securities transactions;
- The Bank of Japan[16] – Responsible for the macro supervision of the banking and financial services to ensure the safety and soundness of the financial system. The Bank conducts examinations of banks with current accounts with the bank;
- Australian Prudential Regulation Authority (APRA)[17] – Having many years ago had the pleasure of working for the Reserve Bank of Australia it is not surprising that I have included APRA here, having long admired their willingness to take a pragmatic approach to regulation covering operational risk. APRA was established in 1998 as an independent statutory authority that supervises institutions across banking, insurance and superannuation. APRA's origins lie with the Insurance and Superannuation Commission, the Reserve Bank of Australia and the Australian Financial Institutions Committee. As we saw earlier, the Australian twin peaks approach to regulation involving APRA and the Australian Securities and Investment Commission (ASIC) provided the blueprint for the current system in the UK.

Readers wanting to improve their knowledge and understanding of the institutions represented on the Basel Committee on Banking Supervision and the observers should access the membership list published on the Bank for International Settlements website.[18] Clicking on a member's name will link you to their website.

PART Two

Operational Risk Management Tools and Frameworks

Every efficient and effective operational risk team has a clear mandate, endorsed by the board and usually articulated in some form of diagram. This diagram depicts the key framework components that enable firms to manage the risk life cycle, an effective explanation of not only what risk teams do but also why (see Figure 5.2). To achieve its mandate and manage risk throughout the risk life cycle, the discipline has created a number of tools and techniques and these are discussed in this part.

Risk identification is, in my view, the key activity undertaken by operational risk teams. It is the starting point of the risk cycle and if we fail to correctly identify our risks everything else we do becomes pointless. It is interesting to speculate how many firms in late 2019 and early 2020 were focusing resources and activity on discussing and managing the usual collection of key risks but had not yet identified the threat posed by COVID-19.

CHAPTER 5

Operational Risk Management – Building Blocks

Many operational risk teams struggle to fully articulate their aims and objectives and, as a result, often create disjointed operational risk management frameworks that fail to work efficiently and effectively or resonate with key stakeholders. One way of seeking to overcome this issue is to begin with a visual representation of the framework. This is best done in one of two ways: the traditional framework diagram, a version of which is shown in Figure 5.1, and the risk life cycle shown in Figure 5.2.

While both have significant roles to play in our understanding of operational risk and our ability to communicate the discipline to our stakeholders, I fear I have spent too many hours in my career drawing framework 'houses' and dealing with seniors who were more interested in the intricacies of the design (the roofs too steep, where are the windows, door, chimney!) than the underlying framework being depicted. As a result, I am grateful to ORX for the diagram on which my figure is based.[1]

Readers will note that I reference information from ORX on a number of occasions in this book, in part reflecting my admiration for the work of the organisation and in part my respect for the staff. ORX is the largest operational risk management association in the financial services sector. The organisation was established in 2002 by financial firms looking to share loss data and committed to improving the management and measurement of operational risk. It is owned and driven by its member institutions, bringing together hundreds of operational risk professionals to share their knowledge, expertise and experience in the financial services industry. They are a not-for-profit industry association. Some lucky readers will discover that their employer is among the (currently) 125 plus financial firms that are members and should be able to access the wide range of information produced by the organisation and its members at no cost. Sadly, some readers will not be working for member firms, although it is possible to buy individual operational risk reports, reference libraries and the reference operational risk taxonomy through ORX Select. In addition, some information is made publicly available. I would urge you to investigate the ORX website.[2] All of the information reproduced in this book is currently available free of charge, although further information may incur a fee.

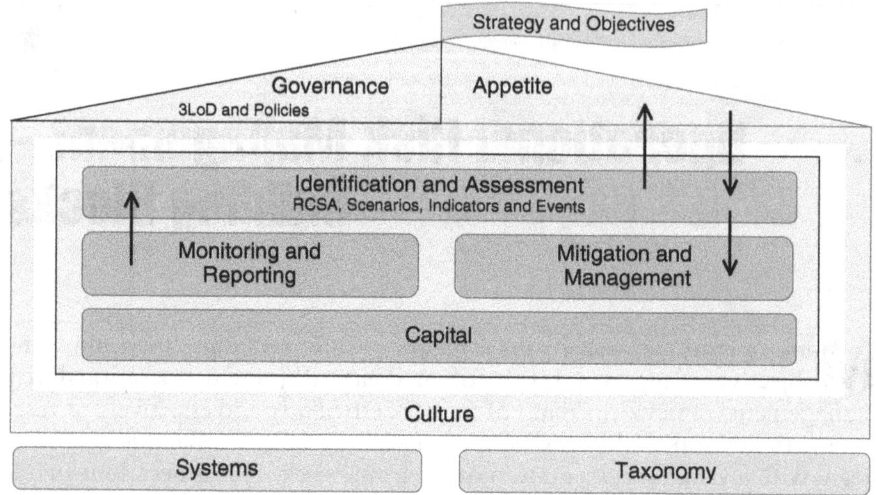

FIGURE 5.1 An Indicative Operational Risk Framework. This Diagram is based on the Framework in the ORX Operational Risk Reference Framework[1]

FIGURE 5.2 The Risk Life Cycle

The risk life cycle often resonates with our stakeholders as it not only offers an explanation of what we do but also why we do the various things we do. The cycle starts with risk identification and assessment; risks are then monitored, followed by their mitigation and management and then finally they are reported. It is an oversimplification to say that once completed the cycle restarts as it is a continuous process and new risks can be identified and risks can be reassessed at any stage. Obviously, if you are incorrectly identifying risks then you are monitoring, mitigating, managing and reporting the wrong risks and effectively threatening the safety and soundness of your firm. This renders your governance arrangements moot. The underlying activities in the risk life cycle include:

- Risk identification:
  - Risk and control self-assessment;
  - Capturing internal events;
  - Capturing external events;
  - Top and emerging risks;
  - Scenarios;
  - Change;
- Monitoring:
  - Control monitoring;
  - Key indicators;
  - Risk appetite;
- Mitigating and managing:
  - Evaluating actions and responses;
  - Management responses;
  - Preventative action plans;
- Reporting:
  - Information;
  - Reporting;
  - Management information;
  - Analysis.

Governance is a key component of any operational risk framework, providing the foundation upon which the indicative operational risk framework in Figure 5.1 sits and the hub around which the risk life cycle circulates in Figure 5.2. Effective corporate governance is critical to the proper functioning of the financial sector and the economy. Weaknesses in governance can result in problems transferring from the financial sector to the economy and the primary aim of corporate governance must be the safeguarding of the safety and soundness of the firm. Corporate governance dictates the way in which the business of the firm is undertaken by the board and senior management and includes:

- The Board – setting the strategy and objectives; setting the firm's risk appetite; overseeing the senior management; protecting stakeholders and setting the firm's culture;
- The senior management – the day-to-day operation of the firm; ensuring the firm's safety and soundness and ensuring compliance with laws and regulations.

Regulatory expectations are best illustrated with reference to the Basel Committee on Banking Supervision (BCBS) Revisions to the Principles for the Sound Management of Operational Risk,[3] with three principles detailing the requirements for the Board and Senior Management.

Board of Directors

Principle 3: The board of directors should approve and periodically review the operational risk management framework, and ensure that senior management implements the policies, processes and systems of the operational risk management framework effectively at all decision levels.

Principle 4: The board of directors should approve and periodically review a risk appetite and tolerance statement for operational risk that articulates the nature, types and levels of operational risk the bank is willing to assume.

Senior Management

Principle 5: Senior management should develop for approval by the board of directors a clear, effective and robust governance structure with well-defined, transparent and consistent lines of responsibility. Senior management is responsible for consistently implementing and maintaining throughout the organisation policies, processes and systems for managing operational risk in all of the bank's material products, activities, processes and systems consistent with the bank's risk appetite and tolerance statement.

Readers should of course note that each principle is supported by a number of paragraphs that provide further insight into how these principles can be achieved. We have seen that some regulators specifically require firms to comply with these principles and they offer an excellent way of evidencing good practice. The South African Reserve Bank, for example, specifically states that 'all banks, branches of foreign institutions, controlling companies, subsidiaries of banks and subsidiaries of controlling companies need to be assessed against the principles contained in the Revisions to the Principles for the Sound Management of Operational Risk'.[4]

Given the important role played by governance in an operational risk framework, firms should regularly assess the effectiveness of their operational risk governance frameworks. Firms should include the following questions in this assessment:

1. **The board:**
   (a) Can the Board demonstrate that they have given full consideration to the operational risk management framework and not simply nodded it through;
   (b) Have the Board ensured that operational risk training is part of the firm's curriculum for the Board, senior management and all other staff and that all these individuals (including the Board) are tested at least annually;
2. **Senior management:**
   (a) Can the senior management demonstrate how they have implemented the operational risk management framework;
   (b) Have the senior management established a hierarchy of risk policies and procedures;
3. **Risk governance:**
   (a) Is the risk governance structure well defined and effective;
   (b) Does information flow efficiently and effectively;
   (c) Can it be demonstrated that over the last six months, key issues have been escalated to senior risk committees and guidance and instructions have cascaded down;
   (d) Can decisions and challenges be evidenced and are they documented;
   (e) Do the governance structure, delegation of authorities and terms of reference all align and are supported by the framework and policy hierarchy;
   (f) Are metrics sophisticated and duplication and gaps in reporting and supporting processes have been removed;
   (g) Is risk appropriately managed through a firm-wide consistent and standardised structure which has the authority to take actions in accordance with the governance requirements established by the overall strategy;
4. **Policies, procedures and guidance:**
   (a) Are the operational risk policies and procedures readily available to all staff;
   (b) Can businesses and functions demonstrate that risk policies, procedures and guidance are read and understood by all staff;
   (c) Does the operational risk policy interface with other risk policies;
   (d) Are policies fully integrated into the business or function;
   (e) Can the senior management evidence that they have promoted good operational risk management throughout the firm;
   (f) Does the risk policy align to risk appetite;
   (g) Is the risk taxonomy applied throughout the firm.

As we can see, BCBS principle 4 requires the board of directors to 'approve and periodically review a risk appetite and tolerance statement for operational risk that articulates the nature, types and levels of operational risk the bank is willing to assume'. The supporting paragraphs for this principle add that:

> **Paragraph 26:** The risk appetite and tolerance statement for operational risk should be developed under the authority of the board of directors and linked to the bank's short- and long-term strategic and financial plans. Taking into account the interests of the bank's customers and shareholders as well as regulatory requirements, an effective risk appetite and tolerance statement should:
>
> **(a)** Be easy to communicate and therefore easy for all stakeholders to understand;
>
> **(b)** Include key background information and assumptions that informed the bank's business plans at the time it was approved;
>
> **(c)** Include statements that clearly articulate the motivations for taking on or avoiding certain types of risk, and establish boundaries or indicators (which may be quantitative or not) to enable monitoring of these risks;
>
> **(d)** Ensure that the strategy and risk limits of business units and legal entities, as relevant, align with the bank-wide risk appetite statement; and
>
> **(e)** Be forward-looking and, where applicable, subject to scenario and stress testing to ensure that the bank understands what events might push it outside its risk appetite and tolerance statement.

> **Paragraph 27:** The board of directors should approve and regularly review the appropriateness of limits and the overall operational risk appetite and tolerance statement. This review should consider current and expected changes in the external environment (including the regulatory context across all jurisdictions where the institution provides services); ongoing or forthcoming material increases in business or activity volumes; the quality of the control environment; the effectiveness of risk management or mitigation strategies; loss experience; and the frequency, volume or nature of limit breaches. The board of directors should monitor management adherence to the risk appetite and tolerance statement and provide for timely detection and remediation of breaches.

Unfortunately, establishing an effective operational risk appetite remains one of the industry's 'holy grails' for many firms. In other words, it is a treasure that is much sought after but not yet found. This is not helped by different firms using the terms risk appetite and risk tolerance in different ways. One interpretation can be found in footnote 16 in the Principles for the Sound Management of Operational Risk that references the FSB's 2013 Principles for an effective risk appetite framework definition of risk appetite:

> the aggregate level and types of risk a bank is willing to assume, decided in advance and within its risk capacity, to achieve its strategic objectives and business plan. Risk tolerance is the variation, around the prescribed risk appetite that the bank is willing to tolerate.

A crucial step for anyone involved in operational risk in any way must be to ensure they understand the way in which their firm uses the terms risk appetite and risk tolerance. If you would like to open the gates of your risk appetite confusion, the next few paragraphs should help. For me, I think about risk appetite and risk tolerance in the same way as I think about driving and motoring speed limits (please do not try this at home). In the UK, the Highways Agency is responsible for determining speed limits on the trunk road network while local traffic authorities are responsible for determining speed limits on the local road network. UK national speed limits are 30 mph in built-up areas, 60 mph on a single carriageway, 70 mph on a dual carriageway and 70 mph on a motorway. Let us assume I am driving on a single carriageway with a speed limit of 60 mph (although some drivers may travel faster or slower than 60 mph). I think of 60 mph as the relevant authority's risk appetite for this road and would not expect to receive a speeding ticket for travelling at 61 mph. Indeed, I understand that many UK police forces only issue speeding notices if a car's speed exceeds the limit for the road plus 10% plus 2 mph. This means that the police force will tolerate me driving at 68 mph on a 60 mph road. Again, please, please do not try this when out in your car, and if you do, on your own head be it.

So, in summary, the risk appetite in my example is 60 mph but the risk tolerance is 68 mph. The diagram in Figure 5.3 is another attempt to explain my terminology.

As I make clear there are alternative views, making it important to fully understand the definitions used within your firm. Some use risk appetite to define the outer boundary at a level above risk tolerance. Some think of risk tolerance as a quantitative measure and risk appetite as a qualitative measure. I have during training asked the question, for your firm, which is higher, risk appetite or risk tolerance. Unfortunately, not everyone knows the answer for their firm, so make sure you do.

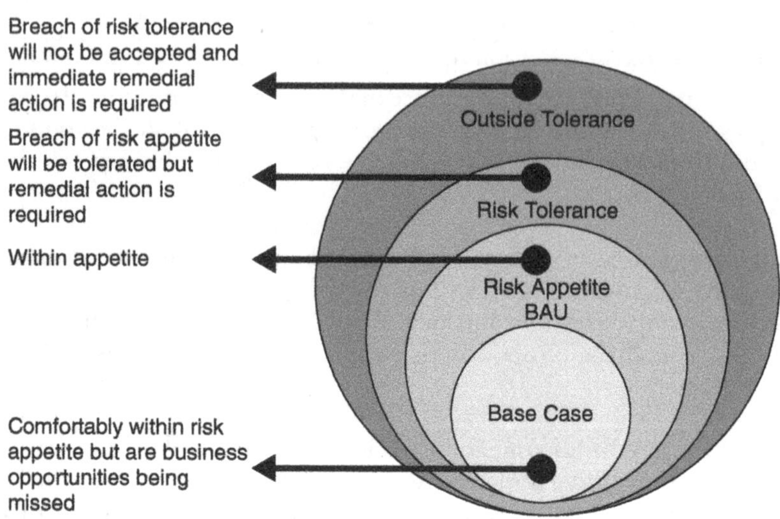

FIGURE 5.3 Risk Appetite

Operational risk appetite plays a central role in the management of operational risk. If we remain within risk appetite then all should be fine and we should achieve our strategic and business objectives. If we exceed our risk appetite, or even worse our tolerance, then action is needed to bring the risk exposure back within acceptable parameters, otherwise, the safety and soundness of the firm may be threatened and we may not achieve our strategic or business objectives. Firms should regularly assess the effectiveness of their risk appetite frameworks and include the following questions in this assessment:

1. Do relevant staff understand how the firm articulates risk appetite and tolerance and can they explain it to a new staff member or a third party, perhaps the regulator or a monitor appointed by the US Department of Justice?
2. Are the risk appetite and high-level measures defined at the Board level, but also cascaded down to the business and function level, where there is consistent execution and management of the risk appetite statements and measures?
3. Is risk appetite fully embedded within every part of the organisation and consistently applied?
4. Are breaches of the Board-approved risk appetite escalated to the highest risk management committee?
5. Is risk clearly measured against appetite at all levels of the organisation?

6. Are qualitative and quantitative analyses used to express risk appetite?
7. Can it be demonstrated that risk appetite has been utilised as a key management consideration with examples available of decisions taken and strategy impacted?
8. Can the firm demonstrate how the risk appetite policy, procedures and implementation have evolved over time and have the risk appetite measures changed over time?

I am sure many of us experienced the 2007–2008 global financial crisis first hand, and those that did not have surely undertaken sufficient research to understand what happened and why. If you have not, the 2015 film the Big Short is a great place to start. In the UK, the government was required to take ownership stakes in some firms to ensure the safety of the UK banking system. A number of measures owe their origins to the financial crisis including the steps taken by a number of regulators to make individuals in the financial sector more accountable for their behaviour and competence. This resulted in the UK in the introduction in March 2016 of the Senior Managers and Certification Regime (SMCR). While the detailed scope and requirements of the SMCR are beyond the reach and size of this book, the UK FCA has published and updated 'The Senior Managers and Certification Regime: Guide for UK FCA solo-regulated firms',[5] which contains a comprehensive explanation of the regime, although those captured by the regime are also advised to read the relevant Handbook requirements.

Other regulators have also introduced senior management regimes, for example:

- The Australian Securities and Investments Commission (ASIC) introduced the Financial Accountability Regime in 2024, for authorised deposit-taking institutions and their authorised non-operating holding companies, and in 2025 for insurance entities and their authorised non-operating holding companies. The regime is jointly administered by ASIC and one of my favourite pragmatic banking regulators, APRA or the Australian Prudential Regulation Authority. The regime replaced the regime with by far the best acronym of them all, BEAR or the Banking Executive Accountability Regime that commenced in 2018. At last, an acronym from someone with some imagination!
- The Central Bank of Ireland's Senior Executive Accountability Regime (SEAR) was implemented in 2023;
- The Hong Kong Security and Futures Commission's Manager-in-Charge regime was implemented in 2017.

These regimes aim to strengthen senior management accountability by: having clear allocations of roles and responsibilities, establishing clear standards for individual conduct and reinforcing the need for senior managers to be 'fit and proper'.

Regulators generally require firms to have clear roles and responsibilities throughout the organisation and the BCBS Revisions to the Principles for the Sound Management of Operational Risk[3] (paragraph 16) require the management 'to set clear expectations and accountabilities to ensure bank staff understands their roles and responsibilities for risk management, as well as their authority to act'. In response, many firms have adopted the three lines of defence, although in some cases, the implementation of the three lines of defence fails to meet regulatory expectations. We should recognise that firms are free to adapt, develop or adopt an alternative approach that meets the requirement to have clear roles and responsibilities.

Many firms adopting the three lines of defence for operational risk generally allocate roles and responsibilities in the following way:

1. The first line comprises the business units and their responsibilities include:
   (a) Identifying and assessing their risk;
   (b) Creating controls to manage those risks;
   (c) Assessing the efficiency and effectiveness of their controls;
   (d) Reporting on operational risk within the business unit;
2. The second line of defence comprises the independent operational risk management team and their responsibilities include:
   (a) Producing, developing and maintaining the operational risk framework, including the policies, standards and guidelines;
   (b) Exercising oversight over the first line risk assessment;
   (c) Challenging the first lines implementation of the operational risk framework;
   (d) Reporting on the firm's operational risk exposure;
   (e) Providing training in operational risk;
3. The third line of defence comprises the internal audit function and their responsibilities include:
   (a) Reviewing all aspects of the operational risk management framework and its implementation throughout the firm;
   (b) Auditing the various framework processes to ensure they comply with the approved policies and procedures;
   (c) Assessing the effectiveness and efficiency of the operational risk framework.

The three lines are not universally endorsed, with critics pointing to their failure to prevent the global financial crisis, complaining of repetition of activities in the first, second and third lines (control assessment is always a good example), expressing concern about hybrid functions that undertake first and second line activities, worried that the approach creates unwelcome friction between the lines and concerns that the approach hinders the second line's ability to understand the business. In April 2024, Lloyds Bank announced plans to reduce the number of roles in its risk management division, feeling the division was a blocker to the company's transformation strategy.

When assessing the implementation of the three lines of defence, a great deal depends on the size of the firm. An organisation with 200,000 staff is likely to have a purer approach with less compromise than a firm with 100 people and several hybrid departments. I am always surprised at the number of medium and small firms that blandly state that they comply with the three lines of defence when, because of their size, it is simply not possible to do so in its purest form. In small organisations single teams like HR, legal, finance and IT often undertake first and second line roles, acting as hybrid functions. In addition, we regularly advocate that operational resilience is an outcome that benefits from efficient and effective operational risk management and that the operational risk and operational resilience frameworks should be fully integrated. In many firms, the operational risk policy is owned by the second line but the resilience policy is, perhaps for pragmatic reasons (the COO had to implement and report operational resilience, but no policy existed so the COO wrote one), owned by the first line. This would not seem to be a consistent application of the three lines. Firms should therefore have clearly defined how they apply the three lines model to their firm (given their size, nature, scale and complexity) and how they ensure that the activities undertaken by hybrid functions are not compromised, rather than blandly copying a description of the roles of the three lines from above or elsewhere.

I have on two occasions been in firms where external parties have challenged random members of staff, first asking them what they do and secondly which line of defence they sit in. The responses were not always reassuring and this would surely be an informative exercise to undertake in your own firm. After all, if you claim to have adopted the three lines your staff must surely know which line they sit in.

During our training, we are often asked what are the key skills and capabilities of successful risk teams. This is perhaps best answered by reference to Figure 5.4. It would be expecting a great deal for each team member to possess all these skills and successful teams have the right combination of individuals so that the team collectively provides the appropriate

FIGURE 5.4 Key Skills and Capabilities of Successful Risk Teams

level of coverage. Technical expertise would include knowledge and expertise in risk management, regulation, finance, strategic thinking, mitigating strategies and problem-solving. Data analysis and modelling require a high level of mathematical knowledge and the ability to quantify risk. Business acumen requires staff to understand the business and be able to both talk the talk and walk the walk. I often feel this is one of the most important skills and it is usually easier to employ someone with business acumen and teach them operational risk, rather than expect an operational risk professional to fully understand the business, particularly when it is highly complex. Leadership and collaboration require good people doing good things and the ability to build relationships. Adaptability includes the ability to be flexible and keep up with developments. Continuous learning covers development and includes striving to be better. In many ways, by reading this book you are showing a willingness to develop your knowledge and skills, and reading and understanding the documents referenced in these chapters is another worthwhile objective. It is always surprising how few operational risk professionals have read one or more of the excellent operational risk books available and operational risk team leaders would benefit from knowing how their teams compare, where the gaps are and how they can be filled. The reference to knowledge and understanding of AI is a relatively new addition. Such is the progress in this field that it will not take many years (or perhaps months) for the ability to use AI efficiently and effectively to become a key skill.

Often in our training, we ask delegates which skills they see as most important and which skills they would most like to develop. Again, this would be another useful exercise for operational risk team leaders.

We frequently encounter firms that do not have comprehensive taxonomies for causes, events and impacts or whose taxonomies are sadly inadequate. Taxonomies play a crucial role in risk management and help firms better understand their risk profile. Without an effective taxonomy, a firm's risk register will fail to identify its risk exposure, for example:

- **Risk one:** Staff are unable to get to the office because of snow;
- **Risk two:** Travel problems are encountered by staff when it snows;
- **Risk three:** If it snows, staff using the railways will be unable to come into the office.

I have seen firms where, in the absence of an effective taxonomy these are seen as three distinct risks, whereas in fact they are identical. Many firms use the seven categories of operational risk contained in Basel 2, and those using other taxonomies must be able to map their losses to the Basel risk categories:

1. Internal fraud;
2. External fraud;
3. Employment practices and workplace safety;
4. Clients, products and business practices;
5. Damage to physical assets;
6. Business disruption and system failures;
7. Execution, delivery and process management.

While the Basel Committee should be applauded for developing these categories in the run-up to the release of Basel 2 in June 2004, we must recognise that operational risk has evolved as a discipline and that perhaps our taxonomy should evolve accordingly. Possibly, the best indicator of how operational risk has evolved is provided by the March 2021 BCBS Revisions to the Principles for the Sound Management of Operational Risk,[3] which include the following principle covering ICT risk:

Principle 10: Banks should implement a robust ICT risk management programme in alignment with their operational risk management framework.

The 2011 version of the principles had identified the need for banks to have a sound technical infrastructure (by which it meant the physical and logical design of information and communication systems) as part of principle 9 dealing with the control environment, but that was all. Clearly, as we have all seen and is demonstrated by the 2021 principles, ICT risk management has grown in importance and continues to do so.

The biggest challenge for those seeking to revise their taxonomies is the need for the taxonomy to be MECE, meaning it must be mutually exclusive, collectively exhaustive. So, the taxonomy should capture everything but each risk should only sit in one category. Speaking as someone who has tried to introduce a new cause, risk and impact taxonomy from scratch, this is extremely difficult to do and sometimes felt impossible. Rather than trying to build a taxonomy from scratch, I would urge readers to download the ORX Operational Risk Reference Taxonomy.[6] Starting with the ORX taxonomies is much better than starting with the proverbial blank sheet of paper, but you should bear in mind that the taxonomy was developed by ORX members and may need some adjustment to reflect the size, nature, scale and complexity of your firm. The ORX Reference Taxonomy is also a useful comparison for those revisiting their taxonomies. The ORX Reference Taxonomy provides level 1 and level 2 categories.

The ORX Reference Taxonomy identifies the following level 1 causes:

- Employees;
- Process failure;
- External;
- Systems.

The following level 1 risks:

- Third party;
- Statutory reporting and tax;
- Business continuity;
- Data management;
- Information security (including Cyber);
- Model;
- People;
- Transaction processing & execution;
- Technology;
- Internal fraud;

- External fraud;
- Physical security & safety;
- Legal;
- Conduct;
- Financial crime;
- Regulatory compliance.

And the following level 1 impact categories:

- Loss or remediation (direct financial impact);
- Indirect financial;
- Non-financial.

As we write this book the European Banking Authority has published a consultation paper on establishing a risk taxonomy that complies with international standards and a 'methodology to classify the loss events included in the loss data set based on the risk taxonomy on operational risk under Article 317 (9) of Regulation (EU) 575/2023'.[7] This consultation paper is discussed further in Chapter 18: ESG.

A few years ago, I worked with my dear friends Ariane Chapelle of Chapelle Consulting and Dr. Jimi Hinchliffe to publish a series of blogs entitled 'Things Not to Tell Your Regulator' designed to identify common mistakes made by firms and explain why the error is damaging and could lead to regulatory sanction, a capital add-on and even a skilled person's review (S166). Two of these blogs are directly relevant to the operational risk building blocks.

<u>Things Not To Tell Your Regulator: 'I have an OR Framework but can't show...'</u>

Many years ago, I was discussing with a firm the use and embedding of its operational risk framework. While the firm was adamant that its framework was being used, it was unable to prove it. I have since had similar experiences with numerous firms covering various elements of operational risk and risk governance frameworks, and have often heard apologetic statements like the following:

- We've taken a decision based on our operational risk framework but I can't prove it;
- Our Board Risk Committee has taken decisions using operational risk information but I can't...;
- We capture all our risks but I can't...;
- We monitor our losses but I can't...;
- We review external events but I can't...;
- We consider controls' effectiveness during the scenario process but I can't...

Let's be clear: *Absence of evidence is evidence of absence*. This means that if you can't provide evidence that you do something, the conclusion can only be that you are not doing it. Certainly, an auditor, regulator or other third party will not take your verbal assertion as confirmation. Proof is required.

So, how can a firm demonstrate that it is using its operational risk or risk governance frameworks? For Governance Committees, including the Board, Board Risk Committee and Executive Risk Committee, the answer is often by recording the issue, discussion and decision in the approved minutes of the meeting.

Of course, some decisions are taken outside of the formal governance and the formal minuting process. For example, the senior management may elect not to introduce a change following a risk analysis. As the proposal had not yet gone through formal governance there is no formal record. Nevertheless, a written record of the decision should be made and retained, perhaps, for example, via email.

The 'absence of evidence' mantra applies beyond the Operational Risk and Governance Framework. For example, it applies to staff captured under the UK SMCR. These staff need to show they have taken reasonable steps to discharge their accountabilities and must provide evidence that they have done so. Once again, the absence of evidence is evidence of absence.

<u>Things Not To Tell Your Regulator (5): 'I didn't read...'</u>

Operational risk practitioners are faced with many rules, speeches, consultation papers and policy documents issued by a variety of supervisors and organisations. While not all the documents will be legally binding, they do reflect regulatory expectations and firms should therefore be aware of anything that is relevant to their businesses. Indeed, in many cases, failure to comply can result in termination, regulatory sanction, a capital add-on and even a skilled person's review (S166). However, despite these potential consequences many practitioners fail to read and understand all the documents that are relevant to them. If you don't read and understand the regulator's expectations, how can you be confident that you comply?

A valuable insight into global regulatory expectations can be found in the paper: *Principles for Operational Resilience* issued by the BCBS.[8] Published in March 2021, the 12-page paper discusses how to create an operational resilience capability and proposes that 'Banks should utilise their existing governance structure' and 'leverage their respective functions for the management of operational risk'. In addition, the paper shows that the approach builds on updates to the BCBS's *Principles for the Sound Management of Operational Risk* (PSMOR),[3] issued at the same time.

When I first left the regulator, I was surprised by the problems many practitioners had navigating and understanding the regulatory rule books. The subsequent evolution of the roles of the UK Prudential Regulation Authority (PRA) and the UK Financial Conduct Authority (FCA), and developments in their rule books have done nothing to simplify this process. Nevertheless, the obligation rests with practitioners to always understand the operational risk rules and requirements imposed on them by their regulators.

To protect against this risk:

- Operational risk teams should generate a library of the regulatory documents that inform and govern how the firm's operational risk framework should operate and ensure that all relevant staff are fully aware of their contents;
- Operational risk staff should be asked to confirm annually that they are fully aware of the listed documents and their contents;
- Operational risk teams should undertake horizon scanning for relevant new documents, and wise practitioners will already subscribe to regulatory alerts where available;
- When new requirements or expectations are published the operational risk function should nominate an individual in the team to present a summary of the contents at the next team meeting.

These activities should be undertaken by the operational risk function, even in firms where a central regulatory compliance or regulatory change team exists. Without this understanding, how can you and your team be confident that you meet regulatory expectations?

CHAPTER 6

Risk Identification and Assessment – RCSA and Other Tools

It should be clear by now that risk identification is one of the most important elements of a firm's ORMF. As we have seen, if we fail to correctly identify our risks everything else we do becomes pointless. From a regulatory perspective, regulators tend to require a firm to have effective processes to identify, manage, monitor and report its risks without specifying the tools to be used. We have already seen that Principle 6 of the BCBS Revisions to the Principles for the Sound Management of Operational Risk[1] states that:

> **Principle 6:** Senior management should ensure the comprehensive identification and assessment of the operational risk inherent in all material products, activities, processes and systems to make sure the inherent risks and incentives are well understood.

In paragraph 24, following Principle 6, the BCBS has provided the following examples of tools that can be used for identifying and assessing operational risk (along with a brief description that I have not reproduced here):

- Event management;
- Operational risk event data;
- Self-assessments;
- Control monitoring and assurance framework;
- Metrics;
- Scenario analysis;
- Benchmarking and comparative analysis.

As we saw in Chapter 5, the risk life cycle is a good starting point for any discussion of risk identification and assessment; it plays an important role in any training and can be applied to any risk discipline. Indeed, if you have attended the Operational Risk training provided by Jimi and I, and not been subjected to a lengthy discussion of the risk cycle, I can only apologise.

Figure 6.1 replicates the diagram shown in the previous chapter and shows the version of the risk cycle we use in training that has four components including risk identification. There are a number of tools that can be used by operational risk practitioners and later in this chapter we will discuss the role of the following tools in the risk identification process:

- Top-down bottom-up;
- Risk and control self-assessments;
- Internal events;
- External events;
- Scenarios;
- Change management;
- Emerging risks and horizon scanning.

There is an interesting state of knowledge in risk management that was best summarised by Donald Rumsfold, at that time the US Secretary of State for Defense; in February 2002, when speaking to the US Department of Defense he said:

> There are known knowns. These are things we know that we know. There are known unknowns. That is to say, there are things that we know we don't know. But there are also unknown unknowns. There are things we don't know we don't know.

FIGURE 6.1 The Risk Cycle

While we accept that there are things we do not know we should constantly strive to ensure we have a comprehensive understanding of the risks faced by our firms.

Firms should regularly review their risk identification process and include the following questions in this assessment:

1. Does the business drive the identification of top operational risks on a regular basis or when there is a material change to the business or risk environment and, in doing so, do they engage with the operational risk function and SMEs;
2. Is the extreme operational risk event management process regularly performed and fully integrated into business activity;
3. Do the risks identified reflect those that could prevent the business strategy and objectives from being achieved and/or relate to material activities and infrastructure and affect Board decisions;
4. Is a thorough post-mortem analysis undertaken of both internal and relevant external events and are the results used for ongoing risk management and resilience planning;
5. Do the risks reflect future predictions and emerging risks;
6. Is all data accurately captured on a GRC system and updated regularly (if not, and you are using spreadsheets, etc., you are managing data not risk);
7. Can you demonstrate that top operational risks are considered.

TOP-DOWN AND BOTTOM-UP

Risks can be considered from two directions. The top-down risks that worry the Board and Senior Management, perhaps even keeping them awake at night, and the bottom-up risks that concern those responsible for the day-to-day running of the firm. Often the Board and Senior Management have a very different perspective on the risks the firm is facing, compared with those managing day-to-day business activities. In some instances, the Board and Senior Management are informed by their involvement with other firms (in the case of non-executive directors or NEDs) or by their participation at one of the various industry senior management forums. It is crucial that these top-down risks are captured in the risk identification process. One technique, which I have found incredibly powerful, is simply to engage directly with the NEDs and senior management. For me, understanding the Board and Senior Management's concerns often involved inviting them to meet for coffee in one of the firm's internal coffee bars. While this generally proved fruitful I always ended up paying for the coffee and in some cases a piece of cake! An alternative approach could involve organising a workshop to identify these risks, although getting time in so many diaries can prove problematic. The primary aim of this top-down risk analysis is to identify important risks to the firm and its activities. Top-down risk assessments can be aided by horizon scanning to identify emerging trends and risks as well as the main threats to the firm.

Bottom-up risk analysis is designed to identify business as usual risks and the processes for exploring these risks, like risk and control self-assessments, are discussed in this chapter.

RISK AND CONTROL SELF-ASSESSMENTS

Risk and Control Self-Assessments (RCSAs) are my favourite tool for bottom-up risk identification, and regulators are likely to expect this tool to be employed by firms. Terminology can become confusing, with some firms, for example, calling the process Risk and Control Assessment (RCA) while others use the term Risk Self-Assessments (RSAs). In addition, different risk silos may have their own risk identification process, perhaps called the Compliance Risk Assessment (CRA) or Legal Risk Self-Assessment (LRSA). This simply emphasises the importance of always being clear about what terms you are using and what they involve. Also, perhaps we should spare a thought for the activities that are required to undertake a RCSA, a CRA, a LRSA and more, particularly as everyone asks very similar questions but in a slightly different way. In these instances, I always urge firms to develop a single self-assessment process or face damaging relationships with those being assessed.

During a recent training session, I asked delegates to select why their firm undertook RCSAs from the following options:

1. To ensure the safety and soundness of the firm;
2. To satisfy the Board and Senior Management;
3. To help senior managers;
4. To satisfy the regulators;
5. To keep the risk team employed.

Needless to say, every option was selected by someone. Readers should ask themselves why is their firm undertaking RCSAs?

The RCSA process involves the six key stages shown in Figure 6.2. A number of different mechanisms exist to help with the initial risk identification. The most widely used are interviews and workshops, which enable individuals to highlight their main concerns. These are most beneficial when

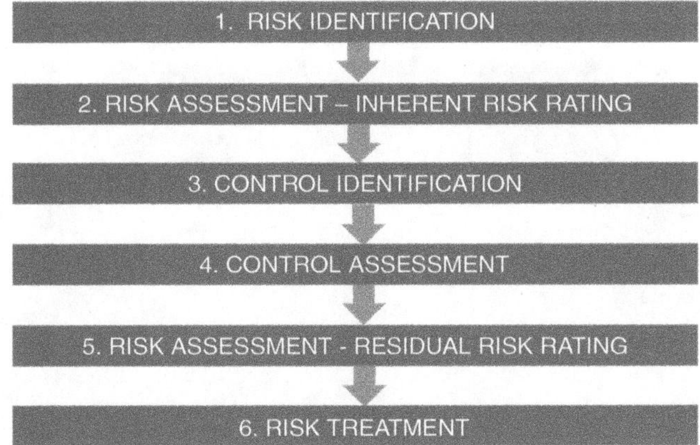

FIGURE 6.2 The Key RCSA Stages

they involve the team or unit completing the assessment as that group will best understand the potential risks they face on a daily basis. RCSA assessment units are determined by the firm and could comprise a team, department, division, product or region. Whichever assessment unit is selected, the RCSA should be constructed so that total risk exposure can be sliced and diced in different ways and specific issues can be identified, for example, operational resilience. The team undertaking the RCSA will also have first-hand knowledge of the incidents that have occurred in the past, including near misses. Some firms use a risk wheel to act as a check process to ensure all potential sources of risk are considered. This wheel has proved very useful, particularly when undertaking RCSAs for the first time as part of brainstorming sessions (see Figure 6.3, for an example). Firms should also consider emerging trends in the external business environment.

Consideration of internal events should include 'losses' experienced by the firm and we should recognise that these are not only financial losses. Financial losses take the form of a monetary amount, perhaps in the form of a regulatory fine, that can be allocated to a specific event. Non-financial losses may take the form of a loss of customer reputation or regulatory censure, perhaps a loss of permissions or restrictions on the activities a firm can undertake.

When assessing the risks faced by the firm we should always keep in mind that the risks faced by the firm are not limited to the first line. Even Internal Audit and Legal Department expose firms to risk, although they may well argue, and often do, that this is not the case. Care should be taken to ensure that risks are identified and not causes or impacts. The benefits of using a taxonomy to ensure this does not happen are discussed in Chapter 5.

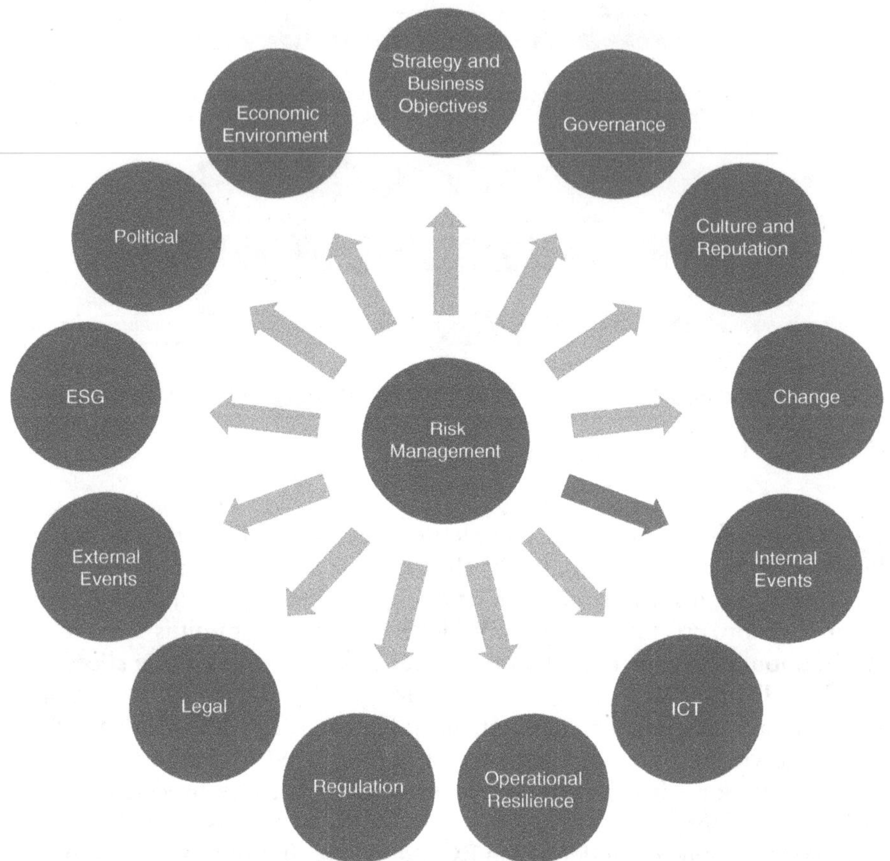

FIGURE 6.3 The Risk Wheel

Once the risks have been identified they will need to be assigned an inherent risk rating. Inherent risk is usually described as the impact of a risk crystallising before the application of controls. This is generally unrealistic and can cause confusion. I have found it better to think of inherent risk as the impact that could be experienced if multiple controls fail, that is, the impact if things go wrong or what is the worst that can happen.

In order to understand the inherent risk, firms develop impact matrices to use as a benchmark. Figure 6.4 is intended as a guide to how to start to construct an impact matrix and should be tailored to the individual firm. Obviously, the level of financial loss a large multinational bank can sustain will, in nominal terms, greatly exceed the amount a small retail bank can absorb. I am always a fan of setting amounts where possible in actual terms,

Rating	Regulatory	Financial	Operational Resilience	Reputation	Customer
Very High	Large fine, formal investigation, removal of licence or permissions	Loss greater than $150,000	Significant breach of impact tolerances (or tolerance for disruption) with potential impact on the safety and soundness of the firm	Sustained national media coverage over a month and long-term impact on the share value	Significant loss of customers
High	Skilled persons review, risk mitigation actions, capital charge	Loss between $50,000 and $150,000	Impact tolerances (or tolerance for disruption) breached and regulator notified	National media coverage over weeks and short-term impact on the share value	Some loss of customers
Medium	Regulatory relationship damaged	Loss between $25,000 and $50,000	Disruption, impact tolerances (or tolerance for disruption) not breached but disruption reported in the media	National media coverage over a few days with no impact on the share value	Minimal loss of customers
Low	No regulatory action triggered	Loss below $25,000	Minimal disruption to important business services (or critical operations) with minimal impact on the firm or customer	Incident receives local or specialist media coverage	No customer impact

FIGURE 6.4 RCSA Impact Scales

for example, the dollar amount of the loss, even if they are originally calibrated as a percentage of annual income or budget. In considering the appropriate impact rating for a particular risk we should always select the highest potential rating. For example, using Figure 6.4, a risk that could result in a large regulatory fine should be assessed as very high even if the resultant financial impact is $100,000, the impact tolerances (or tolerances for disruption) are not breached, national media only covered the story for a couple of days and no customers were impacted.

Once the inherent impact has been determined firms need to consider the likelihood of the event occurring. This is done with the aid of a likelihood scale of the type shown in Figure 6.5, which provides a guide to how to start to construct a likelihood matrix and should be tailored to the individual firm.

Once we have determined the inherent risk impact and the inherent risk likelihood, we can map the risk on a heatmap. For the purposes of this section, we shall assume:

- The inherent risk impact is high;
- The inherent risk likelihood is medium.

Critics of the use of heatmaps complain that they are oversimplified and can provide false comfort by understating the impact and/or likelihood. Nevertheless, they are easy to understand and widely used and, when subject to robust and effective second line challenge, they provide a useful risk management tool. An example heatmap is shown in Figure 6.6. The positioning of the inherent risk in our example is shown with a star in the medium likelihood and high impact cell.

Rating	Occurrence	Description
High	In the next 12 months	The event is expected to occur in the next year and this is supported by empirical evidence.
Medium	In the next 1–5 years	The event is expected to occur while many members of staff are at the firm.
Low	In the next 5–10 years	A significant number of staff will leave the firm before the event occurs.
Unlikely	Greater than 10 years	Most members of staff will have left the firm before this event occurs.

FIGURE 6.5 RCSA Likelihood

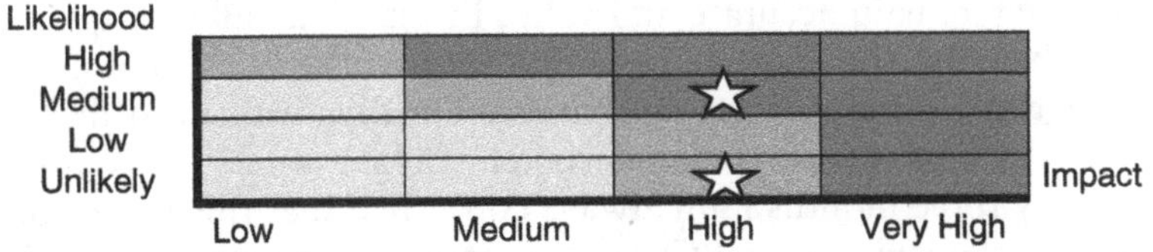

FIGURE 6.6 RCSA Heatmap

The next stage in the RCSA process is to identify the controls and assess their effectiveness and efficiency (this chapter should be read in conjunction with Chapter 7: Controls). Controls should be listed according to their type (preventative, detective, corrective or directive) and then assessed. If we assume for now that our controls pass scrutiny, we can determine the residual risk rating, or the risk with controls in place and operating correctly. Some firms call this business as usual risk. In our example, we shall assume:

- The residual risk impact remains high;
- The residual risk likelihood becomes unlikely.

In other words, our controls have reduced the likelihood of the risk occurring but if the risk does happen the impact will be the same. Controls often only affect likelihood or impact, rather than both. Nevertheless, we can identify some controls that could impact both likelihood and impact. Going back to speed limits for example, if a speed limit is reduced from 60 to 10 mph a crash is less likely to happen, as we have more time to react, and less likely to have the same impact, as our momentum is significantly reduced.

Having now used the RCSA process to determine the inherent and residual risk, we must consider how to respond to the risk. We will see in Chapter 7 that our options are to:

- Accept or tolerate the risk;
- Treat the risk by introducing additional controls;
- Transfer the risk, perhaps by taking out insurance;
- Terminate the risk by stopping taking the risk.

Anything other than accepting the risk will require action by the firm. This action should be contained in an action tracker and the progress should be formally tracked using existing governance arrangements.

There are a number of important considerations to bear in mind when undertaking RCSAs. The first is that impact and likelihood are not constant and can change over time. Secondly, RCSAs should be monitored constantly to ensure they remain accurate and valid. Events that call into question an RCSA, perhaps by showing we have understated the likelihood or impact, should trigger a refresh of the assessment. Thirdly, firms must decide how frequently RCSAs should be undertaken. While some firms undertake RCSAs every three months I am always concerned that this is too frequent. The biggest challenge with RCSAs is keeping the process fresh and frequently undertaking RCSAs raises the spectre of RCSA fatigue, which is ultimately harmful to the process. Lastly, the various impact ratings provide a measure of risk appetite. In our example in the heatmap in Figure 6.6, we would expect that risks in the dark grey cells are outside risk appetite/tolerance and require immediate action to bring within our risk tolerance. Using the approach detailed in Chapter 5, the light grey cells are likely to be within risk appetite and the remaining cells are within tolerance and therefore require some action to bring with risk appetite.

Firms should regularly assess the effectiveness of their RCSA process and include the following questions in that assessment:

1. Is there a fully integrated and standardised RCSA process across the organisation supporting an optimal control framework;
2. Do risk owners, control owners and risk stewards all agree to the scope of the RCSA;
3. Can you demonstrate that RCSA activities (scoping, risk and control identification and assessment, control monitoring, issues and actions, governance and reporting) have been well coordinated across the business units and functions and there is an appropriate balance of cost versus benefit;
4. Does the RCSA process provide forward-looking indicators of current and emerging risks;
5. Can you demonstrate that there is no overlap in activity and excessive controls have been removed avoiding unnecessary constraints on the business;
6. Is the focus of implementation based on risk materiality and does it provide a view of whether a business is in control;
7. Are the risks and controls dynamically updated (e.g. reviews of risks take place when there is a significant or material event).

INTERNAL EVENTS

Internal events, and the operational risk event database in which they are recorded, provide an invaluable insight into the risk profile of a firm and should be aligned to the firm's risk taxonomy. It is important that events are reported promptly and most firms have deadlines for reporting operational risk events. By the time this book is published, the UK should be close to implementing the revisions to the Basel Standards, known as Basel 3.1,[2] while the EU has set an implementation of January 2025. While the contents of the new measures are beyond the scope of this book, readers can access the document free of charge using the endnote above. The new standardised approach methodology includes general criteria on loss data identification, collection and treatment. While the original consultation on this methodology termed it the 'Standardised Measurement Approach' the methodology was renamed the 'Standardised Approach', although many commentators continue to, incorrectly, use the consultation term. I have no idea why the name changed but it is a constant source of frustration when speakers use the wrong title.

Paragraph 25.19 of the BCBS document referenced in the endnote contains the following valuable guidance into the contents of the operational risk loss event database:

> 25.19 Aside from information on gross loss amounts, the bank must collect information about the reference dates of operational risk events, including the date when the event happened or first began ('date of occurrence'), where available; the date on which the bank became aware of the event ('date of discovery'); and the date (or dates) when a loss event results in a loss, reserve or provision against a loss being recognised in the bank's profit and loss (P&L) accounts ('date of accounting'). In addition, the bank must collect information on recoveries of gross loss amounts as well as descriptive information about the drivers or causes of the loss event. The level of detail of any descriptive information should be commensurate with the size of the gross loss amount.

From this paragraph and our own experiences, we can conclude that the loss event database should include:

- A unique incident ID;
- The event classification according to the taxonomy;
- In which unit/function/division/region the event occurred;
- The gross loss amount;
- The date of the event;
- The date of discovery;
- The date of accounting;
- Any recoveries;
- A description of the event;
- Any controls that failed (by type);

- Remedial action taken;
- Whether risk appetite was breached;
- Whether the event impacted the firm's operational resilience;
- Whether any impact tolerances (or tolerances for disruption for non-UK firms) were breached;
- Whether the incident impacted Consumer Duty (UK firms only).

You will see that I have proposed capturing operational resilience events and, for the UK, events that impact the UK FCA's Consumer Duty requirements. It is important that all operational risk events are captured within a single database and can be easily identified. Internal events provide an important mechanism for benchmarking RCSAs and RCSA reviews should be triggered if the impact or frequency of an event calls into question the existing RCSA. The event database must be comprehensive and of course rubbish in means rubbish out.

Firms should regularly assess the effectiveness of their internal event monitoring and include the following questions when undertaking this assessment:

1. Is the event management process fully embedded across the organisation and are risks regularly tested using severe but plausible scenario testing and stress testing;
2. Is there complete internal loss data, seamlessly incorporating internal losses and near misses;
3. Can it be demonstrated that: events are shared across the businesses and functions; formal reviews of RCSAs are triggered by reportable incidents; and businesses or functions have taken decisions as a result of internal events or mitigative action has been taken to prevent the event from reoccurring in a business or function;
4. Is the risk information from internal events consistent, fully retained and readily reviewed;
5. Is there an assessment of the links between key operational risk indicators, loss data and quantitative measures.

EXTERNAL EVENTS

Many years ago, it was often the case that significant operational risk events were subsequently marked by the firm's publication of an assessment of what went wrong. This is much less evident now and often when I see these assessments published, I wonder if the regulator 'encouraged' the firm to take that step. Analysis of external events is crucial and should enable firms to answer the question 'could it happen here'. Often a difficulty in assessing external events is obtaining an accurate understanding of what went wrong and the impact of the event; nevertheless, this does not reduce the value of reviewing relevant external events.

In addition to asking 'could it happen here' firms should regularly assess the effectiveness of their external event monitoring and include the following questions when undertaking this assessment:

1. Can the businesses or functions demonstrate that decisions have been taken as a result of external events or mitigative action has been taken to prevent the event from happening;
2. Is external loss data systematically integrated into all elements of the operational risk framework;
3. Can it be demonstrated that formal lessons learnt reviews are undertaken and considered by the senior management and relevant staff.

SCENARIOS

While scenarios are a widely used capital assessment tool, they also play an important role in the risk identification process. More recently, the publication of regulatory expectations for operational resilience also established an important role for scenario testing as a means of showing firms are able to ensure that disruptions do not result in a breach of their impact tolerances (or tolerances for disruption). In this section, we will focus on the use of scenarios for operational risk management, leaving the discussion of the use of scenarios in operational resilience to Chapter 8, Operational Resilience. While we will focus on risk management scenario testing rather than capital scenario testing the two processes can be run together. I have been surprised in the past by organisations using scenarios solely to generate a capital number for modelling purposes. Often, identified control deficiencies were not addressed, which seemed strange, as surely addressing identified control weaknesses could ultimately reduce the potential capital impact.

Operational risk scenarios involve the creation of a storyline describing an event and aim to identify, analyse, measure and explain the impact on the firm and how the firm would respond. The focus on scenario testing is generally on those high-impact events that are capable of generating significant losses and could threaten the safety and soundness of the firm. Our preferred approach is to organise a scenario workshop attended by the relevant first, second and, in some cases, third line representatives. However, scenario testing could be desk based, perhaps with a questionnaire to individual participants. The inclusion of internal audit will prove contentious in some firms and must be done in a way that does not threaten their independence. Nevertheless, the audit team should possess a holistic view of the firm and also be able to provide insight into any relevant audit reports. The collection of various artefacts for circulation prior to the workshop is a key step and these artefacts should include:

- The name of the scenario owner;
- The storyline;
- Relevant internal events and loss data;
- Relevant external events;
- Relevant RCSAs;
- Control effectiveness assessment;
- Relevant key risk indicators;
- Audit issues and other issues;
- Known vulnerabilities;
- The scenario facilitator.

Once the scenario is completed firms should be able to detail how the firm would:

- Respond to the event;
- Any communications required as a result of the event – both internal and external, including to the regulator;
- The business units and functions impacted by the scenario;
- The effectiveness and efficiency of the controls;
- Any control weaknesses;
- Any remediation/actions required;
- Any lessons learned;
- Whether an RCSA review should be triggered;
- When the scenario should be retested.

As we reflect on the operational risk scenario process a number of challenges and pitfalls come to mind: preparation is key to an effective scenario workshop; generating an appropriate storyline can itself be challenging; scenarios should be severe and plausible and must affect the firm; if an event is considered beyond plausible this should be documented; nothing should be ruled out during the scenario process; no criticism should be intended; and who should be involved in the scenario test.

The entire scenario process must be fully documented. Most firms already have individuals skilled in facilitating the scenario process and these resources should be leveraged. This would seem an appropriate moment to refer again to one of my favourite adages, absence of evidence is evidence of absence. In other words, if you cannot evidence that you have done something then any party not actively involved in that process, including regulators and external audit, can only assume nothing has been done.

Firms should regularly assess the effectiveness of their scenario process and include the following questions when undertaking this assessment:

1. Do formal records show that the testing of severe but plausible scenarios is regularly performed and fully integrated into the organisation;
2. Do formal records show that lessons learned analysis is performed for both internal and external events and included in the artefacts used for scenario testing;
3. Is scenario testing completed annually or reviewed when there is a material change to the internal or external risk and control environment;
4. Can it be demonstrated that management action has been undertaken to improve control deficiencies identified during the scenario process.

Developing an appropriate library of severe and plausible scenarios is a challenge for many firms. As you would expect, locating and accessing independent operational risk scenario libraries can be extremely difficult. I am aware of three scenario libraries, available at a fee or requiring membership, provided by the following organisations:

- ORX Scenarios[3] (available via subscription to members and non-members of ORX);
- RiskBusiness[4];
- ORIC International (a provider of specialist operational risk data, benchmarking services and thought leadership for the insurance, reinsurance and investment management sector). ORIC also maintains a repository of assessment data (frequency & severity) for scenarios and is the only organisation that I am aware of that does so.[5]

CHANGE MANAGEMENT

A firm is often exposed to new, or greater, risk as a result of new and enhanced: products, technology/systems, processes and services. In other words, as a result of change. This means that all change that has the ability to impact the firm's strategy, performance, safety and soundness, reputation and risk profile must be reviewed and assessed using a formal change management process. Such a process is likely to include the following elements:

- Understanding change requests and the reasons for their consideration;
- Prioritising the proposed changes – a firm's ability to effectively and efficiently manage change is likely to be constrained by a number of factors, including the business case or requirements, the resources required to process the change and in business as usual, the cost of the change and the envisaged benefits. This stage should fully involve the second line to ensure that legal, risk and compliance considerations are identified;
- Approved changes should be subject to a clearly defined governance process that has been approved by the Board;
- An assessment of the impact of the change on operational resilience, outsourcing and third-party risk management, and Consumer Duty (in the UK);
- As the governance process moves to a close an RCSA must be completed to ensure that risks are correctly identified and captured;
- The change should then be formally approved, declined or remedial action taken;
- Six months following approval of the change, a review should be undertaken to ensure that the benefits have been realised and all risks identified.

A challenge when considering the implementation of changes within a firm can often arise as a result of the size, nature and complexity of the firm. I can recall a large global organisation that only made changes to its frameworks and activities when a significant change was required. Smaller changes would then be included as part of the implementation of the new change. This reflected the significant cost to the firm of implementing any change, no matter how small.

Firms should regularly assess their change management framework and process and include the following questions when undertaking this assessment:

1. Can the businesses and functions demonstrate that they have complied with the change management policy;
2. Can the senior management demonstrate that they automatically consider operational risk, compliance, operational resilience and consumers during all key management change decisions;

3. Can it be demonstrated that changes are risk assessed from inception and monitored through to implementation with appropriate and cost-effective measures to mitigate any impacts on achieving change objectives;
4. Is there clear evidence through post-implementation reviews of the benefits realised and that the programme assumptions have been met;
5. Are the impacts on business processes well constrained and monitored.

The role of the operational risk function in the change management process is often seen as a sign of the maturity of that function. Usually, the active involvement of the operational risk function during all aspects of the change approval process indicates a mature operational risk management capability.

EMERGING RISKS AND HORIZON SCANNING

It is crucial that firms establish a process for identifying emerging risks and horizon scanning and I am sure there will be some of us that wish we had done a better job of identifying emerging risks in the run-up to the COVID-19 crisis. Regulators are clear that they expect firms to have a process for identifying risk crystallising or any new risks emerging. The BCBS Revisions to the Principles for the Sound Management of Operational Risk[1] include under monitoring and reporting:

Principle 8: Senior management should implement a process to regularly monitor operational risk profiles and material operational exposures. Appropriate reporting mechanisms should be in place at the board of directors, senior management and business unit levels to support proactive management of operational risk.

Paragraph 45: Operational risk reports should describe the operational risk profile of the bank by providing internal financial, operational and compliance indicators, as well as external market or environmental information about events and conditions that are relevant to decision-making. Operational risk reports should include:

(b) A discussion and assessment of key and emerging risks

Clearly, to be able to discuss and assess key and emerging risks firms will need to include in their operational risk frameworks a methodology for identifying, assessing and discussing these risks.

When considering new and emerging risks there are essentially three categories of risk:

- **Early signals:** These may be very numerous and therefore difficult to prioritise in terms of risk assessment;
- **Emerging risks:** These are risks that have been identified and have the ability to cause loss or impact strategic objectives and business plans. They should be reported to the Risk Committees and the Board and be subject to ongoing analysis, for example, how quickly are they likely to impact and is it possible to identify how they can be mitigated at this moment in time. Emerging risks may take some time to emerge and may stay in this category for some time;
- **Mature risks:** These risks are well understood and some may be considered key risks. Mitigating actions may be appropriate.

As part of the methodology for identifying emerging risks, some firms adopt the PESTEL framework. This tool can be used to identify emerging political, economic, social, technological, environmental and legal factors in the external environment. In addition to or as part of this framework, firms should be scanning a variety of publications, including those from the World Health Organisation and the UK FCA business plan. In the past, when teaching about horizon scanning and how to identify emerging risks, I have referenced some of the top risk reports, which provide a useful sense check, including the reports produced by the CRO Forum on Emerging Risks, the World Economic Forum Global Risk Report, Risk Net's top operational risks, the ORX Top Risk Reviews and Operational Risk Horizon reports and AXA's Future Risk Report.

One of the challenges in identifying emerging risks and horizon scanning is simply one of resources. Many of us will already be arriving at work early (either in person or virtually) and leaving late, having only taken an abbreviated lunch, if lunch was taken at all. It is important the firms are adequately resourced to identify these risks. The BCBS Revisions to the Principles for the sound management of operational risk[i] make the senior management's responsibilities for resourcing the Operational Risk Management Function clear:

Paragraph 29: Senior management should translate the ORMF approved by the board of directors into specific policies and procedures that can be implemented and verified within the different business units. Senior management should clearly assign authority, responsibility and reporting relationships to encourage and maintain accountability, and to ensure the **necessary resources are available to manage**

operational risk in line with the bank's risk appetite and tolerance statement. Moreover, senior management should ensure that the management oversight process is appropriate for the risks inherent in a business unit's activity.

Paragraph 32: Senior management should ensure that bank **activities are conducted by staff with the necessary experience, technical capabilities and access to resources.** Staff responsible for monitoring and enforcing compliance with the institution's risk policy should have authority independent from the units they oversee.

It is possible to access information from external providers that will assist in the process of identifying emerging risks and horizon scanning, although this may well incur a cost or require a membership. For example:

- The RiskSpotlight Portal offers an emerging risk monitoring service[6];
- ORX News provides publicly reported operational risk loss events from around the world[7];
- ORIC provides risk events and emerging risks.[8]

I am aware that horizon scanning and identifying emerging risks may require a degree of fortitude that we are not generally required to demonstrate. Imagine you are working for a major UK bank; it is mid-December 2019 and you have become aware that some patients in Hubei Province in China are experiencing symptoms of a pneumonia-like illness that does not respond well to standard treatments. By the end of December, you note that the World Health Organisation's China Office is informed of several cases of the infection in Hubei Province that causes shortness of breath and fever. Hopefully, you will have seen this as a potential emerging risk and committed to monitoring developments closely. As January 2020 progresses reports become more disturbing with the identification of a novel coronavirus, news that the National Centre for Immunisation and Respiratory Diseases in the USA has updated its travel health notice instructing people travelling to Wuhan, China, to 'practice unusual precautions' and the announcement of the first deaths in China. By the end of the month, the USA is screening passengers from Wuhan, China, for symptoms and the US Centre for Disease Control and Prevention has issued quarantine orders to those US citizens who have returned from Wuhan.

Let us speculate on the reception we might have received from the Board Risk Committee in early February had we flagged what we now know to be the impact of COVID-19, including suggesting our firm purchase PPE, make sure all staff have a laptop at home and can log on and work using the firm's network. To cap it all we might have warned that staff could well be instructed to stay at home. Given that at that time it seemed, to me at least, that the UK authorities were underplaying the COVID-19 threat, we might well have been ushered from the Board Room and encouraged to take some time off as we were obviously suffering from stress and impaired judgement. I wonder how many of us would have had the strength of mind to brief an early February Board Risk Committee in this way.

COVID – BLACK SWAN

One of my personal 'triggers', which those who know me will identify, occurs when I hear speakers, including senior risk managers, refer to COVID-19 as a black swan. It seems to me that they simply do not understand what constitutes a black swan, the COVID-19 context or possibly both. The term Black Swan was penned by Nassim Nicholas Taleb in his book 'The Black Swan – The Impact of the Highly Improbable' and a signed copy is one of the most prized books in my personal risk management library. In his book, Taleb notes that before the discovery of Australia, people in the Old World were convinced that all swans were white, an unassailable belief as it seemed completely confirmed by empirical evidence. Taleb continues that the sighting of the first black swan illustrates a severe limitation to our learning from observations or experience and the fragility of our knowledge. Taleb describes a black swan as having three attributes, the event:

- Is an outlier as it lies outside the realm of regular expectations because nothing in the past can convincingly point to its possibility;
- Carries an extreme impact;
- In spite of its outlier status, human nature makes us concoct explanations after the fact, making it explainable and predictable.

While some of you will be wondering why this even matters, it is important to determine whether the failure to identify coronavirus arose because:

- The pandemic lies outside the realm of regular expectations (a black swan) or;
- Of a failure of the risk management framework.

If coronavirus is a black swan, firms and regulators can claim that it could not have been predicted and preventative and detective controls established. This could excuse all parties from failing to prepare for a truly unknown event. However, if it is not a black swan, then deficiencies in the risk management framework prevented the event from being identified and managed/mitigated. In this case, these deficiencies must be addressed to ensure that firms do not fail to prepare for and mitigate similar events.

I would argue that the failure to identify COVID-19 is a failure of risk management, not least because:

- Three worldwide outbreaks of influenza occurred in 1918, 1957 and 1968. The 'Spanish flu' pandemic that began in 1918 is regarded as the deadliest disease event in history with an estimated 500 million people infected with this virus and the number of worldwide deaths estimated to be at least 50 million;
- Severe Acute Respiratory Syndrome (SARS) – This is a species of coronavirus and caused outbreaks of severe respiratory diseases in humans in 2002 and 2003. The virus infected over 8,000 people worldwide and is estimated to have killed almost 800;
- The Western African Ebola virus epidemic in 2013–2016 was the most widespread outbreak of Ebola virus disease (EVD) since it first appeared in 1976, causing major loss of life and socioeconomic disruption in the region. Isolated cases were recorded in the UK and Italy. About 28,000 people were infected and 11,000 died. Another Ebola outbreak began in 2018;
- A few years ago, Bill Gates used a Ted talk to warn that the greatest risk of global catastrophe was most likely to be a highly infectious virus and that the world was not ready for the next epidemic;
- The SARS-related coronavirus was one of several viruses identified by the World Health Organisation in 2016 as a likely cause of future epidemics.

On what many will consider a potentially academic point, the COVID-19 outbreak is considered by many, myself included, to have been a grey rhino. Grey rhinos are not random surprises but occur after a series of warnings and visible evidence. The term had been used increasingly in the Chinese Communist Party's media as a warning to officials to seriously confront the ballooning risks in the Chinese economy like hidden provincial debt.

So, while I am unable to accept that the COVID-19 pandemic was a black swan, I am prepared to accept that the national lockdowns that were initiated in response to the outbreak of COVID-19 do appear to meet Taleb's attributes.

BLOGS

As you will have seen, a few years ago, I worked with Ariane Chapelle of Chapelle Consulting and Dr. Jimi Hinchliffe to publish a series of blogs entitled 'Things Not to Tell Your Regulator', designed to identify common mistakes made by firms and explain why the mistake is damaging and could lead to regulatory sanction, a capital add-on and even a skilled person's review (S166). Two of these blogs are directly relevant to the process of risk identification.

Things Not to Tell Your Regulator : You don't capture all your key risks

A surprising number of firms either do not have a comprehensive framework to identify the key risks they face, or even worse, they have no risk identification framework at all. Risk identification is one of the cornerstones for any risk management framework and the absence of this starting point renders the remainder of the framework effectively null and void. In many cases, a firm's risk assessment processes are incomplete as they either fail to capture top-down risks or bottom-up risk exposure and/or fail to horizon scan for new and emerging risks, the COVID-19 pandemic, for example. To be effective and comprehensive, the risk identification process must seek to capture all of a firm's key risks, whatever their origin. In the UK, under the Senior Management and Certification Regime, the Chief Risk Officer and the Head of the Board Risk Committee could potentially be exposed to regulatory concerns and sanctions if a risk management framework fails to capture a firm's risk exposure.

Nevertheless, many firms struggle with the resources required for establishing a risk management framework that captures all the risks the firm faces. One solution is to ensure that only key risks are comprehensively identified and assessed. The RCSA process provides one mechanism for ensuring that only key risks are subject to a comprehensive review. After all, if a risk is considered to have low inherent risk, it can be argued there is no need to subject the risk to a comprehensive review process.

There are of course some firms, and even some regulators, who argue that there is no need to assess inherent risk. I have never understood this approach as it prevents a firm from understanding its potential risk exposure when controls fail. In addition, the transition from inherent to residual risk must imply something about the quality of the controls established by the firm. If a firm has very high inherent risk, considers its controls to be effective and yet has a very high residual risk, the quality of the control assessment must be questioned.

Things Not to Tell Your Regulator: 'We use scenarios for capital purposes only'

A little while ago I visited a firm to discuss and review its scenario process. The firm's approach was both thorough and efficient and the capital figures generated were accepted by all parties. The comprehensive pre-discussion briefing pack contained a detailed explanation of the scenario, the status of the relevant controls, the firm's previous loss experience under this scenario, external experience and examples of the potential outcomes.

The discussion was very open, involved all the relevant parties, covered all the relevant topics and care was taken by a very capable scenario team not to introduce biases or permit gaming. Finally, all the participants accepted the potential loss generated and everyone was prepared to leave the scenario workshop feeling the job had been well done.

Among the information presented to the workshop was a detailed assessment of the controls impacting the scenario, including controls that were considered to be less than fully effective or had significant weaknesses. Unfortunately, while attendees were prepared to accept the significant loss generated by the scenario, there was no discussion of measures that could be taken to improve risk management, including control efficiency and effectiveness, or to reduce the magnitude of the loss and so reduce the potential capital impact of the scenario. This omission was particularly alarming as the ultimate capital figure generated was allocated to the firm's businesses, including the businesses participating in the scenario workshop.

Recognising this deficiency led the firm to revamp its scenario process and introduce a control improvement component so that when scenarios were discussed in future there was a possibility to reduce the potential loss.

Unfortunately, this experience is not unique and, in many organisations, scenarios focus solely on the loss and capital impact. This omission will certainly cause regulatory concern and could result in sanctions, most likely a capital add-on as the integrity of the scenario process will be questioned. In addition, the regulator's operational resilience expectations require firms to test their ability to deliver important business services within impact tolerances in severe but plausible scenarios.

Scenarios offer a powerful tool that should be used to enhance risk management and improve operational resilience as well as provide inputs to the capital process. When you use a single scenario team to oversee and manage different scenarios within a firm, you encourage efficiency and best practices across the organisation.

The increasing emphasis on scenarios for capital, risk management and resilience raises a question I have been asked many times: 'How many scenarios should a firm have?' The answer depends on a number of factors, such as the size, nature and complexity of the firm. I have seen a firm with three scenarios, which seemed insufficient, while another I met had 300, which seemed too many. I have even heard of a firm with thousands of scenarios. Overall, it is better to do fewer scenarios very well than lots badly.

CHAPTER 7

Controls

In everyday life, we often simply accept controls that deal with risk in some way, usually without thinking. The example I often give relates to car ownership. I guess I should admit upfront that I am old school when it comes to car ownership and, in particular, dealing with the risk of punctures. While the options open to me to prevent punctures from occurring are fairly limited, they would seem to include ensuring my tyres are in good condition, avoiding driving anywhere where the risk of having a puncture is heightened and also not driving at all. Nevertheless, my controls for mitigating the impact of a puncture would seem more numerous leading me to wonder how many people, when purchasing a car, consider the controls in place to mitigate the impact of a puncture. Do would-be car purchasers consider what allowance has been made by the manufacturer and previous owner or consider the steps they might take? The options would seem to include:

- Belonging to a car rescue organisation;
- Fitting run flat tyres;
- Owning tyre sealant that can be squirted into the tyre;
- Carrying a compressor that can pump up a flat tyre and be used to inject the sealant;
- Buying a car with a spare wheel, or purchasing one separately;
- Carrying a car jack and a wrench to remove the wheel nuts, enabling a replacement wheel to be fitted;
- Having a mobile phone to call for help.

We should also recognise that the nature of the puncture will influence the effectiveness of the options we have adopted. For example:

- A can of tyre sealant will not be effective if the tyre is too badly damaged;
- A mobile phone will only be useful in an area with phone coverage, ruling out parts of the country;
- Belonging to a car rescue club, but what if I don't have a phone signal and can't contact them;

- Carrying a spare wheel, jack and wrench assumes you have the knowledge and ability to use them, particularly on a motorway, in the rain, at night.

Hopefully, this example helps us understand some of the controls we have in place to deal with risk in our everyday lives. It is clear, from the options above, that for every risk we have four options:

1. **Tolerate:** We can accept the risk and deal with it if it arises;
2. **Treat:** We can seek to reduce the impact or likelihood of the risk (perhaps by ensuring we care for our tyres, or fit run flats or taking some or all of the steps listed above);
3. **Transfer:** We can move the impact of a risk to another party (perhaps by riding in other people's cars and in taxis, thereby transferring the risk to someone else);
4. **Terminate:** We can remove or avoid the risk altogether (we can simply not go anywhere by car).

So, controls are the most common way in which we treat, and therefore manage, risk, but what is a control? In May 2023, COSO published 'Internal Control – Integrated Framework' and the executive summary[1] contains the following definition of an internal control:

> An internal control is a process, effected by an entity's board of directors, management, and other personnel, designed to provide reasonable assurance regarding the achievement of objectives relating to operations, reporting, and compliance.

We would expect the regulatory community to require firms to organise and control their affairs to ensure the safety and soundness of the firm. The BCBS Revisions to the Principles for the Sound Management of Operational Risk[2] give considerable insight into the regulatory communities control expectations, including:

> **Principle 2:** Banks should develop, implement and maintain an operational risk management framework that is fully integrated into the bank's overall risk management processes. The ORMF adopted by an individual bank will depend on a range of factors, including the bank's nature, size, complexity and risk profile.
>
> **Paragraph 23:** ORMF documentation should clearly:
>
> (e) describe the bank's approach to ensure controls are designed, implemented and operating effectively;

(g) inventory risks and controls implemented by all business units (e.g. in a control library).

Principle 3: The board of directors should approve and periodically review the operational risk management framework, and ensure that senior management implements the policies, processes and systems of the operational risk management framework effectively at all decision levels.

Paragraph 25: Strong internal controls are a critical aspect of operational risk management. The board of directors should establish clear lines of management responsibility and accountability for implementing a strong control environment. Controls should be regularly reviewed, monitored and tested to ensure ongoing effectiveness. The control environment should provide appropriate independence/separation of duties between operational risk management functions, business units and support functions.

Principle 9: Banks should have a strong control environment that utilises policies, processes and systems; appropriate internal controls and appropriate risk mitigation and/or transfer strategies.

Paragraph 47: Internal controls should be designed to provide reasonable assurance that a bank will have efficient and effective operations, safeguard its assets, produce reliable financial reports and comply with applicable laws and regulations. A sound internal control programme consists of four components that are integral to the risk management process: risk assessment, control activities, information and communication and monitoring activities.

It is crucial in any discussion of controls to be clear on the type of control. There are four categories:

1. **Preventative:** These controls are designed to stop the risk from occurring or reduce its impact;
2. **Detective:** These controls identify that the event has happened;
3. **Corrective:** These controls attempt to mitigate the impact of the event;
4. **Directive:** These controls are contained in policies and procedures.

Care should always be taken when assessing and adding controls to understand the control type and its aim. Using the example at the start of this chapter, a can of tyre sealant will not prevent you from having a puncture; it may, however, mitigate the impact of the puncture by reducing the delay to your journey. Unfortunately, I have seen many firms respond to risk events by introducing detective and corrective controls to prevent the event from reoccurring. The control types can be explained by referring to the bow tie (see Figure 7.1), which we will discuss in more detail in Chapter 9.

With controls in place, it is important for firms to be able to gain assurance that they are working efficiently and effectively. This should be done by control testing and control owners should routinely test their internal controls. I have seen instances where it is suggested that only the first line control owners should test their controls but it is important to recognise that controls, and therefore control testing, are not limited to the first line. The risk function should also exercise oversight and challenge over the control testing. In my view, this should not simply mean a repeat of the initial control test but a thematic review of controls for a particular activity, risk or important business service/critical operation. The risk function should also consider testing the relevant controls following a risk incident.

It is important that control owners are able to demonstrate their ability to apply the control. One weekend, a good friend, and knowledgeable risk manager, decided to take advantage of the fine weather and cycle to a nearby place of interest. As an astute risk manager, he realised there was a danger his bicycle would have a puncture so he went online and purchased a cycle repair kit. As luck would have it, he duly punctured enroute and realised he had never before repaired a puncture. In the end, he managed to access a video online showing how to use a puncture repair kit, and he successfully completed his trip. The moral of this tale is that while it is good to have controls you must be able to demonstrate you know how to use them.

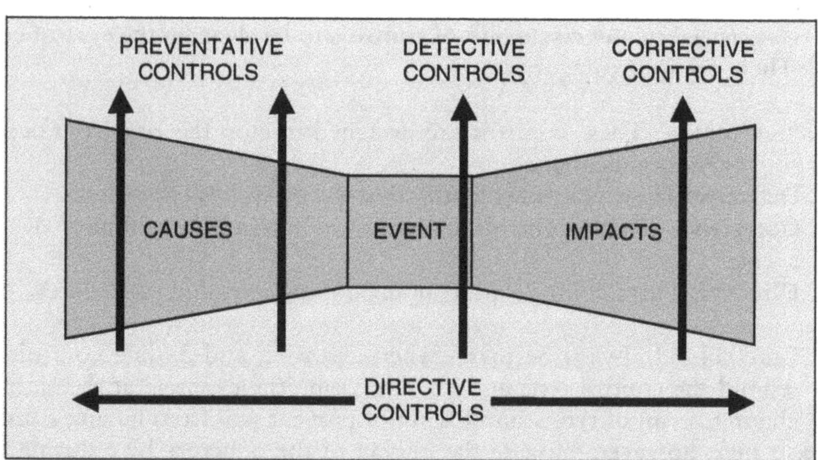

FIGURE 7.1 The Bow Tie

Controls can be tested by:

- Self-certification or enquiry – the control owner attests that the control is working;
- Examination – the control is examined to assess that it is working effectively and efficiently;
- Observation – real-time oversight of the control in action shows if it is working as designed;
- Reperformance – the control is performed again, this is the strongest form of testing.

Having been required to undertake control testing of my own controls in the past, it is clear that the effectiveness of the control testing can be influenced by: the vigour and enthusiasm of the tester, the independence of the tester, the frequency of the testing and the scope and sample size.

Controls are usually assessed for efficiency, design and effectiveness. Efficiency assesses the resources required to undertake the control and the length of time that it takes. I am sure we have all heard of the four eyes principle that might, for example, be associated with payments. One person would produce the payment and check if it is OK and a second individual would repeat the check. Introducing a third or fourth person into the checking process may reduce the risk but it also makes the control less efficient. Nevertheless, I have seen firms where large payments are subject to many sets of eyes. The design focuses on how well the control was conceived and whether the control is fit for purpose. Effectiveness relates to the control's application in relation to the risk it seeks to control.

Unfortunately, increasing the number of controls may not mean less risk. An individual reviewing a payment that is subsequently reviewed by multiple members of staff may not be very diligent as they know others will hopefully spot any errors. In addition, accountability becomes diluted. As we look at poor controls, we recognise that they generally fall into three types: optimistic controls that may not achieve their objectives and may require considerable intervention by the control owner; duplicative controls, where the control is performed several times, usually by different members of staff and finally, more of the same type of control.

In order to assess controls, firms should measure their controls against the following criteria:

(1) Control type, including:
    - What controls are in place, and are they preventative, detective, corrective or directive;
    - What proportion of controls per risk are preventative;

- How long does a detective control take to detect. A detective control that quickly detects an incident enables a firm to respond quickly to that incident;
- Are the controls key controls;

(2) Control effectiveness, including:
- How effective are the controls;
- Have the controls failed previously, are there any incidents or losses;
- Is the control subject to an action plan to ensure or improve its effectiveness and efficiency;

(3) Control performance, including:
- How are the controls performed and does that impact their effectiveness;
- Are the controls manual or automated. Automated controls are usually seen as more effective than manual controls;

(4) Control design, including:
- What about the design of the controls. How were the controls conceived and are they fit for purpose;
- Is accountability for the control clear;

(5) Control effect, including:
- Do the controls impact likelihood, impact or both;

(6) Control testing, including:
- When were the controls last tested and by whom;
- Was the checker independent;
- What is the frequency of testing;
- What was the scope of the test;
- How was the test performed, was it by self-certification, examination or observation or reperformance;
- Have the second line performed a thematic review capturing the control;

(7) Have audit reviewed the control.

Measuring controls in this way will enable firms to fully understand their controls, whether further action is needed to strengthen them and what form that action should take.

In Chapter 6, we examined the way in which controls impact inherent risk, with controls accounting for the difference between inherent and residual risk. I have seen some firms that assess their controls against a numerical scorecard and use the outcome to determine the change between inherent

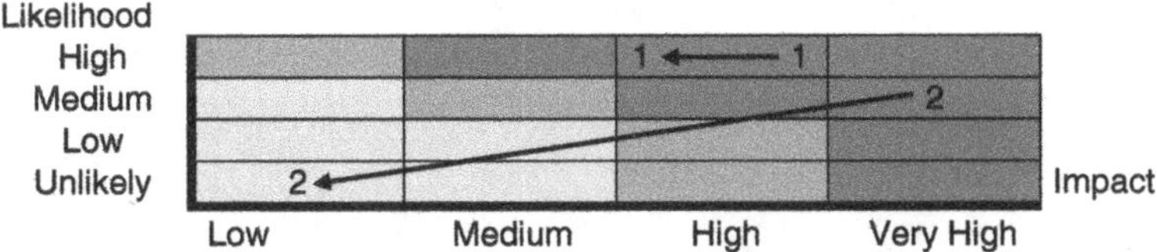

FIGURE 7.2 Inherent and Residual Risk

and residual risk. Unfortunately, this approach is difficult to calibrate and often creates problems when implemented. Nevertheless, there is clearly a relationship between the effectiveness and efficiency of our controls and the difference between inherent and residual risk. This point is illustrated in Figure 7.2. If, for example, as in risk 1, there is no difference between inherent and residual risk, then the controls are not effective. If there is a huge change between inherent risk and residual risk, as in risk 2, then we need to be very comfortable about how well designed and effectively and efficiently our controls operate.

Once firms have assessed their controls against the criteria listed above, they should then reconcile their controls assessment against the difference between inherent and residual risk. This will help identify any inconsistencies.

PART Three

Antifragility, Resilience and When Things Go Wrong

Unfortunately in some firms, operational risk has become a passive activity, usually involving undertaking RCSAs and collecting losses, and often subject to operational risk fatigue within the organisation. Perhaps something a firm had to do to satisfy the regulator, rather than something it wanted to do and saw value in. As a result, some of us feared for the future of the discipline. Fortunately for us all, the regulatory focus on operational resilience and third-party risk management has given the discipline the opportunity to evolve and re-establish itself as a key player within the firm. After all, operational resilience is the outcome of effective operational risk management. In the absence of efficient and effective operational risk management, firms will be increasingly subject to operational disruptions, incurring the wrath of their customers, politicians and regulators.

In this part, we discuss operational resilience, risk incidents, root cause analysis and third-party risk management. Recent regulatory publications globally have focused on these elements, and while we have captured the current position here, readers will need to ensure that they monitor regulatory announcements and expectations going forward.

CHAPTER 8

Operational Resilience – The Outcome of Effective ORM

It's not the strongest of a species that survives, nor the most intelligent, but the ones most resilient and responsive to change.

—Charles Darwin

Operational resilience is the hottest topic in financial services and has been so for some years. Regulators in the UK began focusing on operational resilience in 2016/17 and published a Discussion Paper (DP) in July 2018: **'Building the UK Financial Sector's Operational Resilience'**. Unusually – and positively – this was a joint discussion paper issued by the PRA, UK FCA and Bank of England, in which they set out their thoughts. The DP was reputedly one of the most downloaded ever, and in terms of popularity, it was the Harry Potter of regulatory publications and attracted substantial attention in the industry.

Initially, there was enormous confusion about what the term 'operational resilience' meant. Was it a new risk? A new name or rebranding of business continuity management (BCM)? Was it a new operational risk? Or something else altogether?

Initially, uncertainty abounded in the UK. Following the publication of the DP, some consultants began promoting this as a new risk type and offered services to build new operational resilience functions, tool-kits and so forth. Fortunately, regulators were alert to the risk of creating another conduct 'risk' fiasco and attempted to nip it in the bud. They clarified in speeches (as the DP wasn't explicit) that operational resilience is *not* a new risk but an **outcome** delivered through **effective operational risk management**. Speaking at a conference in 2019, UK FCA's Nick Strange noted: 'Thinking of operational resilience as the **outcome we are seeking**, and **operational risk**

management as the means by which this is achieved gives a clear focus for investment in both… So, to recap, **operational resilience is the outcome** we are seeking, and to do that, we must manage **operational risk effectively**'.[1]

The hugely respected ex-UK FSA and PRA regulator, Lydon Nelson, gave the keynote speech at the **Operational Risk Europe Conference** in June 2018 (shortly before the DP was published). Nelson located operational resilience squarely in the bailiwick of ORM, speaking about the opportunities that the regulatory focus on resilience would present for OR managers. Nelson reflected: 'Recently I was asked to say a few words to a group of new Operational Risk managers. I told them that they would be pioneers. I foresaw that operational resilience would be seen to be on a par with financial resilience and a key part of a firm's risk profile'.[2] In fact, operational resilience is one component of the broader **enterprise resilience** picture (see Figure 8.1).

Given the high-profile failures of multiple banks and numerous costly state bailouts, it's no surprise **financial resilience** was the first area that international regulators sought to address following the GFC as part of a tsunami of new regulations. The stop-gap Basel 2.5 (which addressed immediate inadequacies in the capital framework, especially concerning securitisation) and the more substantive Basel 3 reforms were essentially about improving financial resilience through requiring banks to hold more capital and more liquidity (introducing a new leverage ratio as a backstop to risk-weighted capital ratios). Basel 3 was published in December 2010, and phased implementation began in 2013. Of relevance to ORM – and the ultimate fate of AMA – one of the themes of the post-GRC reforms was an increased scepticism of quantitative capital models.

After addressing financial resilience, regulators turned to **strategic resilience**, focusing on business model viability, governance and accountability.

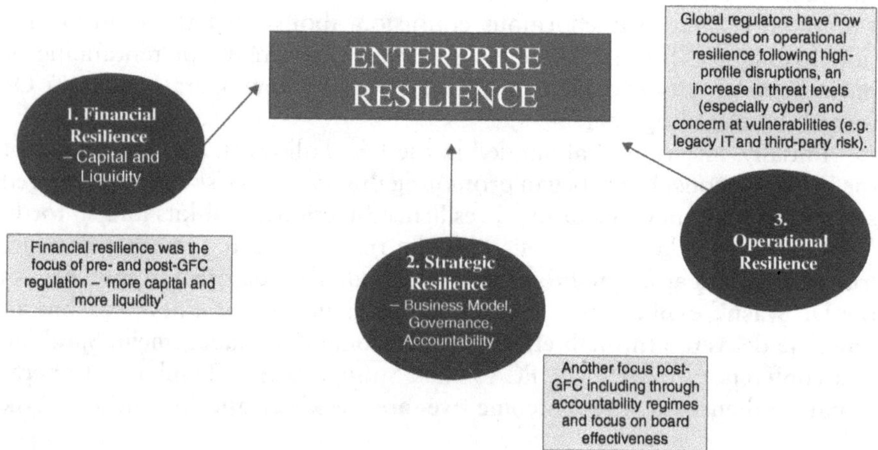

FIGURE 8.1 Enterprise Resilience

In the UK, the **Senior Managers and Certified Persons Regime** (SMCR) was introduced in 2016 for banks (and later extended to insurance and all other UK FCA-regulated firms in 2019) to hold senior people accountable for regulatory breaches. The level of prescription in SMCR was even more significant than in the Approved Persons regime, which it replaced, and it symbolised a profound loss of trust in firms following the egregious misconduct exposed during the GFC.[3] The largest firms were required to create a **Responsibilities Map,** mapping out in detail the assignment of responsibilities across the organisation, including delegations and illustrating clarity on reporting lines. Firms were required to assign and document regulatory **Prescribed Responsibilities** for individual **Senior Managers,** captured in the **Statement of Responsibility.** Senior Managers were held personally responsible with a **Duty of Responsibility** for any regulatory breach in their area of responsibility unless they could demonstrate they'd taken **reasonable steps.** The UK FCA initially proposed adopting a **presumption of guilt,** but this reversal of the normal *presumption of innocence* in English law attracted significant pushback and dropped – much to the relief of many senior managers!

Firms were required to submit detailed applications to regulators for approval of senior manager roles, including skills gap assessments with action plans to address gaps. Some applicants – typically NEDs, CEOs, CROs, CCOs and COOs at medium to large firms – may then be subject to SMF Interviews, whereby, normally, the firm's supervisory team plus a Senior Advisor (known colloquially as 'Grey Panthers') subjected candidates to intensive grilling. Candidates who performed poorly in the first round of the interview would be invited to a second recorded interview; this was a subtle message to the firm to find a better candidate!

After approval, **senior managers** had to demonstrate and document **reasonable steps** in their decisions and judgements. A regulator's favourite mantra – **Absence of Evidence, is Evidence of Absence** – went into overdrive concerning SMCR, with compliance and HR functions in many firms advising senior managers to keep detailed records – day books – of decision-making and where they'd provided challenge in committees and meetings. There were many anecdotes at the time of ***kabuki-style*** committee meetings, where senior managers presented rehearsed and pre-agreed 'challenges' that would be carefully documented in the committee minutes to tick the compliance box – in the knowledge regulators were more than likely to review them.

SMCR also captured **Certified Persons,** which included almost all other staff in the firm (other than catering staff, security, etc.), who were also subject to detailed requirements, including annual certification and training on the **Conduct Rules.** Senior Managers were also subject to an additional set of **Senior Manager Conduct Rules.** The yearly staff certification was a significant compliance exercise in large firms with questionable value.

As part of the focus on strategic resilience and accountability, regulators also addressed the topics of **incentives** and **remuneration**, areas that had previously been considered the sole responsibility of firms and their boards of directors. BCBS published the **Principles for Sound Compensation Practices** in 2009, followed by the **EU's CRD IV** implemented in 2014. The UK implemented a **Remuneration Code** in 2009 before CRD IV but then updated it to reflect the new EU provisions. The new rules in the UK applied to **Identified Staff** who could have a material impact on the firm's risk profile (**'material risk takers'**), including members of senior management, risk-takers and key employees in control functions. The new rules included highly interventionist measures including a bonus cap of 100% of salary, deferral of at least 40% (up to 60% for the most senior or with huge bonuses) of bonuses over a minimum of three years (up to seven years) and clawback rules (meaning bonuses earned in the past seven years could be 'clawed back' in the event of misconduct), a requirement for firms to have a Remuneration Policy and establish Remuneration Committee and public disclosures.

In our time at the regulator, especially before the GFC, supervisors were very wary of taking any actions that could stray into the regulator being seen as a shadow director. The new rules on remuneration put the regulator way beyond this and firmly into the boardroom, with a requirement for the larger firms (banks, building societies and PRA regulated investment firms) to submit their proposed salary and bonuses to the regulators for review and approval.

After addressing Financial Resilience and Strategic Resilience, regulators focused on operational resilience. Regulators in the UK focused on operational resilience for several reasons illustrated in Figure 8.2:

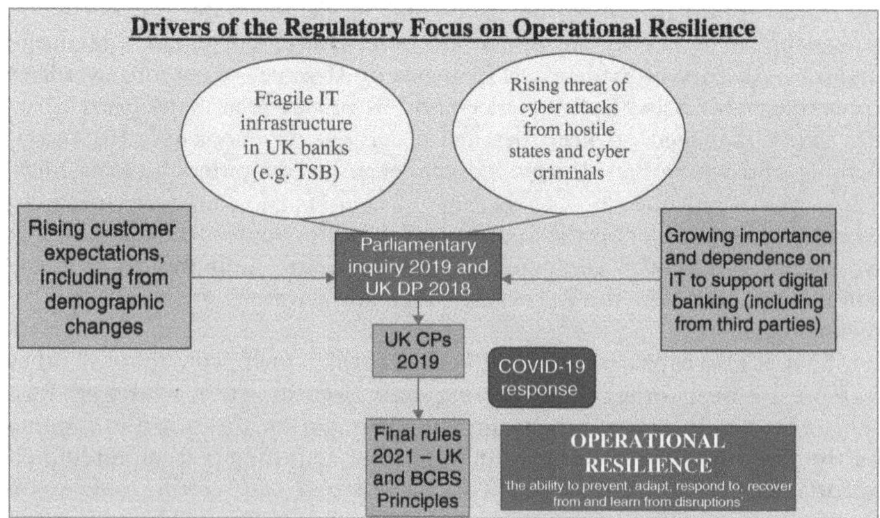

FIGURE 8.2 Drivers of the Regulatory Focus on Operational Resilience in the UK

IT MELTDOWNS IN UK BANKS

Just as the original focus of regulators on ORM was driven by scandals (including especially the Barings collapse), so the focus of regulators on operational resilience was driven by a series of incidents at UK banks driven by mismanagement of IT and IT change and causing significant market disruption and consumer harm.

In June 2012, the **NatWest/RBS IT meltdown** affected millions of customers across the Royal Bank of Scotland (RBS) Group, including NatWest and Ulster Bank.[4] The IT failure lasted several weeks, disrupting customers' ability to access their accounts, process payments and perform routine banking transactions. The issue stemmed from a wrong software update, affecting systems used for day-to-day banking operations. The IT meltdown caused significant public outrage and regulatory scrutiny from UK FCA and PRA and began to attract political attention as MPs received complaints from their constituents. The RBS Group eventually faced heavy fines from the UK FCA and PRA for failing to manage its IT infrastructure properly and causing severe operational disruptions. The incident highlighted the risks of large financial institutions' outdated and complex IT systems and the failure of boards and senior managers to manage IT risk and change.

The NatWest/RBS IT meltdown was surpassed only by the **TSB IT meltdown,** which occurred in **April 2018,** following the bank's attempted migration of its customer data from the systems of its former owner, **Lloyds Banking Group,** to a new IT platform managed by **Banco Sabadell,** which had acquired TSB in 2015. The migration went disastrously wrong, resulting in widespread service disruptions that left **millions of customers** unable to access their accounts, make payments or perform basic banking operations. The disruption at TSB lasted for several weeks and led to significant customer harm, reputational damage and a regulatory investigation. The UK FCA and the PRA launched investigations into handling the IT migration. TSB faced criticism for its poor transition management and failure to test the new system adequately before the rollout.

The meltdown again highlighted the importance of robust IT systems in the financial sector, particularly during change projects involving critical IT infrastructure. The **Slaughter and May report** into the **TSB IT meltdown** of April 2018, commissioned by TSB's parent company **Banco Sabadell** (doubtless after significant pressure from the regulator), identified several key findings regarding the crisis's root causes and poor handling. The independent review, published in **October 2019,** highlighted various issues that contributed to the failed IT migration and the subsequent disruption and harm to consumers.

Some of the key findings in the Slaughter and May report include:

1. **Inadequate testing and planning:** The report found that **TSB** and **Sabadell** failed to conduct adequate testing of the new IT platform before the system migration. Critical problems were not identified or addressed during the testing phase, leading to system failures when the new platform went live.
2. **Complexity of the migration:** The report highlighted that the bank underestimated the IT migration's complexity. TSB was moving from the Lloyds Banking Group IT system, which had supported the bank for years, to a new system (Proteo4UK) managed by Banco Sabadell. The transition proved to be far more challenging than anticipated.
3. **Governance failures:** The report criticised the **governance and oversight** of the migration. It found that senior management at both TSB and Sabadell failed to understand the risks involved in the migration clearly and did not implement adequate risk mitigation strategies.
4. **Supplier management issues:** There were issues with managing **Sabadell's IT supplier,** Sabis, which was responsible for the new platform. The report noted that communication between TSB, Sabadell and Sabis was insufficient, leading to delays in resolving problems during the migration.
5. **Inadequate customer communication:** Handling customer communication during the crisis was another significant issue. The report found that TSB failed to provide clear and timely information to customers regarding the nature and duration of the problems, exacerbating customer frustration and reputational damage.
6. **Board responsibility:** The report emphasised that the TSB board and senior executives bore significant responsibility for the failure, as they were overly optimistic about the migration process and did not respond quickly enough when issues arose.
7. **Cultural and structural issues:** The report noted **cultural differences** between TSB and Banco Sabadell, particularly in IT management and risk appetite, which further complicated the migration process and the response to IT failures.

The findings of the Slaughter and May report resulted in significant criticism of TSB's leadership and **TSB's CEO, Paul Pester,** had already resigned in September 2018. The report also triggered further regulatory investigations by the **UK FCA** and **PRA**. The report emphasised that more significant preparation, governance and transparency could have mitigated the impact of the IT issues and the report recommended stronger oversight for future large-scale IT projects.

The IT meltdowns caused such negative publicity in the UK and doubtless much angry correspondence in UK Parliamentary Members' (MPs) mailbags that the Treasury Select Committee took the unusual step (given the PRA and UK FCA should have been responsible for overseeing this within their firms) of launching a Parliamentary Inquiry specifically on the issue of **'IT Failures in the Financial Services Sector'** in **November 2018.** The inquiry was prompted by the high-profile IT failures in the banking sector and concerns about the resilience of financial services infrastructure in an increasingly digital environment. The main findings of the inquiry are set out below.

Main Findings of the Parliamentary Inquiry:

1. **Frequent and severe IT failures:** The inquiry found that IT failures in the banking sector were frequent and had severe consequences for customers. It highlighted several high-profile incidents, including those already mentioned above at TSB and RBS, as well as Barclays and HSBC, that caused widespread service disruptions, leaving customers without access to banking services for prolonged periods.
2. **Lack of investment in IT infrastructure:** Many banks relied on outdated IT systems that were not fit for purpose in a modern, digital environment. The inquiry criticised financial institutions for underinvesting in IT infrastructure, particularly legacy systems, leading to vulnerabilities.
3. **Insufficient board-level focus on IT resilience:** The inquiry concluded that bank boards and senior executives often did not prioritise IT resilience and operational risk to the extent required. There was a lack of board-level oversight and accountability for IT systems.
4. **Impact on consumers:** The inquiry emphasised the profound effect of IT failures on consumers, notably when they resulted in the inability to access funds, make payments or receive wages.
5. **Regulatory gaps:** The inquiry identified gaps in the regulatory oversight of IT systems in financial institutions. Although the UK FCA and PRA were responsible for supervising financial services firms, the inquiry suggested that regulators needed to take a more proactive stance in ensuring firms had robust IT systems and processes in place.
6. **Recommendations for accountability and oversight:** The committee suggested that senior managers be personally accountable for major IT failures, aligning with the SMCR.

7. **Publish information:** The committee also called for financial services firms to publish information on their operational resilience and IT risk management practices to improve transparency and consumer confidence.
8. **Enhanced compensation and redress mechanisms:** The inquiry recommended that banks strengthen their compensation and redress mechanisms for customers affected by IT failures. It urged firms to respond quickly to ensure customers do not suffer financial losses due to service outages.

The inquiry served as a wake-up call to the UK banking and financial services sector, highlighting the need for more significant investment in IT infrastructure, more robust oversight from both firms' senior management and from regulators, and improved **operational resilience** to avoid such failures impacting consumers and markets in the future.

The Parliamentary Inquiry inevitably played a significant role in the UK regulators' focus on operational resilience and their final policy and, not for the first time, to introduce detailed requirements ahead of the high-level principles being developed by BCBS, which would not publish its final principles until March 2021. Although we can understand the pressure UK regulators were under to move quickly, we believe it would have been better for them to wait until after the BCBS Principles were published and to then publish more detailed rules and guidance supporting those. By taking this approach, the UK regulators would have avoided some of the differences that inevitably developed between the UK rules and the BCBS in terms of terminology and approach.

THE RISING THREAT OF CYBERCRIME

At the same time as the IT meltdowns at major UK banks suggested their IT systems were lacking the necessary resilience, the threat landscape from hostile criminal gangs and state actors was increasing. Between **2018 and 2020**, there was a marked increase in **cybercrime** and **cyber threats**, driven by factors such as the growth of digital banking, the rise of ransomware and the increased risk exposure due to greater reliance on technology. The UK FCA reported a significant increase in the volume of incidents reported to them from 229 in 2017–2018 to 916 in the following year 2018–2019.[5]

Ransomware became one of the most prevalent and destructive forms of cybercrime during this period and reports from **Europol** and **Interpol** in 2019 and 2020[6] indicated that ransomware attacks on businesses and healthcare institutions increased significantly. Attackers increasingly used more sophisticated techniques, demanding large sums of money, often in cryptocurrency, and targeted critical infrastructure.

Data breaches were also becoming more frequent, with high-profile breaches such as Capital One and Facebook in 2019 exposing the personal data of millions of individuals. **Identity theft** also surged, with criminals using stolen data to commit fraud. The UK National Cyber Security Centre (NCSC) highlighted fraudsters targeting consumers and businesses through email phishing and social engineering to gain access to sensitive information. **Phishing attacks** significantly increased between 2018 and 2020, and the Anti-Phishing Working Group (APWG) reported a record number of phishing attacks in 2020, with cybercriminals exploiting the COVID-19 pandemic to trick users into revealing sensitive information. Many phishing campaigns involved the impersonation of healthcare organisations or governments, especially those related to COVID-19 relief efforts.

Targeting of Critical Infrastructure: Cyberattacks targeting critical infrastructure – including healthcare systems, utilities and government institutions – increased. During the pandemic, the NCSC reported multiple attacks on the UK National Health Service and healthcare providers across Europe as criminals sought to exploit vulnerabilities.

Overall, the 2018–2021 period, during which regulators were developing their policy on operational resilience, saw a growing convergence of traditional crime with cybercrime, as criminals increasingly used the methods of cybercrime to commit fraud, identity theft and ransomware attacks.

UK REGULATORS ISSUE CONSULTATION PAPERS ON OPERATIONAL RESILIENCE

UK regulators finally published their Consultation Papers in December 2019, and these reflected the drivers outlined above:

- **UK FCA Consultation Paper (CP19/32):** This paper outlined the UK FCA's expectations for firms to identify their Important Business Services (IBS), set Impact Tolerances for these services, map the services and test their ability to remain within these tolerances during disruptions to prevent intolerable harm to consumers or threats to market integrity.
- **PRA Consultation Paper (CP29/19):** The PRA's consultation also focused on the steps in the UK FCA paper (identifying IBS, mapping, setting tolerances and testing) but emphasised the need to have adequate operational resilience to prevent risks to firm safety and soundness and financial stability.

At the same time BCBS and UK regulators consulted on their new operational resilience policy, the COVID-19 pandemic struck. The pandemic certainly increased the importance and emphasis on operational resilience – it was not just an academic exercise anymore! COVID-19 also broadened the focus from IT resources to all types of resources (including people), and by forcing firms to go through a real disruption, e.g. remote working became the norm overnight for many firms, it revealed the importance of resilience and having the ability to adapt in the event of severe but plausible disruptions.

In addition, remote work mandated by government lockdown policies highlighted the **cyber threats due to remote work.** The shift to remote work in 2020 due to the COVID-19 pandemic exposed many organisations to new or heightened cyber risks (some firms had been cautious of remote working previously for this very reason). A report by McAfee in 2020[7] highlighted that remote work increased vulnerabilities due to the widespread use of insecure home networks, personal devices and insufficient cybersecurity controls in remote settings. Cybercriminals exploited these vulnerabilities with increased phishing attacks, malware and attempts to breach virtual private networks (VPNs). In the USA, according to the FBI Internet Crime Complaint Center (IC3), cybercrime complaints spiked in 2020, with the FBI receiving almost 20,000 COVID-19-related cyber complaints by the end of April 2020 alone.[8]

BCBS CONSULTATION

In August 2020, nine months after the UK regulators had issued their detailed rules for comment, the BCBS issued its Principles for Operational Resilience for comments.

The BCBS published seven principles that are set out in Figure 8.3.

BCBS AND UK REGULATORS ISSUE FINAL RULES

The BCBS Principles were issued in March 2021 at the same time as the UK regulators issued their final policy. The UK regulators issued a suite of documents setting out their detailed new rules.

1. **UK FCA Policy Statement (PS21/3):**
   - Titled **'Building Operational Resilience: Impact Tolerances for Important Business Services'**, this policy statement outlined the UK FCA's final rules and guidance on operational resilience.

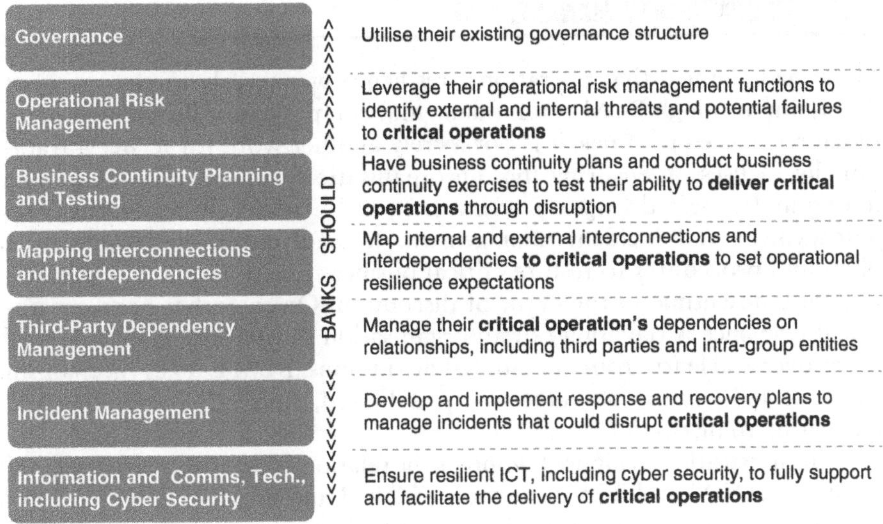

FIGURE 8.3 BCBS Principles for Operational Resilience.[9]

2. **PRA Policy Statement (PS6/21):**
   - The PRA published **'Operational Resilience: Impact Tolerances for Important Business Services'** (PS6/21), which provided similar rules to the UK FCA's for PRA-regulated firms.
3. **Bank of England Policy Statement on FMIs:**
   - The Bank of England published its operational resilience policy statement for **Financial Market Infrastructures (FMIs)**, including central counterparties (CCPs) and payment systems.
4. **Supervisory Statements:**
   - The PRA also issued **Supervisory Statement SS1/21,** which provided more detailed expectations for how firms should implement the operational resilience framework, particularly concerning governance and the role of senior management.

The new UK regulations went way beyond the BCBS Principles by prescribing, in detail, the approach firms must take to deliver the heightened regulatory expectations on resilience. At the same time, regulators issued new rules on third-party risk management (see Chapter 10) and emphasised the need for firms to look at both sets of new rules together as they were intimately related.

RELATIONSHIP BETWEEN OPERATIONAL RESILIENCE AND BUSINESS CONTINUITY MANAGEMENT

Many had claimed that operational resilience was merely a rebranding of BCM, but although BCM is a fundamental component of **delivering** operational resilience outcomes, it is not merely another word for it. BCM traditionally focuses on ensuring that an organisation can continue operations during and after a disruption or incident, and it is closely related to **crisis management** and **incident management**. It involves the development of plans and procedures to restore critical business functions and systems and minimise downtime in the event of disruption. On the other hand, operational resilience is the ability of an organisation to prevent, adapt, respond to, recover and learn from operational disruptions. BCM is a key mechanism by which these **resilience outcomes** are achieved, especially responding and recovering to disruptions.

The illustration in Figure 8.4 shows the relationship between Operational Resilience, ORM and BCM. The tools of ORM and BCM are essential ways to deliver resilience outcomes. Firms must leverage the work done on BCM, including Business Impact Analysis, Recovery Time Objectives (RTOs) and resource mapping, to deliver operational resilience outcomes and meet the heightened regulatory expectations. For example, in BCM testing, it's essential to identify where the tests relate to critical resources (e.g. systems)

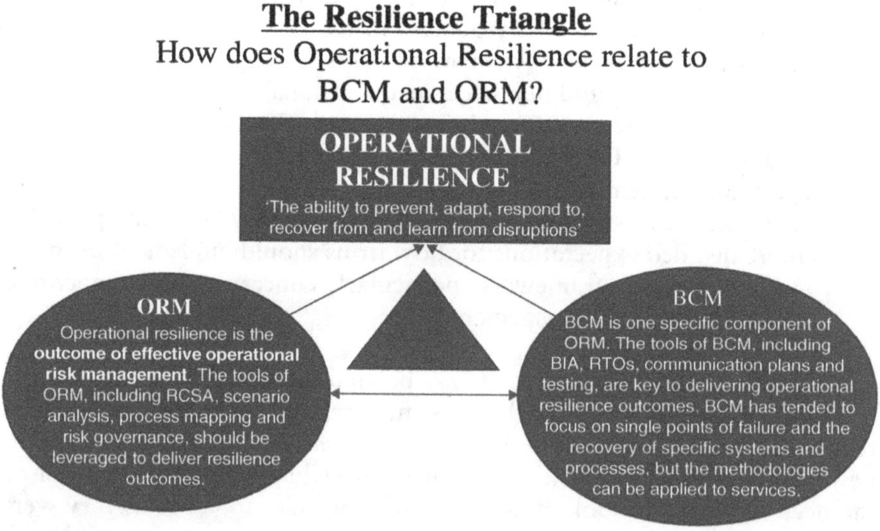

FIGURE 8.4 The Resilience Triangle

supporting IBS and to ensure consideration of impact tolerances when testing against RTOs.

BCM is an essential part of the broader NFR umbrella (Figure 8.5). See Chapter 2 for more on the NFR Umbrella. All the different elements of the umbrella are important for delivering resilience outcomes, but in particular BCM and TPRM (see more on TPRM in Chapter 10).

UK REGULATORY APPROACH AND MEETING REGULATORY EXPECTATIONS

In March 2021, the UK regulators published a comprehensive framework on operational resilience, which set out new rules and guidance for firms. The UK regulators defined Operational Resilience as: **the ability to prevent, adapt, respond to, recover from and learn from disruptions.** This aligned with the BCBS definition. The UK rules require firms to identify their IBS – those that, if disrupted, could cause intolerable harm to consumers, market integrity, firm safety and soundness or financial stability. Firms are required to map their dependencies (i.e. the critical resources required to deliver them) for these services and set impact tolerances. Central to the UK approach is the requirement to test IBS with severe but plausible scenarios to test the firm's ability to remain within impact tolerances. Firms must also have communication plans and learn from disruptions. The regulatory requirement emphasises proportionality; however, all firms have to follow the same basic steps, so the extent to which the rules are proportionate rests on the fact that larger firms are likely to have more IBS.

The UK FCA and UK PRA published detailed rules in March 2021 with an initial deadline (to have completed mapping, identified IBS, set impact tolerances and begun a programme of scenario testing) by the end of March 2022. By, at the latest, the end of March 2025 (four years after the first publication of the rules), firms must ensure their IBS are sufficiently resilient in the event of severe but plausible disruptions that can remain within established impact tolerances. In other words, if a tolerance of T + 1 day is set for an IBS if a disruption occurs, the firm must be able to resume delivery of the service within the T + 1 day tolerance, e.g. implementing 'Plan Bs' or recovering the disrupted critical resources.

Unlike traditional scenario testing for BCM and ORM, the operational resilience tests must assume that disruption has occurred (i.e. likelihood is irrelevant) and focus on identifying vulnerabilities that may compromise the delivery of IBS. When the firm identifies vulnerabilities, it must address them before the end of March 2025. Regulators are unlikely to be forgiving if firms have failed to identify vulnerabilities or taken action to address them, especially given the four year implementation period.

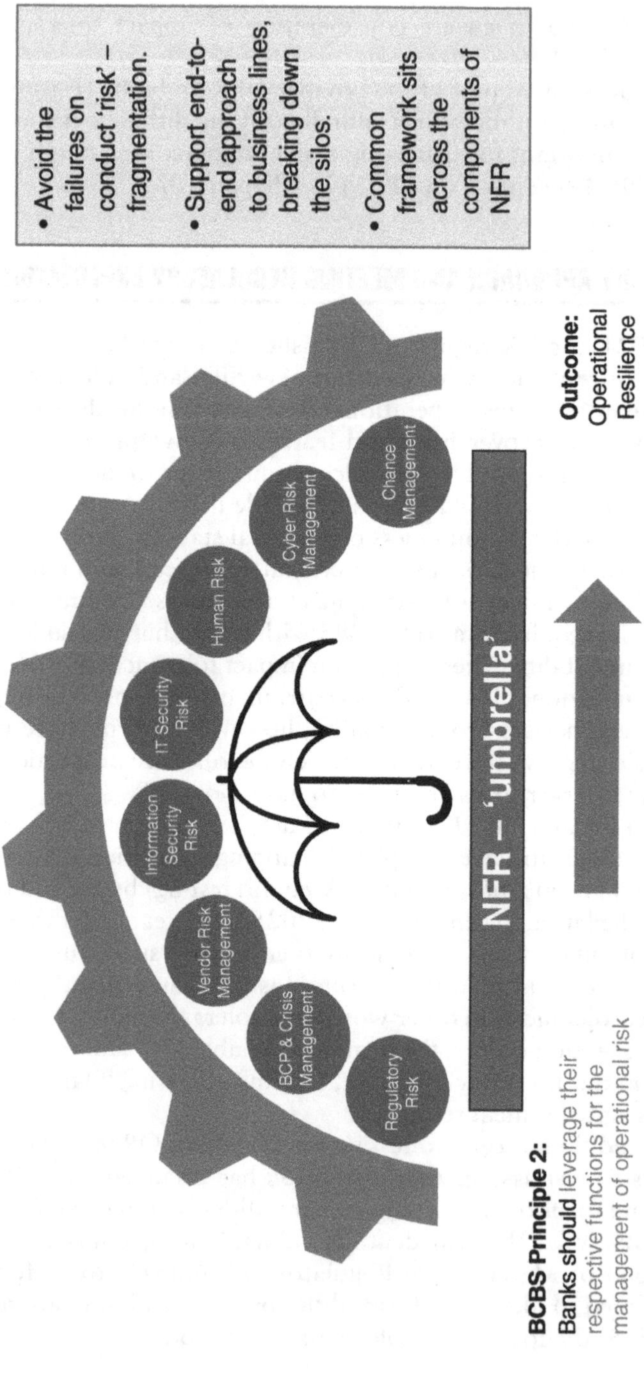

Regulatory Risk

BCP & Crisis Management

Vendor Risk Management

Information Security Risk

IT Security Risk

Human Risk

Cyber Risk Management

Chance Management

NFR – 'umbrella'

- Avoid the failures on conduct 'risk' – fragmentation.
- Support end-to-end approach to business lines, breaking down the silos.
- Common framework sits across the components of NFR

BCBS Principle 2:
Banks should leverage their respective functions for the management of operational risk

Outcome:
Operational Resilience

FIGURE 8.5 The NFR Umbrella

The UK's rules on **operational resilience**, published by the **UK FCA, PRA** and **Bank of England** in March 2021, set out key requirements for financial services firms to ensure they can withstand and recover from significant operational disruptions. These rules are part of a broader regulatory effort to enhance the safety and stability of the financial system by improving enterprise resilience in firms.

The requirements for the UK are shown in Figure 8.6.

Step 1. Create Operational Framework: Governance, Policy and Process

- Operational resilience must be a key priority of the firm's governance, with clear oversight from senior management and the Board.
- Firms must assign responsibilities for managing and implementing operational resilience, and senior managers can be held accountable for failures under the SMCR regime.
- The BCBS and UK regulators expect the Board of Directors to play a key role in operational resilience. The table in Figure 8.7 illustrates the expectations of UK regulators on the Board on approving IBS, impact tolerances and self-assessment.
- In the UK, regulators expect the SMF24/Chief Operations Officer (COO) to be responsible for **implementation** and **reporting** on operational resilience. In our experience, many firms took the pragmatic decision to assign the creation of the policy to the COO. However, we expect ownership of the operational resilience policy to transfer to the second line as part of the embedding journey. Most financial services firms use the three lines of defence or the updated three lines approach, which requires ownership of risk policies to sit in the second line.

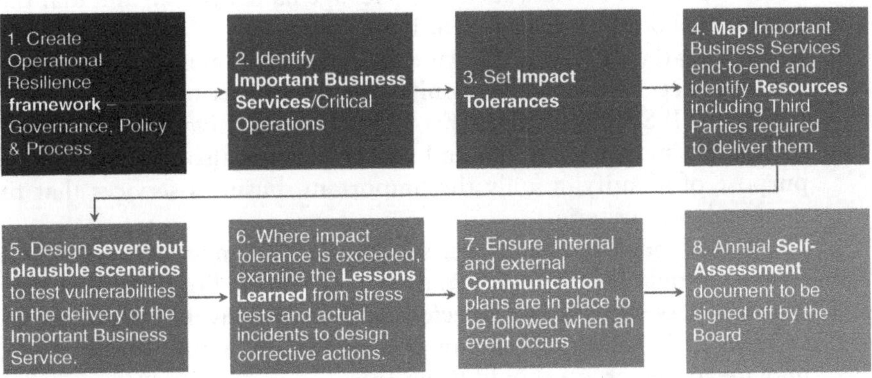

FIGURE 8.6 The Eight Steps to Resilience

What?	When?	Judgements Required
Important Business Services	At least annually or if there is a material change to the firm's business or the market in which it operates.	- What's a 'material' change? - Changes to customer profile – e.g. increase in vulnerable consumers (cost of living crisis)
Impact Tolerances	At least annually or if there is a material change to the firm's business or the market in which it operates.	- What's a 'material' change? - Customer profile re vulnerability and point at which suffer intolerable harm
Self-Assessment document/ Annual Board Review (Basel)	'Regularly'	- What's constitutes 'regularly'? - Regulator: self-assessment must be a 'living document' - Can be requested at any time - Expected to include the compliance journey to 2025 - **Absence of evidence is evidence of absence**

FIGURE 8.7 Requirements on the Board and Judgements Required

Transferring ownership of the operational resilience policy to the second line avoids the unsatisfactory situation where the first line creates the framework, implements it and reviews compliance with it, thereby marking their homework and setting the exam!

Step 2. Identify Important Business Services:

- Firms must identify their IBS, services that if disrupted, could cause intolerable harm to consumers or pose a risk to market integrity, financial stability, or the firm's viability. Each firm was required to assess which services are critical to its operations and the broader financial system and assign these as 'important'.
- Regulators clarified that the IBS should be a separate service rather than a bundle of services such as a package bank account and that the end users should be clearly identifiable.
- Identifying the IBS from the wider population of business services is the first step in this process. Initially, some firms identified a large number of IBS; not only does this commit to a massive burden of work to conduct mapping, testing and so forth, but it also undermines the purpose of identifying only the **'important'** business services that fit the regulatory criteria.
- Firms are required to keep their selection of IBS under review, with at least an annual formal review and approval by the Board. It's essential that business services not selected as IBS are actively monitored, as changes in business volumes or the number or nature of customers may mean the service should be an IBS.

Step 3. Setting Impact Tolerances:

- Firms are required to set **impact tolerances** for each IBS, which is the **maximum tolerable level of disruption** that the firm can accept before it causes intolerable harm to customers or market integrity or threatens firm safety and soundness or financial stability.
- Impact tolerances should be measured in terms of duration (e.g. how long the service can be unavailable before the threshold is breached) and other relevant measures.
- Initially, regulators mandated that firms assign at least one duration-based impact tolerance for each IBS. However, in more recent communication with firms, regulators have requested firms to consider whether other types of tolerances, other than duration, may be appropriate, e.g. the number of vulnerable customers impacted. In the coming years, we expect the large firms, at least, to set other types of tolerances. The challenge of setting non-duration-based tolerances is they need monitoring, and firms must implement mechanisms to, for instance, quickly identify how many vulnerable customers have been impacted by a disruption.
- Figure 8.8 illustrates the relationship between impact tolerance for intolerable harm and other concepts, including RTOs and risk appetite. The key point is that intolerable harm should be a very high threshold beyond mere inconvenience or harm. Intolerable harm is a level of harm from which the consumer cannot easily recover through, e.g. compensation.

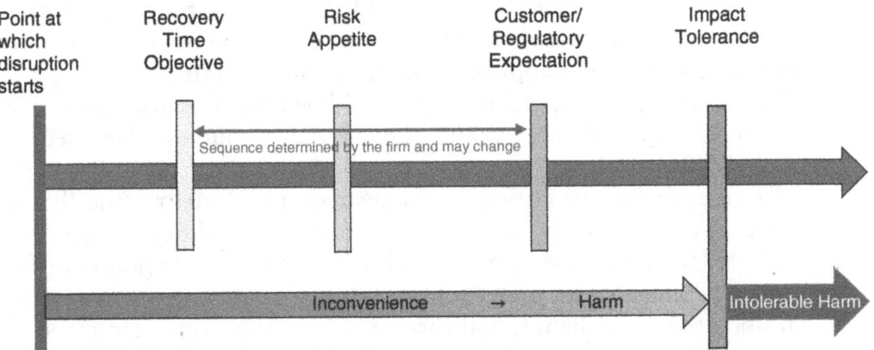

FIGURE 8.8 Impact Tolerances and Intolerable Harm

- In our experience, setting impact tolerances has been the area firms have found most challenging, and it's vital to devote sufficient time and resources (including engaging with board members, including NEDs) to get this right. An approach we've found works well is to hold a workshop with key stakeholders to determine a range, e.g. 1–5 days, and then to present this to a wider group to narrow it down to a specific tolerance.
- In the UK, due to the 'twin-peaks' model of regulation, most firms must set separate impact tolerances for UK FCA and PRA. Although, in principle, regulators have said both tolerances can be the same, it's unlikely this will be appropriate in practice. Regulators are likely to challenge a firm that has adopted this approach, and this is because the time taken to breach the tolerance related to causing intolerable harm to consumers will be much shorter than the time a disruption would take to threaten the firm's prudential safety, given capital and liquidity buffers. It will inevitably raise serious concerns from the regulator if the impact tolerance for the PRA suggests a disruption could quickly threaten the firm's safety and soundness.

Step 4. Mapping Critical Resources:

- Firms must map the critical resources (people, processes, technology, information, facilities and third/nth parties) that support their IBS. Mapping is a fundamental step to gaining a clear understanding of the dependencies and vulnerabilities in delivering IBS.
- In our experience, a top-down approach to resource mapping is the most efficient and effective, utilising SMEs to compile the mapping and then subjecting it to review and challenge through a series of workshops. It's advisable to involve a range of experts in the mapping process so that the mapping is complete and accurate.
- The process for delivering the IBS should be broken down into a series of steps (e.g. 4–6 steps), and the critical resources identified for each step.
- After identifying the critical resources required to deliver the IBS, it's important to identify weaknesses and vulnerabilities, which may include lack of substitutability, high complexity, single points of failure and concentration risk. 'Substitutability' is a fundamental concept in operational resilience, and the absence of substitute resources – in the event one is disrupted – needs to be identified and addressed.
- Given the volume of change in FS, it's advisable to keep the resource mapping up-to-date and to do this formally as part of the annual review of the self-assessment.

Step 5. Scenario Testing:

- Firms must conduct regular **scenario testing** to assess whether they can remain within their defined impact tolerances in the face of severe but plausible disruptions. These tests must simulate a variety of operational disruptions, such as cyberattacks, IT failures or natural disasters. The goal is to ensure firms are prepared for unexpected disruptions and can maintain IBS.
- The UK FCA requires firms to conduct the following five scenarios (these are now included in the UK FCA Handbook), and in our experience, firms have used these as a baseline for their testing programme and added additional scenarios based on events (internal and external):
  - Corruption, deletion or manipulation of data critical to delivery;
  - Unavailability of facilities or key people;
  - Unavailability of third-party services critical to delivery;
  - Disruption to other market participants;
  - Loss or reduced provision of the technology underpinning the delivery.
- Scenario testing for operational resilience has important differences from ORM testing (see below), but it's still important to leverage the results of this other testing in the resilience testing workshops.
- A key output from the testing is the identification of actions to address vulnerabilities, and it's good practice to maintain a vulnerability and action tracker, which should be escalated to governance to oversee and monitor progress.

Step 6. Lessons Learned:

- Where impact tolerances are exceeded, firms should examine **Lessons Learned** from scenario tests and actual incidents to design corrective actions to ensure they aren't repeated.

Step 7. Communication Plans:

- Firms should ensure internal and external **communication plans** are in place to be followed when an event occurs.
- In our experience, firms don't need to reinvent the wheel on communications, as existing communication plans (e.g. BCM and crisis management) can be enhanced to capture operational resilience, e.g. a trigger for the communication must include disruption to an IBS.
- It's important to test communication plans in the scenario testing process, to ensure they are appropriate and there are no gaps.

Step 8. Annual Self-Assessment:

- A requirement that is unique to the UK approach is that firms must create a self-assessment document signed off by the Board at least annually.
- The self-assessment must be a 'living document' and describe what the firm has done to implement the rules and guidance, describing the approach, results and next steps.
- Although the self-assessment is a UK requirement, it's good practice and recommended even for those outside of the UK. Maintaining a self-assessment of progress is a good discipline for those leading the work and extremely useful for second and third lines and regulators as a window on the approach and progress.

BCBS APPROACH AND DIFFERENCES TO THE UK APPROACH

The BCBS published **Principles for Operational Resilience** in March 2021.[10] The BCBS's approach to operational resilience is closely linked to its broader framework on risk management and capital adequacy.

The BCBS guidelines emphasise the need for banks to identify critical operations and interconnected risks that could lead to disruptions. The focus is on ensuring that banks can continue providing critical services during disruptions and have robust recovery plans. The BCBS approach is principles-based and significantly less prescriptive than the UK's approach.

There are several notable differences in terminology between the UK and BCBS policy. BCBS focuses on 'critical operations', which is broader than the UK concept of IBS – critical operations may include services and the critical resources required to deliver them. BCBS also requires firms to set 'tolerances for disruption' rather than 'impact tolerances', but these are synonymous.

Another clear difference is the UK's focus on **harm to consumers** and market integrity, which is not in the BCBS guidelines. The UK's approach is designed to ensure that operational resilience contributes directly to the protection of consumers rather than just the safety and soundness of firms and overall financial system stability.

The UK framework has detailed rules and guidance (including in the original CPs). Conversely, BCBS provides broader guidance, allowing national regulators to interpret and implement the guidelines according to their specific contexts. Many regulators have now developed policies on operational resilience in line with the BCBS Principles, and most have aligned closely with the BCBS. In our experience delivering training to many people based outside of the UK, many firms use UK rules and guidance as a blueprint to operationalise the BCBS Principles.

EU DORA

The Digital Operational Resilience Act (DORA) represents the European Union's regulatory response to the growing importance of operational resilience in the digital age. DORA aims to enhance the operational resilience of financial entities across the EU by setting out uniform requirements for information and communication technology (ICT) risk management. The first explicit mention and formal introduction of DORA as a legislative proposal occurred on 24 September 2020, so it's likely the EU had been doing early work on the proposals around the same time the UK was developing its policy.

DORA builds on existing EU regulations but introduces new requirements that apply across all financial entities, including banks, investment firms and payment service providers. The act requires firms to have comprehensive ICT risk management frameworks, including capabilities for monitoring and responding to ICT-related incidents.

A key component of DORA is the mandatory reporting of major ICT-related incidents to competent authorities, which aligns with the EU's broader goal of improving cyber resilience across the financial sector. DORA also places significant emphasis on third-party risk management, particularly concerning ICT service providers, which are increasingly critical to financial firms' operations. Many of the ICT providers caught by DORA won't have been subject to regulation before. The UK published its policy on Critical Third-Party Providers (CTPs) effective 1 January 2025.

DORA is more focused on digital and ICT risks than the BCBS Principles and UK policy, reflecting the EU's narrower regulatory focus on digital finance.

In their Dear CEO letter of 21 January 2025 on priorities for International Banks,[11] the UK PRA announced their intention to consult (along with UK FCA) on new policy in 2H 2025 on the management of information and communication technology and cyber risks (ICT). It remains to be seen whether this will be a new 'UK DORA', but the new UK regime on critical third-party providers (CTPs), is suggestive of the UK aligning with the EU in approach. We think it unlikely, especially given the pressure from the new Starmer government for regulation to drive economic growth, that the new policy on ICT resilience will be anything like as prescriptive and detailed as DORA. However, taken together with new policy, which at the time of writing, is out for consultation on operational resilience incident reporting (PRA CP17/24 and UK FCA 24/28), it is clear that the subject of operational resilience will continue to be a focus for regulators and therefore for firms.

OPERATIONAL RESILIENCE, INTOLERABLE HARM AND UK FCA'S CONSUMER DUTY

As we have seen, operational resilience is the *ability of firms and the financial sector as a whole to prevent, adapt, respond to, recover and learn from operational disruptions*. Firms must assume that disruption is inevitable and implement an approach (including 'Plan Bs') allowing them to continue providing IBS despite disruption to avoid intolerable harm to consumers or risk the safety and soundness of the firm.

UK FCA's Consumer Duty introduces a new principle, four outcomes and three cross-cutting rules designed to prevent firms from causing *foreseeable harm* to consumers. Firms must ensure they have appropriate systems and controls in place to ensure customers receive fair value in pricing, receive good quality customer support, get products and services that are designed to meet their needs, and that consumers are given the information needed to understand the products or services they're buying. The consumer duty went live in the UK at the end of July 2023.

One of the main themes of this book is the need to take a more integrated approach across the NFR umbrella, and the case of operational resilience and consumer duty is an ideal case in point. While in most firms, these two critical areas of regulatory focus have been considered in isolation (one often by compliance and another by operations), it's crucial that the linkages are considered and a more integrated approach to these two essential aspects of ORM is adopted.

Harm is a key concept and focus for the Financial Conduct Authority and is linked to another key area of focus on 'vulnerability'. The UK FCA's focus on harm will only increase as economic headwinds worsen.

The **'Nexus of Harm'** is illustrated in Figure 8.9. The graphic illustrates the relationship between foreseeable and intolerable harm and the interaction with risk appetite, risk tolerance (as a tolerable buffer beyond appetite) and impact tolerance/tolerance for disruption. You can see that even where a disruption does not cause intolerable harm (the firm can stay within impact tolerance), it may still breach risk appetite by causing foreseeable harm to the consumer – leading to difficult conversations with regulators!

A more integrated approach to harm, through both the lens of operational resilience and consumer duty, is key to ensuring an efficient approach to compliance.

There are four key reasons why an integrated approach makes sense:

1. **Breaking the silos:** We saw earlier how ORM has become increasingly fragmented, especially in the last decade, with new topic areas such as cyber, conduct, climate and financial crime attracting significant attention, including from regulators, and in some firms addressed through

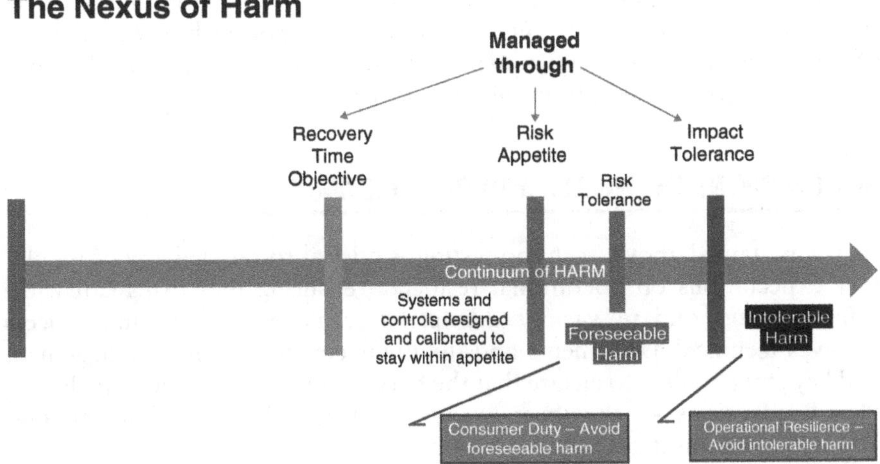

FIGURE 8.9 The Nexus of Harm

new risk silos. By considering both foreseeable harm and intolerable harm through an integrated approach, firms can break down the silos and encourage a more holistic approach across two critical aspects of risk and compliance management.

2. **Efficiency and cost saving:** By adopting a more integrated approach, firms can minimise duplication and maximise the leveraging of existing efforts, achieved by embedding the key regulatory concepts of 'foreseeable harm' and 'intolerable harm' across the various risk and compliance activities, including stress and scenario testing and key operational risk management tools, including RCSA.
3. **Increasing the value of scenario testing:** Firms are now undertaking scenario testing for operational resilience, which tests the ability of firms to stay within impact tolerance in the event of a severe but plausible disruption. By considering foreseeable harm simultaneously, firms may identify plausible scenarios of disruption that, while not causing intolerable harm, cause foreseeable harm. Firms can then take proactive actions to ensure they mitigate such harm.
4. **Regulatory compliance:** An integrated and holistic approach to harm will also reduce the risk of breaching these key regulatory requirements. The concepts of foreseeable and intolerable harm should be embedded in the organisation's DNA and considered across the range of risk and compliance activities. By reducing the risk of regulatory breach, firms can mitigate the risk of fines, S166 reviews and supervisory visits.

By adopting a more integrated approach across the **continuum of harm**, firms can improve efficiency, cut costs and, most importantly, reduce the risk of breaching these key new regulatory requirements, thereby avoiding difficult and costly conversations with regulators.

DON'T REINVENT THE WHEEL...EXCEPT IN TESTING?

As we explained above, scenario testing is critical to the delivery of regulatory expectations on operational resilience, ensuring that firms can withstand and respond to various disruption scenarios. The testing process involves technical assessments and the involvement of senior management and key stakeholders to ensure that the firm's response strategies – including Plan B adaptions – are robust, documented, tested and well understood across the organisation.

As a general rule, firms should leverage existing work (done under the ORM umbrella) to meet the operational resilience outcomes. However, scenario testing for operational resilience differs from the testing most firms have been doing in several ways. Most traditional testing done for operational risk management and BCM focuses on risk **causes**, considers the **impacts** on the firm and critically evaluates the likelihood of the risk crystallising to identify preventative controls. The testing – especially for BCM – is typically also narrowly focused on a particular system or process, and the impacts tend to focus on the firm (rather than the consumer).

Regulators require scenario testing for operational resilience to be **agnostic to the cause of disruption**. Testing must assume disruption has occurred to critical resources, e.g. people, processes, facilities, technology, information and third parties. It must then test the delivery of IBS within impact tolerances. Where the firm identifies vulnerabilities that prevent delivery of the IBS within tolerances, they must be fixed through investment in new systems, expanding capacity or documenting and testing Plan Bs.

Operational resilience scenario testing must also flex the severity of the disruption by extending the duration (including beyond impact tolerance) and adding disruption to additional critical resources. So a typical scenario test might consider disruption to a critical resource for half a day, a full day, then two days, then three days, then add disruption to a second critical resource; this might mean testing disruption to a key facility such as the London branch and then augmenting this with disruption to the remote working technology.

Scenario testing for operational resilience is similar **to stress testing to destruction** or **reverse stress testing.** The approach must assume disruption and test the firm's ability to adapt and respond through Plan Bs and Plan Cs to continue providing the services within impact tolerance. This all means that while the existing testing for ORM and BCM can be a **key input** to operational resilience scenario testing (this is critical to ensure the ORM framework is leveraged and we avoid the fragmentation and inefficiency that's plagued Non-Financial Risk Management), simply taking BCM and ORM testing and rebranding it as 'operational resilience testing' is unlikely to meet regulatory expectations for operational resilience.

EMBEDDING AND FUTURE EVOLUTION

In the coming years, especially after the implementation deadline – in the UK and other jurisdictions as they implement the BCBS Principles into domestic rules – one of the major challenges for firms will be embedding operational resilience in its broader framework and tools. This is essential for efficiency and to avoid unnecessary duplication, but even more so, to ensure the tools of ORM are used to deliver the operational resilience outcomes. This means that core tools of ORM, such as RCSA, should be modified to ensure they can capture risks to IBS and scenario analysis and reports should be augmented to align with new terminology and requirements, e.g. impact tolerances.

Culture, often described as 'what people do when no one is looking', is critical to achieving operational resilience outcomes and to the nirvana of 'resilience by design'. A resilience culture refers to an organisational mindset and set of behaviours where risk awareness, adaptability, and proactive risk management are embedded at all levels in the organisation. It ensures that the bank can prevent, adapt, respond to, recover from and learn from disruptions whether operational, financial, cyber, regulatory or reputational – while maintaining trust and continuity of business services. Regulators talk about a 'resilience mindset' so when disruptions occur, one of the first thoughts is how to continue providing the service, including through adaptations and 'Plan Bs'.

Creating a resilience culture is one of the primary challenges in the embedding process, and the usual tools and techniques for culture building should be deployed, including ensuring 'tone from the top', ongoing 'training' and building key resilience concepts and inculcating and incentivising behaviours (such as 'adaptation') into 'policies, processes (including critically around 'change') and day-to-day activity'.

Inevitably, the approach to operational resilience will continue evolving, driven by advancements in technology, changing regulatory landscapes and emerging risks. As firms become more reliant on digital technologies and third/nth-party service providers, operational resilience will expand to include the requirement for more comprehensive strategies for managing these risks (for example, the detailed requirements in the EU DORA on ICT may well become the de facto benchmark even for UK firms not within the jurisdiction of DORA).

Regulatory expectations will also continue to evolve, with increasing emphasis on resilience in the face of systemic risks, such as climate change and geopolitical instability, and ever-increasing expectations on what firms do, in particular with their third/ nth-party ecosystem, to manage potential vulnerabilities and risks. Furthermore, the rise of GenAI will introduce new challenges and opportunities for operational resilience. While these technologies can enhance risk management capabilities, they also introduce new vulnerabilities that firms must address proactively to meet regulatory expectations (see Chapter 17).

CHAPTER 9

Risk Incidents

It is essential that firms ensure that significant risk incidents are fully and robustly reviewed to enable lessons to be learned, control weaknesses or failures identified, prevent them from reoccurring and also provide assurance that the Operational Risk Framework is working as specified (particularly RCSAs and scenarios). The importance of undertaking a review of significant risk incidents is of course recognised by the BCBS in the Revisions to the Principles for Sound Management of Operational Risk[1] in several sections including:

Paragraph 35: (a) Event management – When banks experience an operational risk event, the process of identification, analysis, end-to-end management and reporting of the event follows a predetermined set of protocols. A sound event management approach typically includes analysis of events to identify new operational risks, understanding the underlying causes and control weaknesses and formulating an appropriate response to prevent recurrence of similar events. This information is an input to the self-assessment and, in particular, to the assessment of control effectiveness.

Paragraph 45: Operational risk reports should describe the operational risk profile of the bank by providing internal financial, operational and compliance indicators, as well as external market or environmental information about events and conditions that are relevant to decision-making. Operational risk reports should include:

(c) Details of recent significant internal operational risk events and losses (including root cause analysis).

Of course, one of the many challenges in this process is to determine what is a significant event. After all, an event that did not incur a cost could have been very damaging in different circumstances. In addition, it is often a challenge to get people to report incidents, particularly near misses, if they fear severe sanction, perhaps even job loss, as a consequence.

As part of the training packages we undertake, Jimi and I often discuss with delegates why specific high-profile events occurred, including the sinking of the *Titanic* and the loss of the *Herald of Free Enterprise*. Everybody knows, or thinks they know, why the *Titanic* sunk; after all, it hit an iceberg. In all of the training sessions we have undertaken, using this event as a case study, only two people have identified a rarely known factor that may have contributed to the sinking of the *Titanic*. Curiously, they both worked for the same firm but had discovered this factor in visits to different Titanic museums. I should, of course, note that experts are still debating the possible causes of this historic disaster and I have less insight than they, so let me explain why I think the *Titanic* sunk.

Just to recap, the *Royal Mail Ship Titanic* was launched on 31 March 1911 and was considered unsinkable. At that time, it was the largest and most luxurious cruise liner of its day. The vessel was 882 feet long and 175 feet high and had an advanced wireless communication system capable of sending and receiving Morse code. On 14 April 1912, only four days after leaving Southampton on its maiden voyage to New York, the *Titanic* struck an iceberg off the coast of Newfoundland and sank.

So let's explore the possible reasons why the *Titanic* sank:
It hit an iceberg
Q1) But why?
It may have been travelling too fast
Perhaps to better the crossing time of its sister ship, the Olympic
Perhaps to control a possible fire in one of the ship's coal bunkers
Q2) But why did it hit the iceberg?
It has been suggested by some that the wireless operator
dismissed a key iceberg warning and did not pass it to the captain
Q3) But why didn't it steer away when it saw the iceberg?
Weather conditions will have created mirages and hazy horizons
Q4) But why didn't they see the iceberg?
The lookouts may have had no binoculars
One suggestion is that the second officer (David Blair) was
transferred off the ship just before it departed and forgot to hand
over the key for the crow's nest locker containing the binoculars
(alternative suggestions include the binoculars being left in Blair's
cabin or taken with him when he left the vessel as they were his
personal belongings)
Q5) But the ship was supposed to be unsinkable?
It has been suggested that the Titanic's builders may have cut costs
Resulting in the rivets containing a high concentration of 'slag.

By far my favourite potential factor is that the lookouts may not have had any binoculars, although this is of course pure conjecture on my part.

However, this factor does show how seemingly relatively minor events could result in major events.

The loss of the *Herald of Free Enterprise* is an equally chilling event. The vessel in question was a drive-on drive-off ferry that capsized just after leaving Zeebrugge in Belgium on 6 March 1967. Unfortunately, the ship left the port with her bow door open, and the sea flooded the decks causing the ship to capsize.

So let's explore the possible reasons why the
Herald of Free Enterprise sank:
The ship sank because it set to sea with the bow doors open
Q1) But why were the bow doors open?
The accepted practice was for the assistant boatswain to close
the door before the vessel left its moorings but it has been
suggested that at that time he may have been asleep
Q2) But why didn't anyone notice and act?
The first officer was required to stay on deck to ensure the
doors were closed but he may not have done so
Q3) So why did the vessel depart with the bow doors open?
The captain may have assumed that the doors had been closed
but could not see them from the wheelhouse and had no way of
knowing the doors had not been shut

As you would expect, albeit too late for those lost, some significant lessons were learned, including the need for indicators to show if the bow doors were open.

Readers will have noticed that a key element to understanding why events occur is to keep asking the question, why. It is generally accepted that asking why at least five times will uncover the cause but, as we can see, it may be more or less than that number.

Incidents can take the form of either internal or external events. As we discussed in Chapter 2, many firms define operational risk as the risk of loss resulting from inadequate or failed internal processes, people and systems or from external events. For our purposes, we can consider internal events to comprise inadequate or failed internal processes, people and systems or perhaps alternatively the things we do to ourselves. As a result, external events are the things that others do to us. There is often a debate, particularly when discussing internal and external fraud, over the difference between the two when both internal and external parties are involved. In cases of fraud, I always feel that events involving the participation of one or more members of staff should be considered to be internal events, particularly if the fraud could not have been undertaken without the knowledge and participation of one or more members of staff. When a bank implements changes to its system and the system crashes, we should consider that an internal event. When a bank's system crashes as the result of a cyberattack we should consider that to be an external event. Probably, the highest profile external event of recent times was COVID-19.

There are a number of techniques available to help us understand why risk incidents occur. The approach we shall discuss here is the 'Bow Tie', although those seeking alternatives can investigate decision tree analysis, SWIFT (Structured What-If Technique) analysis and fishbone diagrams.

We first introduced the bow tie in 'Chapter 7: Controls' to help illustrate preventative, detective, corrective and directive controls. In Figure 9.1, we have produced an augmented bow tie diagram that will help us understand why events happen, using the following stages:

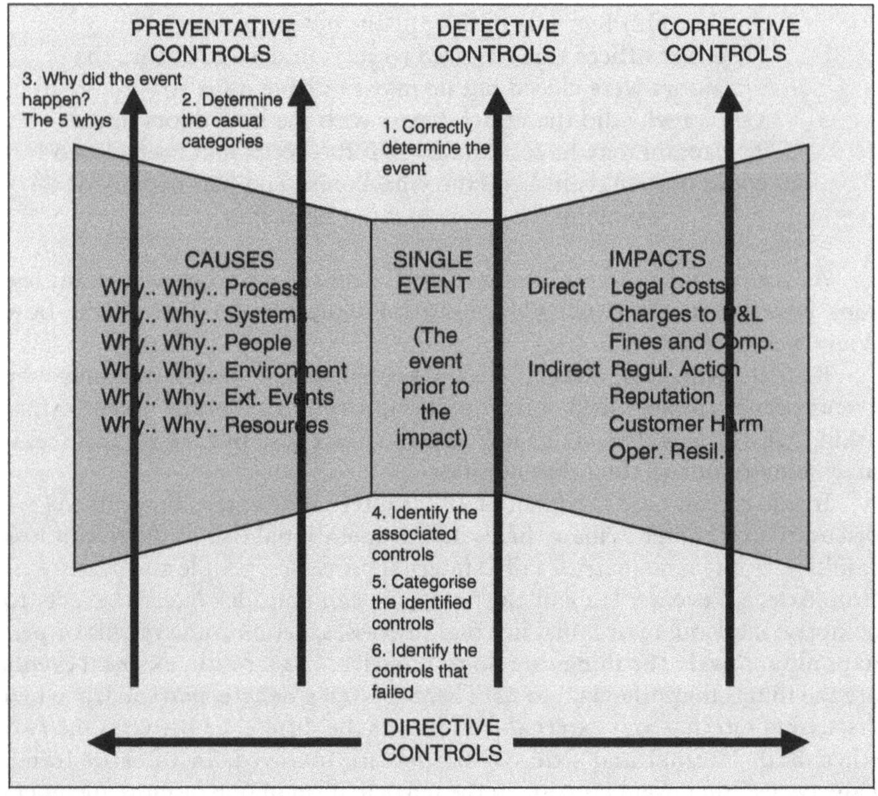

FIGURE 9.1 The Bow Tie

1. **Identify the event:** It is important to correctly understand the event and this can often result in some considerable debate. I always advocate identifying the event that occurred immediately prior to the impact. Nevertheless, this is not always straightforward as some impacts, regulatory fines for example, take some time to happen and may be imposed long after the event has been analysed and mitigating action taken.
2. **Identify the causes:** Once the event is correctly identified, then the causes must be determined. You will see that in the diagram we have added two more causes than is often the case (environment and resources) particularly for those using the generally accepted definition of operational risk. Just because an initial cause is identified does not mean that the subsequent cause should remain in the same causal category.
3. **The five whys:** Keep asking why a cause happened until you have exhausted the causes. I am sure many of us have (occasionally) annoying children, grandchildren or nephews who keep asking why something is being done or happening. This is your opportunity to take on that annoying persona.
4. **Identify the associated controls:** At this stage identify the controls that are in place to prevent, detect, correct or direct the activity that resulted in the event.
5. **Categorise the controls:** Allocate each of the controls to the appropriate category (preventative, detective, corrective or directive). At this stage you need to ensure that you have an appropriate spread of controls.
6. **Identify the controls that failed:** Which of the controls identified failed and why?

Let us apply this technique to a hypothetical event. A software update is downloaded that matches addresses on envelopes with the address on the bank statement, to ensure that statements are sent to the appropriate account holder. Unfortunately a few days after the update, clients complain that while they have not received their statement, they have instead received the statement for another customer. This incident is reported on social media and Bank's reputation is damaged. So applying the six stages above, and using swim lanes to follow the approach:

1. **Identify the event:** The reputational damage is attributable to sending statements to incorrect addresses.
2. **Identify the causes:** In this instance, the event occurred because of an error in the software.
3. **The five whys:** But why was there an error in the software. Let us use the swim lanes in Figure 9.2 to help us identify the root cause:

Event: Statements were sent to the wrong address due to a system error that mismatched the statement and envelope addresses. In reality, every envelope contained the statement for the next person on the print run

Q1) But why wasn't this error identified in the buddy checks undertaken in the department that developed the updated software?

Buddy checks are required by the software team's policies and procedures but these were not followed

Q2) But why weren't the standard procedures applied?

The software team were experiencing resourcing issues and were under pressure to deliver the update, so the decision was taken not to complete the buddy checks

Q3) But why were they experiencing resource issues?

The software team were operating below approved headcount

Q4) But why were they operating below approved headcount?

Salaries in the software team had fallen considerably below industry norms and the firm was unable to attract or retain staff.

So in our hypothetical example, the event occurred because the firm was not paying industry-level salaries. (When we have run through examples like this in senior management training, the Finance Director often starts to protest at this stage.)

4. **Identify the associated controls:** The key control associated with this process was the requirement for buddy checks.
5. **Categorise the controls:** While the requirement for buddy checks is contained in the teams' procedures and could therefore be considered to be a directive control, the control purpose was to prevent events from occurring, and so we will consider it to be preventative.
6. Allocate each of the controls to the appropriate category (preventative, detective, corrective or directive). In this hypothetical instance, there would have been a significant benefit from establishing an additional preventative control by checking some of the statements before posting, to ensure they would be sent to the appropriate individuals. As this control takes place before the despatch of the statements, we will consider it to be preventative. If the statements had been despatched, with only some held back for verification this would have been a detective control.
7. **Identify the controls that failed:** The control that failed was the buddy check and the root cause for the failure was the inability to retain or recruit staff due to a failure to match industry salaries.

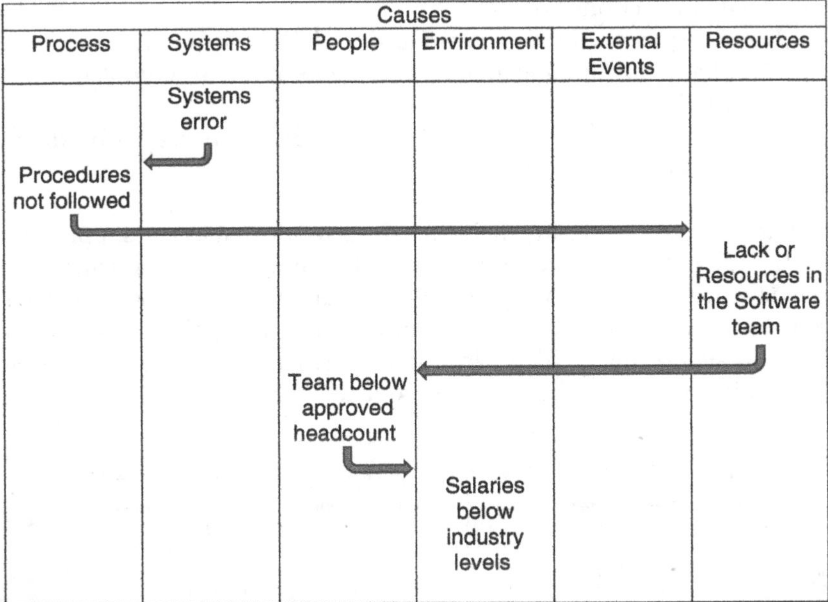

FIGURE 9.2 Causal Analysis Using Swim Lanes

As we have seen at the start of this chapter, the regulator expects firms to undertake root cause analysis for significant operational risk events. While we can utilise the bow tie approach described above to facilitate an understanding of the event, firms will need to complete and retain a root cause analysis template to ensure the event is comprehensively recorded. We would expect this template to include the following components:

- Unique incident reference number;
- When did the event occur;
- What was the event;
- How was the event discovered;
- Describe what went wrong, the circumstances and subsequent events;
- Has this event occurred previously in the last 12 months, if so, give details;
- Detail the impacts;
- Show which of the following causes were evident: process, people, systems, environment, external events and resources;
- For each of the six causal categories identified, undertake the five whys (use a swim lane);
- Identify the associated controls by category: preventative, detective, corrective and directive (include the control owner);
- Identify the controls that failed, including their category;

- Detail any actions taken;
- Detail any new controls introduced, including their category;
- Detail any outstanding actions and the deadline for completion;
- Identify lessons learned;
- Was a review of other framework components triggered by the incident, if so, provide details.

Naturally, exposing all incidents to 'bow tie' analysis, supplemented with the use of 'swim lanes' to help identify the root cause, is neither effective nor efficient. At the beginning of this chapter, I mentioned the need to ensure 'significant risk incidents are fully reviewed' begging the question of what is a significant incident. In Figure 6.4, I provided a spreadsheet of potential impact scales and this is reproduced in Figure 9.3.

Significant incidents
Significant incidents

Rating	Regulatory	Financial	Operational Resilience	Reputation	Customer
Very High	Large fine, formal investigation, removal of licence or permissions	Loss greater than $150,000	Significant breach of impact tolerances (or tolerance for disruption) with potential impact on the safety and soundness of the firm	Sustained national media coverage over month and long-term impact on the share value	Significant loss of customers
High	Skilled persons review, Risk Mitigation actions, capital charge	Loss between $50,000 and $150,000	Impact tolerances (or tolerance for disruption) breached and regulator notified	National media coverage over weeks and short-term impact on the share value	Some loss of customers
Medium	Regulatory relationship damaged	Loss between $25,000 and $50,000	Disruption, impact tolerances (or tolerance for disruption) not breached but disruption reported in the media	National media coverage over a few days with no impact on the share value	Minimal loss of customers
Low	No regulatory action triggered	Loss below $25,000	Minimal disruption to important business services (or critical operations) with minimal impact on the firm or customer	Incident receives local or specialist media coverage	No customer impact

FIGURE 9.3 Using RCSA Impact Scales to Determine Incident Significance

This would mean that 'significant risk incidents' requiring a full review comprise all those incidents with one or more of the following impacts:

- Regulatory:
  - Large fine, formal investigation, removal of licence or permissions or;
  - Skilled person's review, risk mitigation actions, capital charge;
- Financial:
  - Loss greater than $150,000 or;
  - Loss between $50,000 and $150,000;
- Operational Resilience:
  - Significant breach of operational resilience impact tolerances (or tolerance for disruption) with potential impact on the safety and soundness of the firm or;
  - Impact tolerances (or tolerance for disruption) breached and regulator notified;
- Reputation:
  - Sustained national media coverage over a month and long-term impact on the share value or;
  - National media coverage over weeks and short-term impact on the share value;
- Customer:
  - Significant loss of customers or;
  - Some loss of customers.

Obviously, the senior management of individual firms will need to determine the appropriate RCSA impact scales for their firm.

CHAPTER 10

Third-Party Risk Management – The Elephant in the Room

Hand in hand with the increasing focus on operational resilience discussed by Jimi in Chapter 8 comes an increasing focus on third parties, particularly as firms increase their reliance on such arrangements. Regulators will always point out that failures of third-party risk management can threaten the safety and soundness of individual firms, the financial system and also threaten a firm's ability to deliver good outcomes for consumers. Trust in the reliability of the financial system is crucial for its proper functioning and is a prerequisite if it is to contribute to the economy as a whole, as was demonstrated by the global financial crisis. As a result, third-party risk management has become a major issue that is obviously present but is avoided by some firms as a subject for discussion, thereby becoming 'the elephant in the room'. It is important to recognise that firms remain responsible and accountable for all the regulatory responsibilities that apply to their third-party service arrangements. Firms cannot delegate any part of this responsibility to a third party.

For UK financial firms, the potential consequences of a disruption at a supplier are not limited to an operational resilience event that results in them breaching their impact tolerances and causing intolerable harm to customers or threatening their safety and soundness. At the end of July 2023, the UK Financial Conduct Authority's rules for a new Consumer Duty[1] came into operation for existing products and services. As a result of these consumer duty requirements, firms must deliver good outcomes for retail customers and as part of the new regulation firms must comply with three cross-cutting rules:

- Act in good faith;
- Avoid causing foreseeable harm;
- Enable and support retail customers to pursue their financial objectives.

In complying with these three rules firms must deliver four outcomes relating to:

- Products and services;
- Price and value;
- Consumer understanding;
- Consumer support.

It is easy to envisage scenarios where a disruption at a third party causes a firm to cause foreseeable harm to customers, perhaps by impacting the firm's:

- Ability to conduct business with retail customers to a standard that ensures an appropriate level of protection for retail customers;
- Ability to act in good faith with retail customers;
- Ability to enable and support customers;
- Ability to communicate and engage with customers so that they can make effective, timely and properly informed decisions about financial products and services and can take responsibility for their actions and decisions, including the:
  - Quality of post-sales support;
  - Ability to answer questions from a prospective customer;
  - Ability of a prospective customer to apply for a new product or service;
  - Ability to provide good outcomes to vulnerable customers who may not have access to alternative solutions.

Unfortunately, we regularly see operational disruptions caused by third parties, or even nth parties, with the CrowdStrike outage in July 2024 probably the most infamous. Before we progress with this topic, it would be wise to agree on some definitions:

- **Third party:** An organisation that has entered into a business relationship on a contract with a firm to provide a product or service;
- **Third-party risk management (TPRM):** The management of a third-party relationship throughout the outsourcing life cycle, including the review, analysis and control of unforeseen circumstances;
- **Outsourcing:** 'An arrangement of any form between a firm and a service provider, whether a supervised entity or not, by which that service provider performs a process, a service or an activity, whether directly or by sub-outsourcing, which would otherwise be undertaken by the firm itself'[2];

- **Sub-outsourcing:** A situation where the service provider under an outsourcing arrangement further transfers an outsourced function to another service provider;
- **Materiality:** Assesses the potential impact of a given outsourcing or third-party arrangement on a firm's safety and soundness;
- **Intragroup third party:** A third party that is part of the same group and provides services predominantly to entities within the same group.

We should also clarify the relationship between third parties and outsourcing. Outsourcing is a subset of a firm's third-party relationships, a relationship I have attempted to illustrate in Figure 10.1, which is taken from our training slides.

To further clarify the relationship between third-party arrangements and outsourcing, it is worth considering third-party arrangements that a firm would not consider undertaking itself. For most firms this list would include: security, software purchases, catering, printing and cleaning. A number of firms, particularly smaller firms, employ an external party to act as the third line internal audit function and I have had some interesting, and unresolved, discussions on whether these arrangements should be considered outsourcing or third-party arrangements. My view is that this is an important activity that firms would generally undertake themselves and should therefore be considered to be outsourcing. The alternative argument is that these specific firms would never undertake the internal audit function, so these arrangements are third-party arrangements.

The G7, EBA and PRA define a **third party** as an organisation that has entered into a business relationship or a contract with a firm to provide a product or service.

Outsourcing is an arrangement of any form between a firm and a service provider, by which that service provider performs a process, a service or an activity, whether directly or by sub-outsourcing, which would otherwise be undertaken by the firm itself.

Materiality assesses the potential impact of a given outsourcing or third-party arrangement on a firm's safety and soundness.

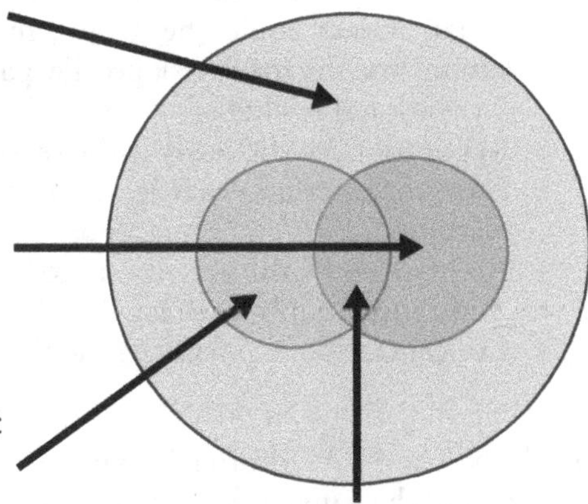

FIGURE 10.1 TPRM vs Outsourcing

A key factor in Figure 10.1 is the assessment of the materiality of a third-party arrangement, be it a third-party exposure or more specifically outsourcing. For me, this is a key consideration as materiality must surely rate above whether the activity is considered outsourcing or not. In December 2024, the UK FCA published a Consultation Paper CP24/28, Operational Incident and Third Party Reporting.[3] In that consultation paper the regulator proposes to adopt a single definition that encompasses outsourcing and third-party arrangements. As a result, the UK FCA proposes to define a third-party arrangement as an arrangement of any form between a firm and its service provider. Whether or not the product or service is:

- One which would otherwise be provided by the firm itself;
- Provided directly or by a sub-contractor;
- Provided by a person within the same group as the firm.

While I interpret this as a very welcome refocus that can only benefit the third-party risk management process, any revision will come after publication of this book. As a result, I will continue to make the distinction between outsourcing and third-party risk management contained in the definitions above, and as they are expressed in the approved regulatory requirements at the time of drafting this chapter.

Before entering into an arrangement with a third party, firms must determine the materiality of the arrangement. We saw in the definitions above that materiality 'assesses the potential impact of a given outsourcing or third-party arrangement on a firm's safety and soundness'. Any materiality assessment should therefore assess the impact of the arrangements on a firm's:

- Business – How important to the firm is the activity;
- What impact could the arrangement have on profitability, liquidity, capital and the firm's risk profile, particularly if the service is disrupted?
- Operational resilience;
- Reputation, particularly if the service is disrupted;
- Customers, counterparties and clients, particularly if the service is disrupted;
- Ability to take the activity in-house or whether there is a substitute;
- Ability to comply with legal and regulatory obligations;
- Concentration exposure to the third party.

Materiality can change over time and firms should reassess materiality regularly. The PRA's approach to materiality is discussed further later in this chapter and the Authority's materiality criteria are reproduced in Table 10.3.

We should also consider why firms engage in third-party arrangements. In many cases, the arrangements result in significant cost savings and improve flexibility and efficiency, enabling firms to concentrate on their core business. In some instances, third-party arrangements give the firm access to increased capacity, skills and knowledge that they may not possess. A number of firms undertake intragroup outsourcing as they are required to use the group's expertise and resources.

Not surprisingly the regulatory community has focused attention on TPRM with the following publications among those that may impact readers:

- Basel Committee on Banking Supervision, Consultative Document, Principles for the sound management of third-party risk (issued for comment by 9 October 2024) was published in July 2024[4] (readers referencing this document should check to see if the final version has been published);
- Prudential Regulation Authority Supervisory Statement, SS2/21 Outsourcing and third-party risk management March 2021[5];
- European Banking Authority Revised Guidelines on Outsourcing Arrangements[6];
- Financial Stability Board, Third-Party Risk Management and Oversight, a toolkit for financial institutions and financial authorities[7];
- IOSCO Principles on Outsourcing Final report[8];
- Office of the Superintendent of Financial Institutions Canada (OSFI) Third-Party Risk Management Guidelines.[9] OSFI's Third-Party Risk Management Guidelines and their Operational Resilience and Operational Risk Management – Draft guideline (2023) are extremely well written and well worth reading, irrespective of whether you are Canadian or not.

As we consider and evolve our third-party risk management frameworks (TPRMFs), we should do so in the context of the third-party risk management life cycle shown in Figure 10.2, which is also taken from our training slides.

Governance sits at the heart of TPRM and oversees the outsourcing life cycle. In many firms, TPRM governance operates at two levels:

- Governance by the Board or appropriate body and senior management who approve the framework within which governance takes place and includes formal approval of the outsourcing and third-party risk management policy;
- The detailed oversight governance arrangements whereby the firm exercises governance over the third-party activities and process. The detailed oversight governance process often sits in a programme or relationship management office.

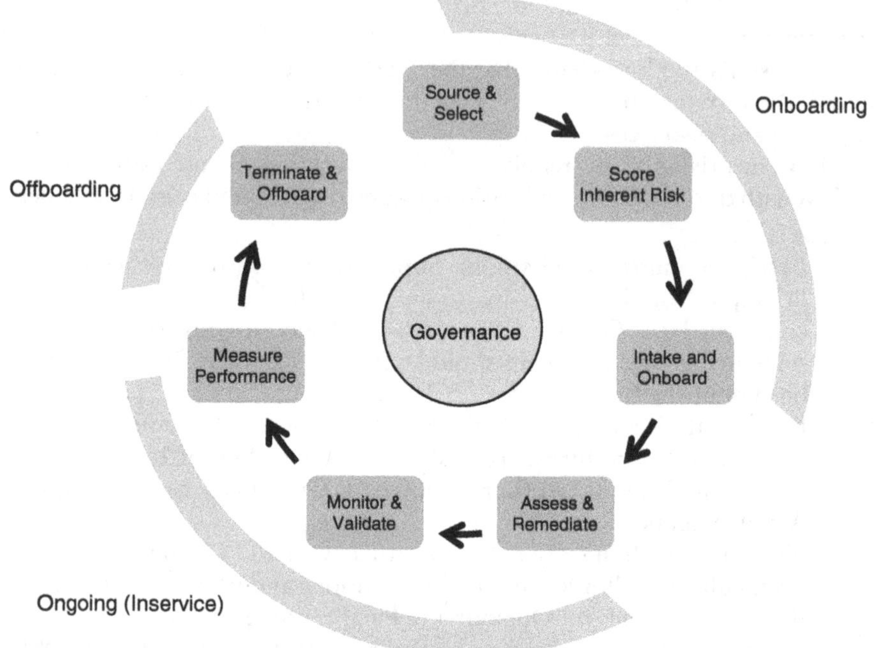

FIGURE 10.2 TPRM Lifecycle – The Three O's

The detailed oversight governance arrangements require a clear understanding of the objectives and strategy behind the outsourcing decision and ongoing assessment process. The involvement of the outsourcing end users in this process is crucial. Clear roles and responsibilities are essential and this ongoing oversight process will usually focus on performance, objectives and service-level agreements. Should issues be identified, a problem escalation mechanism is needed along with a dispute resolution process.

Firms should make sure that all third-party providers are aware of their relevant internal policies. Obviously, if the policy contains information that is either not relevant or sensitive, firms can redact or remove the information. Nevertheless, a word of warning. I have in the past received redacted statements where the originating firm had merely blocked out the information using the Word highlight facility in black and then shared a Word version, making it easy to simply remove the highlighting. I have also received documents where the originating firm has coloured the text in white and again shared the document in Word. I would expect the outsourcing policy to include:

- **Governance:** Including a general introduction; the roles and responsibilities of the Board, senior management, first, second and third lines; business continuity, consumer duty (if relevant) and operational resilience requirements; links to any other relevant policies; details of how intragroup outsourcing is treated; whether there are differences in the approach to material and non-material third-party arrangements and how third-party arrangements are impacted if the supplier is either unregulated but the activity takes place in the firm's regulatory jurisdiction or the activity takes place outside the jurisdiction;

- **Onboarding:** Including how the provider is sourced and selected, together with how the criteria used in the selection process are developed; who approves the new provider and the various arrangements; how the initial risk assessment is undertaken and the onboarding process;
- **Ongoing:** Including the detailed oversight governance arrangements; how incidents are captured and reported; how the performance of the arrangement is assessed and what is the independent review process;
- **Offboarding:** Including the basis for exits in both normal and stressed conditions.

In SS2/21 (table 4) the PRA includes suggested minimum contents of the outsourcing policy and UK firms would be wise to ensure that their outsourcing policy aligns with the PRA's expectations. I am always surprised when firms elect to ignore guidance of this type when provided by the regulator. The contents of that table are reproduced in Table 10.1.

Obviously, readers are advised to benchmark their own outsourcing policy against these contents.

The allocation of roles and responsibilities is key, and in the UK, firms are required to allocate a prescribed responsibility for regulatory obligations in relation to outsourcing to an SMF. This is usually the Chief Operations Officer or SMF 24, who sits in line 1. Allocating specific responsibility for third-party arrangements to a senior manager would seem a practice worth adopting for all firms globally. Nevertheless, we are often asked what are the roles of the three lines and generally propose the roles and responsibilities shown in Table 10.2 as a starting point. Responsibility for individual outsourcing arrangement must rest with the users of the service.

Readers will notice that I have shown responsibility for the policy as moving from the first line to the second. This reflects a compromise, as in some firms, in the absence of an existing policy, the COO has produced and currently owns the TPRM Policy. As a consequence, the COO is effectively drafting the requirements (or the exam question) and then providing the answers. My starting point for the allocation of responsibility for all risk policies, including the TPRM Policy, is that they should be owned by the second line. I feel that firms where the policy is owned in the first line should enter a transition period where responsibility for the policy is initially shared between the

TABLE 10.1 Contents of the Outsourcing Policy

General	• The responsibilities of the board, including its involvement, as appropriate, in decisions about material outsourcing
	• The involvement of business lines, internal control functions and other individuals (in particular, SMFs) in respect of outsourcing arrangements
	• Links to other relevant policies
	• Documentation and record-keeping
	• Procedures for the identification, assessment, management and mitigation of potential relevant conflicts of interest
	• Business continuity planning (BCP)
	• Differences, if any, between the approach to:
	  • Intragroup outsourcing vs outsourcing to external service providers
	  • Material vs non-material outsourcing
	  • Outsourcing to service providers regulated or overseen by the Bank, PRA or UK FCA vs unregulated service providers
	  • Outsourcing to service providers in specific jurisdictions outside the UK

Pre-outsourcing and on-boarding	• The processes for vendor due diligence and for assessing the materiality and risks of outsourcing arrangements (including notification to the PRA where required) • Responsibility for signing-off new outsourcing arrangements, in particular material outsourcing arrangements
Oversight	Procedures for the ongoing assessment of service providers' performance, including where appropriate: • Day-to-day oversight, including incident reporting, periodic performance assessment against service level agreements and periodic strategic assessments • Being notified and responding to changes to an outsourcing arrangement or service provider (eg to its financial position, organisational or ownership structures or suboutsourcing) • Independent review and audit of compliance with legal and regulatory requirements and policies • Renewal processes
Termination	• Exit strategies and termination processes, including a requirement for a documented exit plan for material outsourcing arrangements where such an exit is considered possible, explicitly catering for the unexpected termination of an outsourcing agreement (a stressed or unplanned exit), and taking into account possible service interruptions (and the firm's impact tolerance for important business services).

Source: Reproduced from PRA Supervisory Statement 2/21 table 4.[5]

first line authors and the second line risk team, before transitioning to become the sole responsibility of the second line, hence the ugly compromise in Table 10.2. It is always interesting to see firms that claim in their published material (Annual Reports, for example) and to the regulator that they follow the three lines of defence, but ownership of the TPRM Policy and/or the Operational Resilience Policy sits in the first line, in contradiction to the three lines of defence.

Key governance challenges often comprise:

- Ensuring the arrangements are robust and include escalation processes;
- Developing appropriate Management Information;
- How metrics are escalated and to whom;
- What does second line oversight and challenge look like in practice;
- The involvement of the third line;
- Ensuring clear roles and responsibilities.

The TPRM process should be enshrined in the outsourcing and third-party risk management policy and as you would expect the BCBS Basel Committee on Banking Supervision, Consultative Document, Principles for the Sound Management of Third-Party Risk[4] devotes its first two principles to governance, risk management and strategy:

> **Principle 1:** The board of directors has ultimate responsibility for the oversight of all third-party service provider (TPSP) arrangements and should approve a clear strategy for TPSP arrangements within the bank's risk appetite and tolerance for disruption.

TABLE 10.2 Allocating Responsibilities Across the Three Lines

Activity	1st Line	2nd Line	3rd Line
Overall framework	✓		
Policy	✓ ⟶	✓	
Systems and controls	✓		
Reporting	✓		
Oversight and challenge		✓	
Review			✓
Responsibility for individual outsourcing arrangements	✓	✓	✓

Principle 2: The board of directors should ensure that senior management implements the policies and processes of the third-party risk management framework (TPRMF) in line with the bank's third-party strategy, including reporting of TPSP performance and risks related to TPSP arrangements, and mitigating actions.

In their Supervisory Statement 2/21,[5] the UK Prudential Regulation Authority articulates its governance expectations, which include:

- Boards and senior management, in particular individuals performing SMFs, cannot outsource their responsibilities:
- Firm's boards should:
  - Set 'the control environment throughout the firm, including the appetite and tolerance levels in respect of outsourcing' and third-party risk management;
  - 'Bear responsibility for the effective management of all risks to which the firm is exposed', including by:
    - Appropriately 'identifying and [having an] understanding of the firm's reliance on critical service providers';
    - Ensuring that the firm has '(from board level downwards) appropriate and effective risk management systems and strategies in place to deal with outsourced service providers'.

The first stage in any third-party arrangement must be for a firm to decide whether to outsource or not, particularly as some regulators prevent the outsourcing of some activities. Once this decision is taken then firms must decide whether there are any deal breakers, for example, environmental, social and governance (ESG) considerations or limits on fourth and nth parties. As part of the onboarding process, firms need to source and select an outsourcing provider that meets their requirements, including operational resilience. Vendor due diligence will need to assess the materiality and risks of the outsourcing arrangements. Only once these processes are completed to the satisfaction of the bank should they commence selection and then onboarding.

In SS2/21, the PRA notes that their rulebook defines 'material outsourcing' as the outsourcing of 'services of such importance that weakness, or failure, of the services would cast serious doubt upon the firm's continuing satisfaction of the threshold conditions or compliance with the Fundamental Rules'. They also note that although the term 'material outsourcing' in the PRA Rulebook is limited to outsourcing arrangements, the concept of materiality itself and the criteria in chapter 5 of SS2/21 apply to all third-party arrangements.

The PRA adds that a firm should generally consider an outsourcing or third-party arrangement as material where a defect or failure in its performance could materially impair the:

- Financial stability of the UK;
- A firm's:
  - Ability to meet the Threshold Conditions;
  - Compliance with the Fundamental Rules;
  - Requirements under 'relevant legislation' and the PRA Rulebook;
  - Safety and soundness, including the firm's:
    - Financial resilience, i.e. assets, capital, funding and liquidity;
    - Operational resilience, i.e. its ability to continue providing important business services;
  - For insurers only, the:
    - Ability to provide an appropriate degree of protection for those who are or may become policyholders in line with the PRA's statutory objectives;
    - Requirement not to undermine the 'continuous and satisfactory service to policyholders' in line with Conditions Governing Business;
- Operational Continuity in Resolution (OCIR) and if applicable, resolvability.

In addition, in table 5 of the PRA's Supervisory Statement 2/21 (Materiality criteria), the PRA details other materiality criteria to be taken into account. That table is reproduced in Table 10.3.

There are a number of tools and techniques that can be employed during the risk assessment process, including:

- Fully assessing the risks arising from the third-party activity to ensure they are fully understood. In completing this risk assessment, firms should apply the risk and control assessment methodology and also undertake testing of severe but plausible scenarios;
- While the third-party arrangement will generate risks not faced previously in this respect, it may also reduce or even eliminate other risks. An assessment should be undertaken to evaluate the positive and negative impacts on the firm's risk profile and decide whether the 'new' net position is acceptable;
- Evaluating the impact of the arrangement on the firm's third-party concentration risk, including overall exposure to the third party and geographic concentration.

TABLE 10.3 Materiality Criteria

Criterion	
Direct connection to the performance of a regulated activity.	
Size and complexity of relevant business area(s) or function(s).	

The potential impact of a disruption, failure, or inadequate performance on the firm's:	• Business continuity, operational resilience, and operational risk, including:
	  • Conduct risk
	  • ICT risk
	  • Legal risk
	  • Reputational risk
	• Ability to:
	  • Comply with legal and regulatory requirements
	  • Conduct appropriate audits of the relevant function, service, or service provider
	  • Identify, monitor, and manage all risks
	• Obligations under
	  • The PRA Rulebook
	  • The protection of data and the potential impact of a confidentiality breach or failure to ensure data availability and integrity of the institution or payment institution and its clients, including but not limited to GDPR and the Data Protection Act 2018
	• Counterparties, customers or policy holders
	• Early intervention, recovery and resolution planning, Operational Continuity and Resolution, and resolvability

The firm's ability to scale up the outsourced service	
Ability to substitute the service provider or bring the outsourced service back in-house, including estimated costs, operational impact, risks, and timeframe of an exit in stressed and non-stressed scenarios.	

Source: Reproduced from PRA Supervisory Statement 2/21 table 5.[5]

Many regulators require formal notification of the bank's intentions and selected supplier at this stage. Once the decision to outsource is taken and a vendor selected, then the contract negotiations should commence and include:

- The contract invitation;
- Who is the provider and what due diligence is required;
- What are the service-level agreements;
- Who will sign the contract;
- How will the agreement be communicated to stakeholders, including staff.

The BCBS Principles for the Sound Management of Third-Party Risk[4] are clear that:

Principle 3: Banks should perform a comprehensive risk assessment under the TPRMF to evaluate and manage identified and potential risks both before entering into and throughout a TPSP arrangement.

Principle 4: Banks should conduct appropriate due diligence on a prospective TPSP prior to entering into an arrangement.

Principle 5: TPSP arrangements should be governed by legally binding written contracts that clearly describe rights and obligations, responsibilities and expectations of all parties in the arrangement.

As we can see from Figure 10.2, once a supplier is onboarded, the bank will enter the ongoing or in-service phase that involves assessing and remediating any risks and issues that are identified or arise and monitoring, measuring and validating the performance of the outsourcing arrangement. The BCBS Principles for the Sound Management of Third-Party Risk[4] are clear that:

Principle 6: Banks should dedicate sufficient resources to support a smooth transition of a new TPSP arrangement in order to prioritise the resolution of any issues identified during due diligence or interpretation of contractual provisions.

Principle 7: Banks should, on an ongoing basis, assess and monitor the performance and changes in the risks and criticality of TPSP arrangements and report accordingly to board and senior management. Banks should respond to issues as appropriate.

Principle 8: Banks should maintain robust business continuity management to ensure their ability to operate in case of a TPSP service disruption.

The ongoing oversight of third-party suppliers is an important activity and firms could base the level of ongoing oversight on their materiality assessment. This oversight should include:

- Reporting of incidents by the supplier – some firms provide third-party providers with their incident reporting form to ensure adequate and consistent information is received;
- Desk-based reviews of information relevant to the supplier and the quality of service, including the annual report and accounts, news and social media items, reports of performance against SLAs and responses to questionnaires;

- Periodic meetings with the supplier to discuss the service;
- Onsite visits (an extremely powerful tool);
- Pooled third-party visits.

Some firms experience problems utilising all these tools, particularly where their use is not part of the agreed documentation. In addition, some suppliers or users of a product or service form user groups, which meet regularly to discuss any issues arising. The value of actively participating in these user groups should not be underestimated.

A key component of any third-party framework must be management reporting and it is an area where some firms struggle. As we would expect, regulators are not prescriptive about the actual management information that should be generated and submitted to the senior management and board, although it is not a surprise that they would expect it to be:

- Clear;
- Consistent;
- Robust;
- Timely;
- Well targeted;
- Containing an appropriate level of technical detail.

Certainly, firms are expected to keep an up-to-date register of all their third-party arrangements, detailing material and non-material relationships. We would expect the third-party register to include:

- A unique reference number for each third-party arrangement;
- When the arrangement started;
- The contract renewal date;
- The notice period;
- A description of the third-party arrangement;
- Whether firm and/or customer data is involved in the arrangement;
- Where the data is held;
- Which function has been impacted by the arrangement;
- Who is the service provider;
- Is the arrangement material;
- When was materiality last assessed;
- Is the outsourcing to a cloud service provider;
- Who within the firm owns the relationship.

The UK FCA Consultation Paper 24/28, mentioned earlier, proposes that firms should submit details of their material third-party arrangements to the regulator, ensuring the register is submitted and updated annually, using a template provided by the UK FCA. The CP highlights the following information that will need to be submitted:

Data on the regulated firm;
Data on third parties including intra-group arrangements;
Data on types of services being performed by the third-party;
Data on products and services used;
Information on the supply chain;
Information on firms' assessments of their third-party arrangements.

The CP contains a link to the proposed third-party reporting data table[10] which requires the completion of up to 53 data cells for each material third-party arrangement. As this table appears on a consultation paper it may well have been revised by the time this book is published.

Our first recommendation when working with clients to scope and design the management information needed for the Board and senior management is, as always, to engage with the Board and senior management. Find out what they want to see rather than simply telling them what you think they need to know. While hopefully there is a significant overlap between the two, by engaging the Board and senior management you effectively make the content of the regular reporting their problem, although you should not rule out a lack of Board expectation, creating a void you will have to fill. If I was a Board member I would want to see:

- The extent of our third-party exposure;
- The extent of our outsourcing exposure;
- Material exposures vs non-material exposures;
- Any third-party concentrations, both by firm and location;
- Dependence on fourth to nth parties;
- Which third-party arrangements are impossible to substitute in a stressed exit;
- Details of any relevant events (internal within the firm, at the provider and also in industry);
- Any developments or disruptions that could impact the firm's operational resilience;
- Any developments or disruptions that could impact the firm's ability to comply with the Consumer Duty requirements;
- The effectiveness assessment of the relevant controls;
- Any action plans, including how they are being monitored, possible mitigating actions and any additional or different controls that are required.

Firms already have multiple sets of management information being generated that could contribute to understanding third-party exposure, for example:

- Operational risk management information – including monthly operational risk reports, loss events, near misses, RCSA's showing potential disruptions and risks outside appetite;
- Cyber and IT risk management – including any breaches or data loss incidents, IT incidents, patching and IT downtime;
- Business Continuity, Incident Management and Disaster Recovery – including BCP test outcomes, historical incidents, open actions, audit findings and training.

The Management Information required as part of the TPRMF contains all of the challenges and issues associated with management reporting in general:

- What to report;
- Good reporting is key; otherwise, why bother;
- Knowing how the information will be used;
- Informed decisions require good information;
- How much is enough, it is difficult to find the right balance – pass me the phone book? Not everything you monitor has to be reported;
- Reporting must be relevant to the audience. The Board is unlikely to be interested in the detail;
- Understanding risk terminology used;
- What are the key messages;
- Data quality (the quality of data collected in year 3 is usually significantly better than that collected in the inaugural year; if it isn't, you are either a genius or may have a problem);
- Quantitative and qualitative information;
- How to consolidate information.

Firms should always be aware of the possibility that the third-party arrangements may come to an end at some stage. The exit arrangements should be negotiated as part of the legally binding initial agreement specified in the BCBS principle 5 and must ensure an orderly end to the outsourcing arrangements. Firms should be aware of and mitigate the possibility that the risk exposure may continue beyond the life of the outsourcing relationship. Exit strategies should be clearly documented with clear roles and responsibilities and refreshed as appropriate.

On several occasions, during the outsourcing training Jimi and I provide, there are discussions on the importance of having exit, particularly stressed exit, strategies. Some delegates have explained that their firm had outsourced a significant part of their operations to a company and that the company had notified them that they were entering administration, citing increasing costs as the cause. The various firms had wrestled with the implications over the next few days as they came to recognise that there was no simple substitute available and that if the service provider ceased to operate they would be unable to offer a significant part of their product offering. Fortunately, the third-party provider had entered into discussions with another party to help in the search for potential buyers and that party had apparently obtained interim funding to enable the service provider to continue operating while a buyer was found. In the end, creditors took control of the company and the various delegate firms continued to operate. While I expect that even firms with robust stressed exit strategies would have struggled in these circumstances, firms must endeavour to ensure they are protected in extreme circumstances.

The BCBS Principles for the Sound Management of Third-Party Risk[4] are clear that:

> **Principle 9:** Banks should maintain exit plans for planned termination and exit strategies for unplanned termination of TPSP arrangements.

Intragroup outsourcing poses one of the big third-party challenges. Having worked in the UK subsidiary of a very significant international bank, the use of the group systems was not optional. Regulators expect firms to subject intragroup third-party arrangements (including outsourcing) to the same regulatory expectations as arrangements with a third party. In the UK, the PRA[2] permits firms to comply proportionately with the requirements according to their level of 'control and influence' over the entity that is providing the outsourced service, and we have worked with firms to develop a control and influence assessment.

Finally, there are a number of key challenges and opportunities associated with third-party risk management, including:

- There is a general regulatory expectation that firms:
  - Entering into third-party arrangements should retain the necessary skills to exercise effective oversight over the service provided. While both understandable and laudable, the reality is that staff who have seen their roles and responsibilities outsourced often leave the firms involved, perhaps even moving to the third-party provider;

- Should be able to substitute the service provider or bring the service back in-house. For a variety of reasons, including cost, this may be easier to say than do;
- Knowing and understanding your third parties. Surprisingly, some firms still struggle to identify all their third-party exposures. Every firm using third parties must have an inventory that:
  - Details all the third-party relationships throughout the organisation;
  - Enables the firm to quickly identify third-party relationships and contracts;
  - Establishes and documents who is accountable for individual supplier relationships;
  - Tracks contract terms, including key events such as renewal and expiration dates;
- Tracking activity – firms should document and track engagements and activity, including:
  - Knowing exactly how and why third parties are being engaged;
  - Identifying any inherently high-risk third-party products or services;
  - Using notifications and reporting to provide transparency into third-party relationships;
  - Monitoring and mitigating third-party-related audit and regulatory findings;
- Volume and complexity of third-party relationships:
  - Many firms have hundreds or even thousands of third-party relationships;
  - These relationships are often complex;
- Understanding fourth to nth-party exposures;
- Regulatory and Compliance challenges:
  - Data privacy and cybersecurity regulations increase as digital data becomes ingrained into business operations. These regulations can indirectly affect your organisation if you work with a third party that must comply with them;
  - General Data Protection Regulation.

PART

Four

Monitoring, Reporting and Taking Action

We see many examples where firms complete RCSAs periodically but then do not monitor and report on risks and controls or take appropriate action when issues are identified. The operational risk management activities are academic if they do not lead to action, and failure to take action will lead to crystallised risks and undermine the value of ORM within the firm. Part Four of the book considers three crucial areas: risk monitoring, risk mitigation and risk reporting.

In Chapter 11, we examine how to monitor risks and controls on an ongoing basis using risk indicators and metrics. Predictive KRIs are the 'holy grail' of ORM, and we will explore progress towards this Eden. Chapter 12 will explore taking action to mitigate and manage identified risks, including critical decisions around the trade-offs involved in decision-making. Finally, in Chapter 13, we consider the crucial area of risk reporting. Effective risk reporting is fundamental to proactive action-focused ORM and is often given too little attention by firms. We review the main types of ORM reports and some key principles to help design reports that meet the needs of those using them.

CHAPTER 11

Monitoring Risks and Controls – The Holy Grail of ORM

The tools and techniques discussed in Chapter 6 (Risk Identification and Assessment) enable us to understand and mitigate our firms' potential exposures to operational risks and also to identify when things have gone wrong. This is perhaps similar to thinking about what might go wrong before undertaking a long road trip and taking actions to reduce the likelihood of a breakdown (perhaps by checking our tyres, fuel and coolant).

Once we depart and commence driving, we then have a number of ways of monitoring the performance of the car. We all have a speedometer, and fuel and temperature gauges to ensure no unforeseen developments and most modern cars also offer a sometimes bewildering array of dashboard warning lights, from the dreaded engine management light to the frustrating tyre pressure light that is often triggered by the impact of temperature changes on our tyre pressures. These lights tend to fall into two categories: lights that warn us but enable us to continue driving and those telling us to stop driving immediately. In the UK, some of these lights can cause your car to fail its annual roadworthiness test.

In operational risk management, there are a number of metrics that enable us to monitor the performance of our organisation and reduce the likelihood or impact of an operational risk event. Most firms have developed metrics to assess and monitor their operational risk exposure and any firms that have not should begin to do so without delay. These metrics can be very simple indicators, for example, how many events, or be more sophisticated. In an ideal world, metrics provide an early warning by monitoring the ongoing performance of the organisation and the control environment while also reporting the operational risk profile.

The metrics utilised to monitor risks and controls in operational risk management comprise:

- **Key risk indicators (KRIs):** A metric that indicates whether a potential key risk could crystallise. KRIs must by definition be aligned with key risks;

- **Key control indicators (KCIs):** A metric that measures the effectiveness of key risk controls;
- **Key performance indicators (KPIs):** A metric that measures performance.

Unfortunately, one category of indicator can often morph into another. For example:

- A KPI that captures the number of foreign exchange transactions processed by a back office function can morph into a KRI if it shows activity has grown to such an extent that transactions can no longer be processed safely and efficiently;
- A KCI that shows weaknesses in a particular control can morph into a risk indicator.

Some of the common indicators collected and monitored by firms include:

- Number of loss events;
- Impact of the loss events;
- Events that did not result in a loss;
- Customer complaints;
- Customer satisfaction surveys;
- Department headcount below approved levels;
- Staff turnover – which is best by department and key management;
- Staff absence;
- Failures to complete mandatory training;
- Employment satisfaction surveys;
- Control failures;
- Near misses;
- IT downtime;
- Missed system patches;
- Failure to meet service-level agreements;
- Outstanding audit issues;
- Cyber incidents.

Setting indicator levels is a difficult task. KRIs must be aligned to a risk but what is the appropriate metric. Many years ago, when operational risk was in its infancy, I introduced KRIs into an organisation that had not previously captured any operational risk metrics. The question immediately became at what level should the actual metric itself be set. If we consider the appropriate metric for external frauds in a small retail bank, what is the appropriate number. Initial effort must focus on collecting or reviewing the external fraud data and then taking a judgement as to the appropriate metric (how many internal fraud events are enough, for example per month, is it 0, 1, 5 or 100). Clearly, once a metric has been established, effort will focus on monitoring external frauds, thereby validating if the metric is appropriate. I would expect a large domestic bank in the UK to have a great many external fraud events each month while a small retail bank may have very few, if any. The size, nature and complexity of a firm are therefore an important consideration when compiling a library of metrics. Practitioners, senior management and boards should also accept that if they are capturing and setting a metric for the first time the likelihood is that it will need to be revised in due course, and this should not be seen as a criticism of the individual who proposed the original metric.

In the past, I have been asked by firms looking to introduce KRIs for the first time whether it is best to start with the proverbial clean sheet of paper, use existing information or base the indicators on existing RCSAs. While much will depend on the organisation involved, it is important that our KRIs are aligned with our key risks, making the RCSAs a good place to start, but we should not discard existing information as it is already collected and available. Firms in this position should also review the existing KRI libraries from external sources.

When setting KRIs from scratch there are 10 key steps:

1. What are the organisation's key risks;
2. What causes can result in these key risks crystallising;
3. Review existing information to see if it reflects these causes;
4. Identify any key risk causes that do not have an associated KRI;
5. Establish a process for collecting and capturing key risk causes that do not have an associated KRI;
6. For each KRI, establish a trigger that when breached results in a review and reporting of the underlying risk;
7. Create a KRI database and mechanism for recording the metrics;
8. Establish governance arrangements for the reporting and oversight of the indicators;
9. Constantly review the KRIs to ensure the KRI and associated thresholds are appropriate;
10. Take action when triggers are breached.

Some of these key steps can be applied to existing metrics and I would urge readers to benchmark their existing metrics against the following criteria:

- Do all key risks have KRIs;
- Do the metrics reflect the key risk causes;

- Does the KRI database capture all KRIs;
- When a KRI trigger is breached is a review undertaken and the breach reported;
- Are the governance arrangements for the reporting and oversight of the indicators effective and efficient;
- Is action taken when triggers are breached;
- Can you provide examples of action being taken as a result of trigger breaches;
- Are KRIs regularly reviewed to ensure the KRI and associated thresholds are appropriate;
- How is this review evidenced.

If we set triggers for a particular metric we are effectively setting a risk appetite. If the indicator is below the trigger the risk is within appetite and no action is needed. If the trigger is breached action will be required to ensure the risk does not crystallise or, if it does, the impact is mitigated. I would expect breaches in KRIs, KCIs and KPIs to be subject to formal governance arrangements and reported to the relevant risk committees and senior management, both as part of the regular management information pack and as a specific standalone escalation if warranted by the breach.

Since operational risk emerged as a distinct discipline, practitioners have searched for a number of 'holy grails' including leading KRIs (indicators that will enable practitioners to predict and therefore prevent operational risk incidents). Obviously, KRI indicators are most valuable when they are forward looking as they warn that a risk may crystallise and enable the firm to take corrective action. Nevertheless, we must recognise that there is not usually a direct, consistent, automatic link between a leading indicator being breached and the risk crystallising. By that I mean, although an indicator trigger may be breached, that may not automatically result in the risk crystallising. Also, I have found that sometimes it is only after an event has crystallised that it is possible to connect the performance of the KRI and the event. For example, when I ran a treasury back office, staff absenteeism was an indicator of potential risk events crystallising. However, there were other considerations that also contributed to back office failures. Staff absence could well be high during the flu season but if treasury activity was low (perhaps because of flu in the dealing room) there was generally not a problem.

To be truly leading, an indicator must address the causes of an operational risk. In Figure 9.1, we discussed the causes of operational risk events and our leading KRIs must reflect causal issues. Lagging KRIs would identify that a risk has crystallised. In Figure 9.1, we also identified the four types of controls as preventative, detective, corrective and directive. When monitoring and reporting on KCIs it is important to identify the control type being measured. A defective preventative control is potentially more damaging than a corrective control.

Many years ago, a branch I was responsible for experienced a significant risk event. When we undertook a post-mortem, the branch responded by pointing to one of the several 100 risk indicators they submitted to head office on a daily basis, noting that this event was flagged in the metrics. Of course, the branch had not reported the indicator's performance at the time! This incident raises the issue of how many KRIs should you collect. We have already seen that a KRI must be linked to a key risk so in some ways this limits the number of KRIs we could collect. Nevertheless, if we collect a high number of KRIs and cannot review them as necessary then we are not enhancing the risk management process. KRIs must be aligned to a key risk, actionable and reviewed in a timely manner (which is determined by the nature of the risk and the indicator).

We should therefore strive to avoid creating a KRI, KCI or KPI cottage industry. Manually collecting, collating, reviewing and reporting metrics is extremely burdensome and usually fails to identify potential risk events. Many firms use GRC systems for the collection, collation, review and reporting of indicators and their risk management process is enhanced as a result. Moving from manual spreadsheets to using a GRC system for indicators will enable you to stop managing the data and start managing the risk. It will also release valuable resources from your indicator cottage industry and enable them to focus on the resultant risks.

While the general issue of operational risk reporting is addressed by Jimi in Chapter 13, the subject of how to report metrics to the various risk committees and the Board warrants attention here. As we would expect the BCBS Revisions to the Principles for the Sound Management of Operational Risk addresses the issue of monitoring and reporting[1] in principles 2 and 8 and some of the supporting paragraphs (the italics are mine and are used to draw attention to the relevant statements):

Principle 2: Banks should develop, implement and maintain an operational risk management framework that is fully integrated into the bank's overall risk management processes. The ORMF adopted by an individual bank will depend on a range of factors, including the bank's nature, size, complexity and risk profile.

Paragraph 23: ORMF documentation should clearly:

(h) *establish risk reporting and management information systems (MIS) producing timely, and accurate data;*

Principle 8: *Senior management should implement a process to regularly monitor operational risk profiles and material operational exposures. Appropriate reporting mechanisms should be in place* at the board of directors, senior management and business unit levels to support proactive management of operational risk.

Paragraph 43: A bank should ensure that its *reports are comprehensive, accurate, consistent and actionable across business units and products*. To this end, the first line of defence should ensure reporting on any residual operational risks, including operational risk events, control deficiencies, process inadequacies and non-compliance with operational risk tolerances. *Reports should be manageable in scope and volume* by providing an outlook on the bank's operational risk profile and adherence to the operational risk appetite and tolerance statement; effective decision-making is impeded by both excessive amounts and paucity of data.

Paragraph 44: Reporting should *be timely and a bank should be able to produce reports in both normal and stressed market conditions. The frequency of reporting* should reflect the risks involved and the pace and nature of changes in the operating environment. The *results of monitoring activities should be included in regular management and board reports, as should assessments of the ORMF performed by the internal/external audit and/or risk management functions.* Reports generated by or for supervisory authorities should also be reported internally to senior management and the board of directors, where appropriate.

Paragraph 46: Data capture and risk reporting processes should be *analysed periodically with the goal of enhancing risk management performance as well as advancing risk management policies*, procedures and practices.

In summary, therefore the metric reports to the relevant risk committees should be able to satisfy the following requirements:

- Timely;
- Accurate;
- Regular;
- Monitor operational risk profiles and material operational exposures;
- Comprehensive;
- Consistent;
- Actionable across business units and products;
- Manageable in scope and volume;

- Capable of being produced in normal and stressed market conditions;
- Analysed to enhancing risk management performance.

In many firms, metric reporting takes the form of a spreadsheet with cell colours reflecting within appetite (green), within tolerance (orange) and above tolerance (red) with each metric evident in the report. If the colouring process is undertaken manually there is always scope for error, thereby failing to satisfy our checklist. There is also a tendency to swamp the report recipient with too much information, making it difficult, if not impossible to identify the real issues. But surely not everything we monitor needs to be reported to the relevant risk committee. If everything is fine (green) then why report that metric. As a board member I would only want to be notified if there is a potential issue or concern.

Often metrics are consolidated across business units, for example, operational risk incidents may be collected from each relevant department and a consolidated report submitted to the risk committee. It is often at the point of consolidation that a key error is made. As an enthusiastic salmon fisherman, but nervous wader, I often find myself standing in a river wondering how far I can wade before the water becomes too deep (a process I have tried to illustrate in Figure 11.1). Obviously knowing the average depth of the river creates a false impression as in parts the river is deeper than the average.

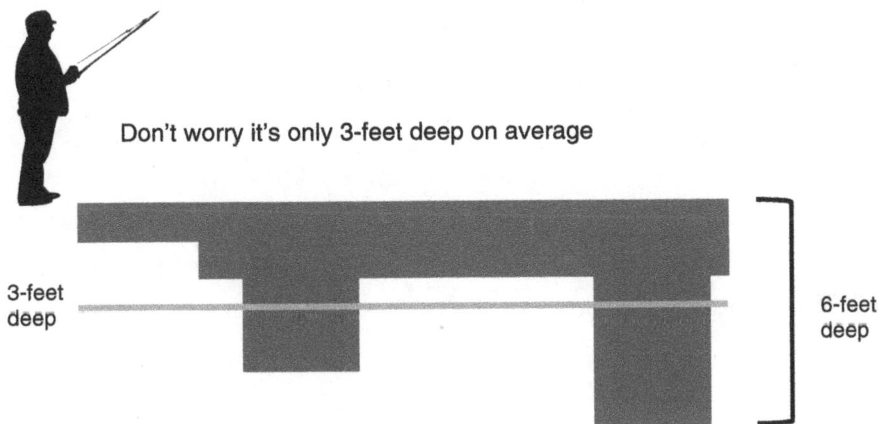

FIGURE 11.1 A Fisherman's Tale

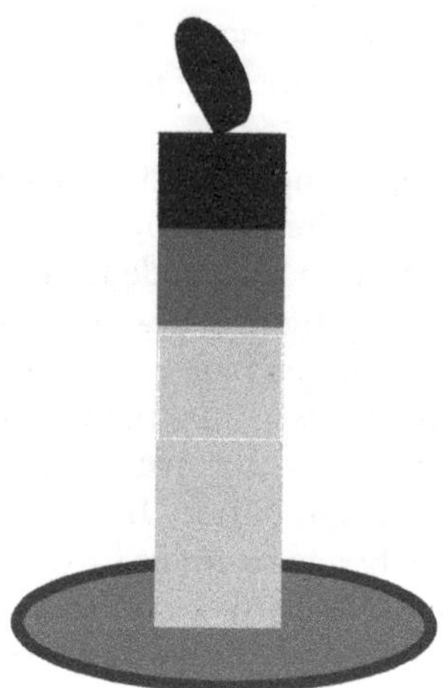

FIGURE 11.2 The Candlestick

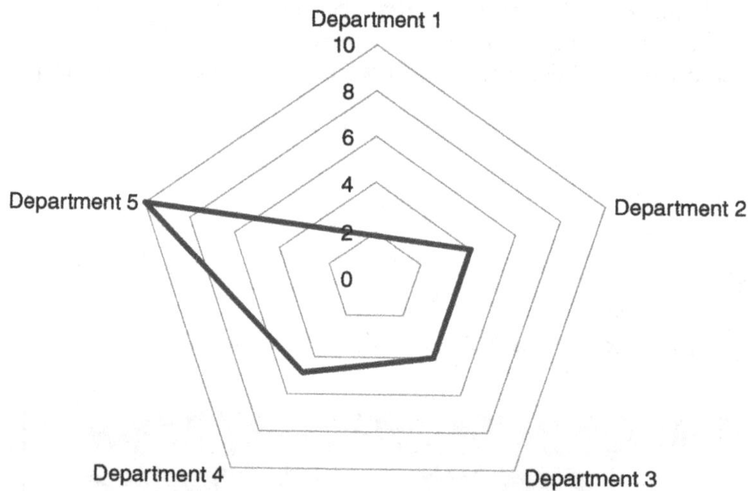

FIGURE 11.3 Risk Spider Gram

The same can be said of monitoring risk and control metrics. Let us consider the following risk metrics, which are captured by departments. A score of 1–4 is within appetite, 5–8 is within tolerance and 9–10 is outside appetite. How then should we report the following situation:

Department 1	2
Department 2	4
Department 3	4
Department 4	5
Department 5	10
Average	5

Reporting the situation as a 5 is incorrect as one particular department is recording the worst possible score, a 10. In these situations, I would rather report the position as a 10 to ensure that the report recipients are fully aware of possible issues. A better solution, if the reporting framework permits, would be to present the metrics in a way that conveys the true story and I have attempted to illustrate this in Figure 11.2, although I am unable to use green (hence light grey), orange (hence medium grey) or red (hence black). This would enable report recipients to better understand the true picture. An alternative to my candlestick could be a risk spider gram of the type shown in Figure 11.3. I have seen these used very effectively recently.

CHAPTER 12

Mitigating and Managing Operational Risks

In Chapter 5, we explored the importance of risk appetite. Risk appetite is a fundamental component of the ORM framework, and the absence of a clear statement of risk appetite and supporting measures is like driving a car without any speed limits. The risk appetite should drive the calibration of controls such that residual risk is within the Board-approved risk appetite. Therefore, risk appetite statements and metrics are essential when deciding how to address identified operational risks. Indeed, such decisions are only possible when made in the context of risk appetite! The appetite statement must go beyond qualitative statements and include measurable metrics and limits that can be used, returning to our motoring analogy, to drive the car safely.

TAKING ACTION

The tools and activities described in Chapter 6, including RCSA, should not be ends in themselves; they are means to an end – the end being to **manage operational risks.** As outlined in Chapter 5, there are four different possible responses (4Ts) to an identified risk:

- **Treat:** This means taking **action** to reduce the risk of exposure; this could be the inherent risk exposure and/or the residual risk exposure. In most cases, actions are taken in relation to the residual risk by implementing preventative controls that reduce the likelihood of the risk occurring or controls that mitigate the impact if the risk crystallises (e.g. new detective controls that may mitigate the size of the loss through rapid detection, or new corrective controls such as insurance).
- **Tolerate:** Just as the name suggests, another option is to do nothing and, as such, tolerate or accept the risk exposure. Operational risks, which are unlikely to be zero, can be tolerated when within risk appetite. When a decision is made to tolerate a risk exposure beyond risk

appetite, it's important to be explicit, gain approval through governance and document it. We will explore this type of risk acceptance below.

- **Transfer:** Another option is to transfer the risk. Two common examples of how risk can be transferred are through insurance (where the risk crystallises, the insurance company will mitigate the loss in return for the premium) and through outsourcing or using third parties, where activities and risks are transferred to a third party. The firm remains accountable for outsourcing or using third parties and must manage the new risks associated with the third-party arrangements.
- **Terminate:** Finally, the firm can terminate the risk exposure. For example, if a firm is uncomfortable with third-party risk exposure, e.g. a vendor compromises customer confidential data, it may bring the outsourced activity back in-house. As risk is part and parcel of doing any activity or business, there will be limits to the extent to which terminating risk will be possible.

The response to an identified risk will depend on several factors, as shown below.

First is the **severity and impact of the risk**, which could include the potential impact on business operations: Firms need to assess how the risk might affect day-to-day operations, customers, financial markets and overall business performance. Given the increasing importance of **operational resilience**, it's essential to consider how significantly the risk could disrupt IBS. When considering the impact of operational risks in RCSA, many firms now explicitly rate the potential impact of the risk on resilience/IBS, which allows easy identification and mitigation of risks that may threaten resilience.

The **financial impact**, which includes estimated potential financial losses from the risk, including direct and indirect losses (e.g. reputational damage and regulatory fines). Since the GFC, regulators have increasingly emphasised **customer impact**, including understanding how the risk might affect clients such as delays in payments, data breaches or service interruptions. Under the UK FCA Consumer Duty, firms must consider the potential for foreseeable harm and ensure this is prevented. Customer harm can lead to long-term reputational damage, and failure to mitigate identified foreseeable harm to consumers could lead to severe regulatory sanctions.

Second is the **likelihood of occurrence**. The likelihood of the risk materialising is a key determinant of how the firm should act. Highly likely risks but with a moderate impact may require immediate action to reduce the residual risk, e.g. adding preventative controls. In contrast, low-likelihood, high-impact risks that might be considered in scenario analysis (e.g. a financial crisis or pandemic) may demand contingency planning to help manage the potential impact.

Third is **regulatory and compliance requirements.** Banks must comply with an array of regulatory standards, rules and guidance from local regulators (FCA and PRA in the UK) and international standard setters. Regulators often require specific actions for risk mitigation, such as enhancing capital buffers or tightening controls for particular risk categories. An additional dimension that can be more difficult to assess is **regulatory expectations.** Understanding what regulators expect in terms of what's appropriate and proportionate given their scale, nature and complexity is key. Requirements are frequently not black or white and require judgement on what is appropriate. Failing to meet these expectations can result in fines or restrictions on operations. Chapter 14 has more on how to manage expectations.

Fourth is the relationship between risk exposure and **risk appetite and impact tolerance.** Banks must align their responses with their risk appetite – the level of risk they are willing to accept in pursuit of their objectives. Where risks that are outside the bank's risk tolerance are identified, they must be addressed with high-priority actions. We explored **impact tolerance** in Chapter 8 in relation to operational resilience, which refers to the maximum level of disruption a bank can withstand while continuing to provide IBS. Banks must establish actions that keep them within these tolerances during severe but plausible disruptions.

Fifth is the critical issue of **cost–benefit analysis.** It's essential to evaluate the costs of implementing risk controls or mitigation strategies (e.g. cybersecurity upgrades, enhanced monitoring systems) compared to the potential losses if the risk materialises.

Sixth is **time sensitivity and urgency.** Determine whether the risk requires immediate action (such as containment or mitigation) or long-term strategic initiatives (like revising risk management frameworks or investing in new technologies). In cases where risks present immediate threats (e.g. cyberattacks, market crashes), banks need to implement crisis response plans including communication strategies and incident response.

Finally, **stakeholder considerations.** Involve senior management, risk committees and other key departments (e.g. legal, compliance, IT) in the decision-making process to ensure a comprehensive approach to risk response. Also, consider the position of **external stakeholders,** including the expectations of external stakeholders such as regulators, investors, clients and partners. Transparent communication with these groups is critical, especially if the risk may impact them. We consider this increasingly hot topic much further in Chapter 18 on ESG.

MANAGING TRADE-OFFS

As the old saying goes, *you can never have too much of a good thing*. This may be true for guitars, cars and even handbags, but too much control can be inefficient, costly and counterproductive. Controls impose costs, and these can be **direct** costs, such as resource time taken to operate the control (specialists may be hired just to operate controls), systems costs and **indirect** costs, such as the impact on the ability to meet customer deadlines or on staff satisfaction levels and morale (increasing staff turnover and knock-on risks such as key person risk).

Controls may also be counterproductive if people don't see their value; they may simply ignore them or find ways to get around them. We have probably all seen rules in firms that are more honoured in the breach than in observance. Not only is this a significant issue when internal audits or regulators conduct reviews, but it can also cultivate a toxic culture of non-compliance that ultimately leads to patchy compliance across the organisation – not just for the rules that don't make sense!

As we saw in Chapter 7, determining the optimum level of control can be challenging. An important consideration will be the mix of controls between, on the one hand, preventative, detective, corrective and directive, but also concerning the independence of controls (i.e. the Swiss Cheese concept) so that controls are not highly correlated with each other but provide independent mitigation. The fundamental point is to recognise the trade-offs that are part and parcel of an integrated approach to risk management.

RISK ACCEPTANCE

After assessing and identifying residual risk, risk owners must judge whether the level of risk is acceptable or not. We saw above in the '4Ts' that one of the options is to tolerate the risk. A special category of tolerating risk is risk acceptance, where the risk exposure is beyond risk appetite. Where a decision is made to accept a risk outside the Board-approved appetite, it must implement robust safeguards to mitigate potential adverse impacts. The following measures are crucial to ensure adequate control and monitoring:

First, it's essential to establish a **clear governance framework for risk acceptance** of risks above risk appetite, including obtaining approval from senior management or the Board. The absence of evidence is evidence of absence, so decisions on acceptance must be documented. It's also critical to establish accountability at appropriate levels for managing and monitoring the elevated risks that were accepted and for any compensatory risk mitigation strategy. An important consideration will be whether to inform the regulator about the decision – it will be essential to consult with the compliance/regulatory engagement team as to whether the decision meets the criteria in UK FCA Principle 11 and PRA Fundamental Rule 7 concerning informing regulators of things *they might reasonably expect to be made aware of.*

Second, where risks above appetite are accepted, conducting an **enhanced risk assessment is important**, including potential financial, operational, reputational and regulatory compliance impacts. Stress testing and scenario analysis can be helpful tools to evaluate the possible effects under adverse conditions.

Third, it's critical to establish **clearly defined escalation procedures** and to develop **clear guidelines for escalating risks** to higher management and the Board, ensuring timely reporting and communication of deviations from the risk appetite.

Fourth, **mitigation plans** should be developed to address the heightened risk exposure. Compensating controls can be implemented, such as increased capital reserves or liquidity buffers and identifying and planning mitigating actions to reduce the risk over time. Strengthening internal control systems to detect, monitor and manage the heightened risk effectively and conduct frequent reviews (compliance or risk reviews) or audits to ensure compliance with the approved approach.

Fifth, the **time frame of risk acceptance and exit strategy must be established quickly.** Where a risk is being accepted that's above the Board-approved appetite, it's important to establish a strict time frame for review and, ideally, a strategy and documented plan for bringing the risk back within the appetite.

Sixth, developing and implementing **increased monitoring and reporting is essential,** ideally through real-time data analysis and more frequent risk reports during acceptance. Regular reporting should be carried out to relevant governance committees, the Board and appropriate regulators, who may request additional reporting during heightened risk.

Finally, it's important to ensure **training and awareness**, train relevant staff to understand the nature of the elevated risk and the controls in place, and foster a culture of risk awareness and accountability.

The above safeguards can help ensure that accepting risks above the appetite is a deliberate, controlled and documented decision, minimising potential adverse consequences if risks crystallise.

CASE STUDY: COVID-19 LOCKDOWNS

The dangers of failing to recognise the potential costs of actions and ensuring these don't outweigh any possible benefits have been illustrated numerous times in recent history, but perhaps most starkly with the lockdown policies deployed by many countries in response to the COVID-19 pandemic.

COVID-19 lockdowns were initially implemented as an emergency measure ostensibly to curb the virus's rapid spread, protect healthcare systems from collapse and save lives. While they may have succeeded in slowing transmission rates, the broader consequences of these policies have raised significant concerns. Growing evidence suggests that the harms caused by prolonged lockdowns – economic, social, educational and psychological – may have outweighed their intended benefits.

Economic devastation: Lockdowns resulted in unprecedented economic disruption worldwide. Businesses, particularly small and medium enterprises, were forced to shut down, leading to mass layoffs and financial insecurity. The World Bank reported a sharp increase in global poverty, reversing decades of progress, with an estimated 97 million people pushed into extreme poverty in 2020 alone. The informal sector, on which many low-income families depend, was disproportionately affected, leaving millions without a livelihood. While the intention was to protect lives, the economic fallout caused hunger, homelessness and long-term financial instability for millions of individuals and families. The economic impact on developing countries was even more devastating than in the developed world.

Educational inequalities: One of the most profound impacts of lockdowns was on education and children. School closures disrupted learning for millions of children, particularly those in low-income families who lacked access to online learning tools. A report by UNESCO highlighted significant learning losses, with many students failing to regain lost ground even after returning to in-person education. Moreover, marginalised communities faced widening educational gaps, further entrenching inequality. The long-term consequences of these disruptions – reduced lifetime earnings, diminished social mobility and lower overall productivity – are likely to reverberate for decades.

Mental health crisis: Lockdowns exacerbated a global mental health crisis. Social isolation, job losses and uncertainty about the future triggered significant increases in anxiety, depression and stress-related disorders. A meta-analysis published in *The Lancet*[1] found a consistent rise in mental health issues across all demographics during lockdowns, with young people and the elderly particularly affected. Suicide rates spiked in some regions, while access to mental health services was curtailed due to restrictions. For many, the psychological scars of prolonged isolation and economic hardship may endure long after the pandemic.

Health system disruptions: Ironically, lockdowns designed to protect healthcare systems disrupted non-COVID-19 healthcare services. Routine medical appointments, preventive screenings and elective surgeries were delayed, worsening health outcomes. A report from the World Health Organisation[2] indicated a decline in vaccination rates and increased mortality from preventable diseases. Additionally, the rise in sedentary lifestyles during lockdowns contributed to a surge in obesity, diabetes and cardiovascular conditions, placing further strain on healthcare resources.

Unintended consequences: Lockdowns had unintended social consequences as well. Incidents of domestic violence surged as victims were trapped with their abusers, and support systems were overwhelmed. Social cohesion frayed as individuals faced isolation from family and friends. In some communities, the enforcement of lockdown measures disproportionately affected marginalised groups, exacerbating social inequities and tensions.

While COVID-19 lockdowns may have been necessary initially when the nature of COVID-19 was unknown, their widespread and prolonged implementation created a cascade of harmful impacts. The economic devastation, educational losses, mental health crisis, healthcare disruptions and social issues they caused highlight the need to consider the full range of costs, benefits and trade-offs when determining what actions are appropriate. The use of lockdowns is a case study of the dangers of taking action without adequately considering the potential impacts (including unintended consequences).

CHAPTER 13

Reporting Risks

Operational risk Management Information (MI) and reporting are critical components of the ORM cycle for identifying, assessing, mitigating and monitoring risks while being essential for ensuring transparency and accountability across the organisation. This chapter explores the key components, principles and best practices for producing operational risk MI reports. It also examines the challenges and technological advances in this domain.

The revised BCBS Principles for the Sound Management of Operational Risk set out the expectations for internationally active banks on risk MI and reporting in principle 8:

> **Principle 8:** Senior management should implement a process to regularly monitor operational risk profiles and material operational exposures. Appropriate reporting mechanisms should be in place at the board of directors, senior management, and business unit levels to support proactive management of operational risk.[1]

To identify **potential risks and vulnerabilities**, operational risk MI should include **risk identification data**, including internal audit findings, RCSA, KRIs, incident reports and external events. Risk assessment data should be included to evaluate the likelihood and impact of risks and prioritise mitigation actions, including quantitative data such as loss data and exposure metrics, qualitative data, expert judgement, scenario analysis and survey-based assessments. To help the organisation learn from past incidents and improve future risk preparedness, risk MI and reporting should include **Risk Mitigation and Control Information**, including reports on the adequacy of risk controls in mitigating identified risks and documentation of planned or ongoing measures to reduce risk exposure. MI should feature **incident and loss data**, including records of actual operational risk events and their financial impact, and industry-wide events to benchmark and anticipate emerging risks. We considered KRIs and monitoring metrics in Chapter 11, which are essential in operational risk MI and reporting. Finally, risk MI and reports should include regulatory compliance data, and it is important this now includes MI on operational resilience concerning the status of IBS in relation to impact tolerances.

The **objectives** and **purposes** of ORM reporting should be to inform decision-making at all levels in the organisation, to ensure transparency and accountability, to inform management of current risk levels versus risk appetite, to provide assurance, to facilitate the control processes, to provide evidence of compliance with internal and regulatory requirements ('absence of evidence is evidence of absence'), to enable proactive responses to emerging risks and to allow decision-making around the active management of risks.

It is essential when designing operational risk MI reports to ask and answer a series of questions:

- What are we trying to achieve?
- What are the objectives of the report?
- Who are the reports for?
- What level and who in the organisation?
- Are they reports that we anticipate may be shared with regulators?
- What are the expectations of the Board and Senior Management?
- Can we leverage existing information?
- What should we report?
- How frequently should the reports be produced?

The **frequency of reporting** is critical and requires some careful judgements to be made – too infrequent and decision-makers and governance committees will be acting on outdated information, which could mean taking inappropriate action or failing to act quickly enough given an emerging threat; on the other hand, too frequent and there is a danger risk reporting becomes a cottage industry and the risk team ends up managing the data/ and producing risk MI reports rather than managing and overseeing risk. Moreover, unless the reported data are volatile and likely to change often, there is no point in expending great effort to produce the same information. Some types of data need to be timely, and advances in technology and the widespread use of Governance, Risk and Compliance tools (GRCs) are making this more practical:

- **Real-time:** For critical risk indicators, incidents requiring immediate action, the status of IBS;
- **Weekly/monthly:** Routine updates for ongoing monitoring and decision-making, status reports on actions and RCSA results and risk incident reports;
- **Quarterly/annually:** Comprehensive reviews for strategic planning, regulatory compliance and aggregated data.

THE REPORTING PYRAMID

There are various reporting levels, first at the **strategic level**, including high-level reports for senior management and the Board of Directors focusing on risk appetite, emerging risks and overall trends. Reports at the **tactical level**, including more detailed reports for business unit heads highlighting specific risks, incidents and mitigation plans, and reports at the **operational level**, featuring even more granular reports for frontline teams addressing day-to-day risks and control issues.

The reporting pyramid is a structured approach to organising and presenting operational risk management information to ensure that stakeholders at various levels of the organisation receive relevant and actionable insights.

Figure 13.1 illustrates the reporting pyramid by reference to operational resilience.

The three levels of the reporting pyramid are:

A. Day-to-day (operational)
- **Purpose:** Focused on day-to-day risk identification and management activities;
- **Audience:** Frontline managers and operational staff.
- **Content:**
    - Detailed incident reports, near misses and risk event logs;
    - KRIs showing early warning signs;
    - Status updates on risk mitigation actions and control effectiveness.

Who are the reports for?

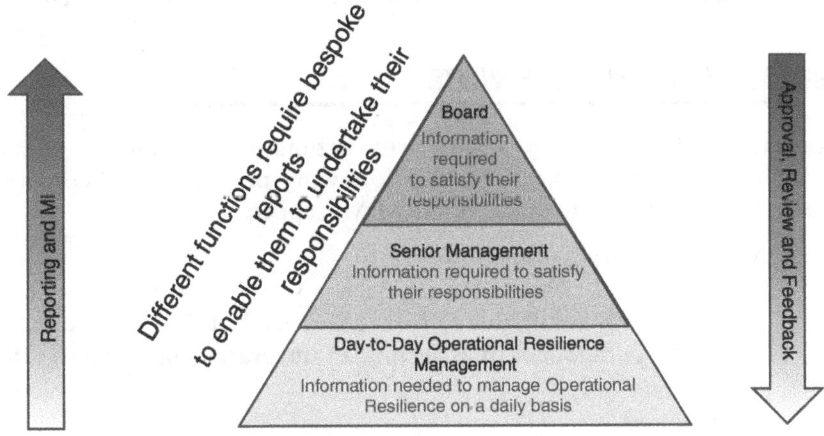

FIGURE 13.1 The Reporting Pyramid

B. Senior management (tactical)
- **Purpose:** Monitors risk trends and evaluates the effectiveness of controls within business units or departments;
- **Audience:** Business unit heads, department managers and risk teams.
- **Content:**
  - Aggregated risk data from multiple business units/IBS;
  - Heatmaps and dashboards highlighting emerging risks;
  - Analysis of control weaknesses and mitigation plans.

C. Board (strategic)
- **Purpose:** Provides a high-level overview of the organisation's risk exposure and alignment with risk appetite;
- **Audience:** Senior management and the Board of Directors.
- **Content:**
  - Summary of significant incidents and their organisational impact;
  - Trends and forecasts for significant risks;
  - Assessment of the organisation's adherence to their risk appetite.

The pyramid ensures a flow of information from detailed operational data to high-level strategic insights, enabling informed decision-making at every level in the organisation. There must be approval, review and feedback, as well as information flowing up the hierarchy. Too often, we have heard board members complain that the MI they receive is not fit for purpose, but at no point have they provided this feedback to those producing it! The result is a guessing game by the people creating the reports about what the audience actually wants, which can result in wasted time and effort. The content and design of MI should be driven by what the Board (or other committee) members need to be able to discharge their responsibilities, so it is critical to engage with them and get feedback when producing them.

BUILDING EFFECTIVE ORM REPORTS

Effective ORM reports provide clarity, actionable insights and alignment with organisational objectives. The following principles and components are critical for building effective ORM MI reports:

- **Integration across functions**
  - A perennial concern for regulators is where organisations operate in silos and are unable to form an integrated view of risk. A fundamental component of achieving an integrated approach to ORM is

consolidating risk information across various functions, including finance, IT, compliance and operations, into a unified reporting framework with a common language and criteria.

- **Focus on actionability**
  - A fundamental precept in effective integrated risk management is that it drives action. Therefore, it is essential to design risk MI reports that provide actionable insights rather than raw data dumps – the 'so what' is vital, where key findings can be highlighted and recommendations clearly articulated.
  - Perhaps the most powerful concept in the Basel 2 capital regime was the 'use test'; in the context of Basel 2, this was that capital models should be used to manage risk and not just be for calculating capital, in the context of risk MI reports, the MI must be capable of informing and driving action.

- **Leverage existing reports**
  - It is crucial to leverage or modify existing reports to the extent possible rather than *reinvent the wheel.* A good example is operational resilience, where there should be massive scope to leverage existing MI reports, as illustrated in Figure 13.2.

Can we leverage existing information?

Multiple sets of MI and reporting are currently being generated that can help a firm understand its resilience

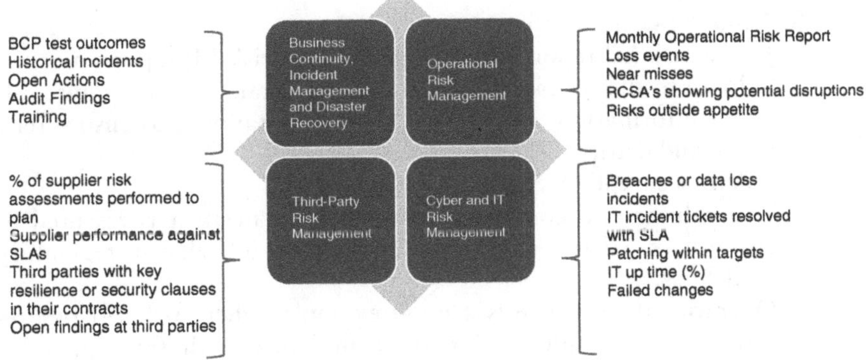

FIGURE 13.2 Leveraging Existing Reports

- **Make use of technology and tools**
  - Producing risk MI reports manually, using spreadsheets and PowerPoint, can be an extremely laborious process and, at worst (and this is something we have seen!), can consume the lion's share of the risk team's resources. With modern GRCs and business intelligence tools (e.g. Power BI), leveraging the available technology tools and analytics platforms to streamline data collection, analysis and reporting is essential.
  - Firms are increasingly incorporating GenAI to generate predictive risk analytics and more significant insights and improve efficiency in collection and production – more on the use of technology in Chapter 17.
- **Data quality and consistency**
  - Inaccurate risk reports that provide false or misleading information can be even more dangerous than no reporting – they are literally worse than useless! The complete mismanagement by TSB of the IT migration to Sabadell's IT platform is a good case in point, where the risk reporting on the change project failed to convey the potential for catastrophic failure. The focus on meeting deadlines overshadowed the acknowledgement of risks, and preliminary testing phases revealed flaws, but these were downplayed in risk reporting. For instance, incomplete integration and inadequate stress testing were not highlighted, leaving the Board and senior management overly confident in the change project with disastrous consequences.
  - It is vital to focus on data quality and consistency and to implement robust data governance to ensure accuracy, completeness and timeliness.
- **Stakeholder customisation**
  - Just as risk MI reports must be actionable, risk MI reports must be tailored to the recipient's needs. Different stakeholders require different information, and reports should be tailored to ensure relevance and clarity.
- **Regulatory compliance**
  - The volume and complexity of regulation mean it is essential to ensure risk MI reporting frameworks meet all relevant regulatory guidelines.
  - Operational resilience is a good example, where risk MI reports should include information on compliance with the regulatory requirements, e.g. maintaining IBS within impact tolerances, having the board review and approve the IBS, tolerances and self-assessment at least annually and so forth.

It is rare to find organisations genuinely satisfied with their risk MI reports, reflecting the significant challenges in producing high-quality risk MI reports.

Some of the key considerations and challenges include:

- You must know how the information will be used – otherwise, it is a lottery of whether it will meet the users' expectations.
- Informed decisions require good quality information – focusing on quality and accuracy is key to the usefulness of risk MI.
- But how much information is enough? It is difficult to find the right balance – we have all seen board risk committee reports that resemble War and Peace, and it is unlikely any board members have read them.
- Not everything you monitor should be reported! Especially given the ease of producing impressive-looking reports in modern GRCs, it can be tempting to include everything in the risk reports. The risk team must carefully judge what to include, which should not be everything! Setting a maximum page limit can be helpful to ensure only necessary information is included – additional materials can always be included in an annexe or appendix.[2]
- Reporting must be relevant to the audience. Board members are unlikely to be interested in very granular details, whereas members of the Operations Committee will be.
- Understand and use risk terms consistently and avoid a word salad of acronyms. Too often, we see casual use of risk terminology that can result in confusion and error (e.g. using risk appetite and risk tolerance interchangeably, which have very different meanings in the firm).
- What are the key messages in the risk MI reports – the 'so what'? This is where the risk team can demonstrate their value, including expertise and understanding, by providing expert commentary and key messages, not just the raw data.
- It is vital to get the right mix of quantitative and qualitative information in MI reports and to be creative in how complex information is presented – select the graphics and charts based on the data presented and feedback from the recipients (modern GRCs have vast capabilities to present data in multiple ways and formats and time should be taken to select the right approach for the specific data being presented, whether this is a simple graph, pie chart, scatter chart, heatmap or Harvey Balls).
- Decisions need to be made on consolidating information, such as the different legal entities, geographies and functions within an entity.

Although many larger organisations operate on business lines with support functions that do not sit neatly in regulated legal entities, regulators will expect legal entities to have risk MI reports that allow them to understand risk for the legal entity. Organisations often produce numerous cuts in risk MI, including by geography, group, regulated entities and business lines.

- One of the significant challenges to producing risk MI reports is fragmented data systems. Modern GRCs have powerful capacities to draw data from many data sources. The big challenge remains where end-user computing solutions are used, including spreadsheets, making producing holistic consolidated information challenging.
- Aggregate or escalate? It can be tempting to use average indicators to produce aggregate metrics (e.g. average risk scores, average control scores and average KRI scores). However, this is extremely dangerous, as it can conceal high scores that should prompt action (sometimes, this is a deliberate consequence of avoiding reporting lousy news to governance committees, an all too common characteristic reflecting significant cultural flaws). Escalation should be utilised rather than aggregation and candlestick reporting, as popularised by Ariane Chapelle.

KEY ORM RISK REPORTS

No two organisations are exactly alike regarding their suite of risk reports. Still, there are some key reports that almost all firms produce that provide an essential foundation for effective risk reporting.

- **The risk register:** This key report should capture all risks (often just operational risks, but sometimes financial ones). The Risk Register should be stored on the GRC system if used, or if the organisation does not use a GRC, a spreadsheet. However, be warned, maintaining a Risk Register on a spreadsheet can be challenging and lead to the problem of **managing data, not risk.** The main potential issues with the Risk Register include:
  - **Granularity:** Getting the right level of granularity is key. Too much, and the Risk Register can become unwieldy and difficult to manage, especially where it is being housed on a spreadsheet.

- Maintenance costs can become a huge problem, especially when large spreadsheets are used and must be manually updated monthly.
- **No causes or impacts:** The Risk Register often excludes causes and impacts (these are captured in RCSA), which can limit its usefulness, especially since there is limited ability to drill down to the underlying risk, which is a challenge when spreadsheets are used.
- Lack of control adequacy assessment.

- **RCSA Heatmaps:** Risk Heatmaps can be a powerful risk MI report as they are multi dimensional, illustrating the risk profile, the effectiveness of controls in mitigating inherent risk and the status of risks in relation to risk appetite. An example of a risk heatmap is shown in Figures 13.3 and 13.4, with a 5 × 5 matrix. The colours in the heatmap reflect the firm's risk appetite.

Figure 13.4 shows the Risk Heatmap that plots individual risks in a risk appetite matrix by their inherent and residual risk (as scored in RCSA). The heatmap can also help illustrate the effectiveness of controls and their preventative power and impacts.

Risk heat maps can be produced effortlessly in modern GRCs in stark contrast to the laborious task of producing these in spreadsheets and PowerPoint. There are numerous benefits, including being widely understood, offering a simple visual approach, and being useful for various risk types. On the other hand, it is essential to decide how many risks to include (if there are too many risks, the heatmap can become too busy to compre-

Impact					
5. Ext. High	5	10	15	20	25
4. Very High	4	8	12	16	20
3. High	3	6	9	12	15
2. Medium	2	4	6	8	10
1. Low	1	2	3	4	5
	1. Remote	2. Unlikely	3. Probable	4. Most Likely	5. Likely
			Likelihood		

FIGURE 13.3 A Risk Heatmap Matrix

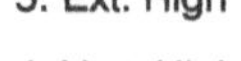

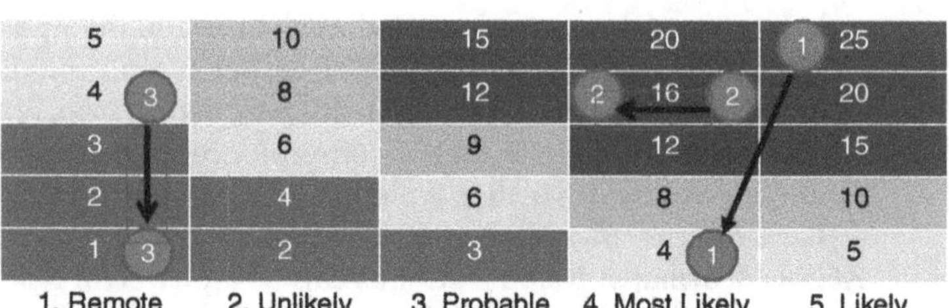

- What does the difference between inherent and residual risk say about our controls?
- What do the three examples say about the controls?

FIGURE 13.4 The Risk Heatmap

hend easily); it is also important to be clear on the assumptions and to articulate these on the heatmap and finally to use the heatmaps together with more detailed reports and tools that answer the 'so what' questions by providing explanations and expert judgement and analysis from the risk teams.

- **Risk events database/incident reports:** Collecting risk events is the first stage in maturity in operational risk, and risk events constitute powerful information for assessing a bank's exposure to operational risk and the effectiveness of internal controls. A Risk Events Database is required to store the events. Firms with a GRC will use the system, and those without a GRC can use a simple spreadsheet or database. Analysis of loss events can provide insight into the causes of significant losses and information on whether control failures are isolated or systematic, and root cause analysis should feature the risk MI reports.
- **Top Risks Report:** Another commonly used report is the Top Risks Report. As its name suggests, this report highlights the top risks (often 10–20, depending on the organisation's size). Top Risks reports can be extremely helpful in focusing the attention of boards and senior managers on the top risks and avoiding getting lost in the weeds. The report also helps answer a key question that boards and regulators frequently ask, namely,
  - What are my top risks?
  - What are the risks that keep you awake at night?

A decision needs to be made about the number of risks to include. Is 10 the magic number? A further key issue is how to score the risks, in other words, how do you move from likelihood and impact to a single measure of risk? One option is to multiply likelihood and impact. However, this may conceal the characteristics of the risk and lead to inappropriate action or inaction, e.g. a high-likelihood low-impact risk may have the same score as a high-impact low-likelihood risk, but the latter is arguably of much greater concern.

- **Risk dashboards:** Risk dashboards provide significant value to senior management by offering a consolidated, visual representation of critical risk-related information. Modern GRCs have revolutionised the production of risk dashboard reports. Figure 13.5 illustrates the power of dashboards, providing a rich array of information on top risks, the risk heatmap, risk indicator trends and a narrative from risk owners and the second line risk team.

  The key benefits of risk dashboards include:

  - **Communication:** The simplified display of risk information through the use of risk dashboards makes it easier to communicate complex risk information to non-technical stakeholders or board members (especially NEDs), improving understanding and awareness of risk and decision-making.

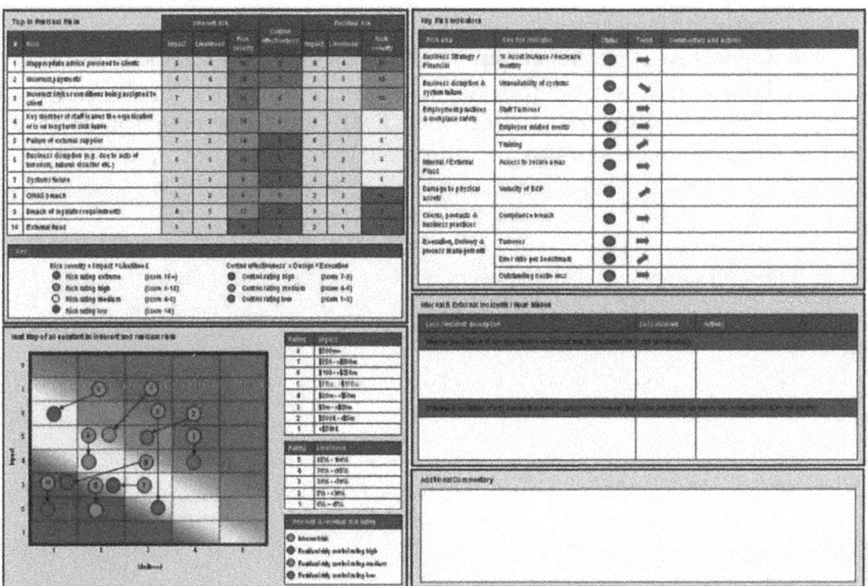

FIGURE 13.5 Risk Dashboards

- **Enhanced decision-making:** Dashboards can help provide timely insights, including where modern GRCs are used, as well as real-time or near-real-time data, enabling senior management to make prompt and informed decisions. Dashboards support strategic prioritisation by highlighting the most critical risks, allowing senior management to allocate resources effectively and focus on what matters most.
- **Improved risk oversight:** Dashboards can help provide a holistic perspective on risk, offering a platform to monitor risks across functional departments, processes or geographies. Dashboards can also provide powerful trend analysis, which helps risk managers understand patterns and anticipate future challenges.
- **Regulatory compliance:** Absence of evidence is evidence of absence! Risk dashboards can provide evidence of active risk management practices essential for audits or regulatory reviews.
- **Drives proactive action-focused risk management:** Risk dashboards help identify emerging risks that might be overlooked in static reports and highlight mitigation action plans and strategies.
- **Cost efficiency:** Automated data aggregation and reporting save time and reduce the risk of human error. Risk managers can focus on risk management and oversight rather than managing data.
- **Customisation and scalability:** Through modern GRCs, risk dashboards can be easily customised to reflect the most relevant metrics to the organisation's strategy and profile.
- **Operational resilience reports:** Increasingly crucial due to the regulatory focus on operational resilience are reports on the status of IBS in relation to impact tolerances (see Chapter 8 for more on operational resilience, including MI).

PART Five

Hot Topics and the Future

ORM is undergoing a renaissance, propelled by profound changes in financial services (driven in large part by dramatic improvements in technology) and by regulators, particularly their focus on operational resilience (Chapter 8) and TPRM (Chapter 10). However, these are not the only hot topics in the ORM universe, and in this book's final section, we consider some of these.

In Chapter 14, we consider the art of regulatory relations management. A corollary of the ever-increasing scope and activities of regulators is the need to manage regulators effectively, including regulatory visits or inspections. Chapter 15 explores the now defunct AMA and the controversy over modelling operational risk, while in Chapter 16 we consider the applications and risks of GenAI. Chapter 17 examines ESG, a cause célèbre of supra-nationals and governments over the last decade and a topic that has had growing importance in financial services. Finally, we explore some future challenges and opportunities and consider the future prospects for ORM as a discipline and for ORM professionals.

CHAPTER 14

The Art of Regulatory Relations

Banking and financial services is a highly regulated sector, and the burdens of regulation and the number of regulators have increased dramatically in the last 40 years. As Andy Haldane explained in his excellent speech, 'Turning the Red Tape Tide':

> In the UK, the Banking Act (1979) covered 52 sections and 75 pages. By the mid-1980s, the Financial Services Act (1986) and an updated Banking Act (1987) had expanded primary legislation to 110 sections (106 pages) and 212 sections (299 pages), respectively. The Financial Services and Markets Act (2000) took this to 433 sections or 321 pages. And the new Financial Services Act (2012) takes this to 695 sections or 534 pages – a tenfold increase in primary legislation in a generation.[1]

The number of regulators in the UK increased from around 2,000 staff in the year 2000[2] to around 5,000 in 2024 (the UK FCA and PRA combined staff) as regulations' scope, complexity and volume have risen inexorably.

As the volume of regulation and the number of regulators have increased, the costs of failing to satisfy the growing expectations of the regulators have also grown. In addition to the high-profile tools such as issuing fines, regulators have a wide array of **tools** they can deploy, including:

Non-Firm-Specific Tools
These tools address industry-wide concerns and ensure general compliance across all regulated firms.

1. **Handbook rules:** The regulatory handbook (PRA and FCA in the UK) sets the rules and guidance for authorised firms. The volume of regulations in the UK is vast and dynamic, and despite regulators often saying they will simplify them, they remain challenging to navigate, even for professionals. The combined handbooks of the PRA and UK FCA amount to many thousands of pages and millions of words. The challenges – and operational risks – of being aware of the rules, understanding them

and complying are significant. New technology, including GenAI, is increasingly being deployed to help manage the enormous challenges of complying with the rules, including keeping up-to-date with changes.

2. **Dear CEO letters:** Formal letters sent to CEOs of regulated firms to highlight specific risks, expectations or areas requiring attention. Dear CEO letters are often used to highlight thematic concerns affecting multiple firms. When receiving a Dear CEO letter, it is good practice to capture the key concerns, findings and recommendations in a system or simple spreadsheet and record any gaps and actions required to address them.
3. **Press and media (including speeches):** Public statements or speeches by regulators to communicate priorities, risks or focus areas to the industry and the public. Regulators are generally now less willing to speak at events than they were 20 years ago, in part due to the large number of internal hoops and approvals they need to navigate to get approval to speak at events. Nonetheless, when regulators do speak – which tends now to be only the senior ones – the content can be invaluable for adding meat to the bones of what they expect in relation to new regulations. In the case of operational resilience, for example, in speeches, they clarified this was an outcome of ORM and not a new risk type.
4. **Enforcement:** Legal or disciplinary actions taken against firms or individuals to address breaches of regulations and deter future misconduct.

Firm-Specific Tools

These tools target individual firms to assess and enforce compliance with regulations.

1. **Desk-based reviews:** A firm's submitted documentation, reports or compliance data are analysed without an onsite visit. Supervisors will do so-called baseline monitoring of firms based on desk-based reviews. This is often supported by using technology and accelerators to quickly identify areas where a firm may be an outlier against peers, prompting further investigation.
2. **Liaison with other agencies or regulators:** Cooperation with other national or international bodies to exchange information or coordinate action. As we saw in Chapter 3, Basel 2 established the international college system, and there is now close cooperation between international regulators. In the UK, where there are two primary bank regulators, this also means close cooperation, regular contact and information sharing between domestic regulators.

3. **Meetings with management and representatives:** Direct engagement with firm leaders, board members and senior management to discuss compliance issues, risks or specific incidents. One of the trends we have seen post-GFC in the UK is that regulators are conducting interviews and meetings with more junior staff members, e.g. the certified staff reporting to SMs. By meeting more junior staff, regulators can better understand the strength of the function in-depth and, more broadly, of the organisation's resilience if the SMs were unavailable or left.
4. **Onsite visits:** Physical inspections at a firm's premises to review processes, systems and compliance in real time, often involving several days of interviews and file/document reviews. Supervisory visits are considered an expensive tool by regulators as they involve multiple staff members for a prolonged period – pre-visit preparation and review of materials, onsite visit write-up and post-visit letter and actions. As such, visits are deployed prudently. However, the utility of the supervisory visit is unparalleled as a way to understand a firm and its issues and risks.
5. **Reviews and analysis of periodic returns and notifications:** Routine analysis of regulatory submissions (e.g. financial returns, notifications of key events). Regulated firms submit a panoply of returns, usually through an automated reporting portal. In addition, they may be required to submit ad hoc submissions, for instance, on the progress of a project or to mitigate an identified risk. Analysis of submissions is a key firm-specific tool in the regulators' armoury.
6. **Transaction monitoring:** Reviewing transaction data to identify suspicious activities or breaches of financial crime regulations.
7. **Use of skilled persons (S166) in the UK:** Independent reviews are conducted by experts appointed under Section 166 of the Financial Services and Markets Act (FSMA). These reviews provide detailed insights into specific issues within a firm. They can be highly costly for firms that must pay a skilled person, and the skilled person and the regulator will control the scope and approach, meaning the firm has very little control. Where a firm is concerned, the regulator may commission an S166 or they may commission their own review by a consultant (often a 'Big 4' firm). The advantages of this so-called 'own initiative S166' are that it is likely to be much lower cost, and, importantly, the firm has control of the review and findings. In addition, using a consultant in this way mitigates the potential reputational risk of an S166.
8. **Enforcement:** The worst case is where regulators initiate firm-specific legal actions to address serious compliance breaches or systemic risks, e.g. the enforcement actions taken by the UK FCA between 2012 and 2015 concerning LIBOR manipulation.

The 'softer' impacts of failing to manage regulatory relations effectively can be very significant, including:

1. **Greater scrutiny and challenge to applications:**
   - Regulators may apply heightened scrutiny to applications submitted by the firm, such as new authorisation requests or changes in permissions, model approvals, new material outsourcing arrangements or changes in business models. This can lead to prolonged evaluation processes, additional data requests and increased resource burden.
2. **Unsuccessful regulatory applications:**
   - Failing to meet regulatory expectations may result in the outright rejection of critical applications, hindering business growth or strategic plans. Examples include the denial of permissions for new services, acquisitions or expansions into new markets.
3. **Increased discretionary liquidity and capital add-ons:**
   - Regulators may require the firm to hold additional capital or liquidity buffers beyond standard requirements. This can restrict financial flexibility, reduce profitability and affect competitiveness.
4. **Remedial work/projects required by the regulator:**
   - Firms may be mandated to undertake costly and resource-intensive remediation projects to address identified weaknesses or gaps in compliance. These projects often divert attention and resources from core business activities.
5. **Reduced likelihood of using the firm's tools for review or mitigation:**
   - Regulators may perceive internal controls, such as the risk management function, internal audit or compliance teams, as ineffective or unreliable. This can lead to external parties being mandated to conduct reviews or implement remediation, which can be both intrusive and expensive.
6. **Loss of trust and damage to the regulatory relationship:**
   - A poor relationship with regulators can result in diminished trust, leading to increased oversight and monitoring. Regulators may become less inclined to provide leeway (e.g. supervisory forbearance) in complex or borderline cases, potentially worsening outcomes for the firm.
7. **Increased intrusion and oversight:**
   - A lack of trust may result in more frequent and intrusive regulatory interventions, such as onsite inspections, enhanced reporting requirements or direct monitoring of specific activities, adding operational strain.

8. **Damage to reputation:**
   - Negative perceptions of a firm by regulators can harm its reputation in the industry. This may affect relationships with clients, investors and other stakeholders, leading to a loss of confidence and potential business erosion.

FOR FIRMS WITHOUT A DEDICATED SUPERVISOR

For larger firms with dedicated supervisors, the face of the regulator is the supervisory team – in the UK, all PRA-supervised firms have a dedicated supervisor. However, for the vast majority of firms at the UK FCA that are too small to have a dedicated supervisor, their interactions are primarily with the call centre or email mailbox for their portfolio supervision team. Although smaller firms without a dedicated supervisor may feel fortunate to be *below the radar* concerning regulatory attention, there are at least two significant challenges for such firms.

First, without a dedicated supervisor, smaller firms find it extremely difficult to build any kind of relationship with the regulator, meaning that when a firm inevitably has problems or questions about the rules, it is much more challenging to get informal guidance or answers to questions. Firms without a dedicated supervisor are most likely to interact with the regulators where they are included in thematic reviews. Because they are largely unknown to the regulator, the risks from such thematic reviews can be significant.

There are two essential tools that firms without a relationship can use to mitigate this risk (of course, large relationship-managed firms also use both of these types of resources, but often for different reasons):

- Trade associations such as UK Finance, the Association of Foreign Banks and the Building Societies Association;
- Consultants.

The trade associations do some excellent work to support their members, providing training, briefings and fora for members to join to discuss hot regulatory topics and to support lobbying efforts. We have worked with many different trade associations over the years, and they are an extremely valuable and powerful resource, especially for smaller firms for whom it is not economical to employ large regulatory affairs teams. Trade associations have excellent relationships with the regulators and will organise events for their members to hear from regulators and have the opportunity to ask questions.

The other tool for smaller firms without a dedicated supervisor is using consultants. Consultants can be used to provide advice on a range of issues. They can be especially valuable in providing guidance on regulatory expectations and suggesting how to respond to regulatory communications, especially if they are former regulators. Consultants can also prepare firms for visits and regulatory interviews (e.g. by reviewing materials and conducting mock interviews/meetings) and provide expert guidance on rules.

Second, all too often, we see firms that have been below the regulatory radar pass one of the thresholds to become relationship-supervised (e.g. such as passing a scale threshold to become an enhanced SMCR firm) and suffer a very rude awakening in terms of the step change in attention, scrutiny and demands. Resourcing with additional specialists in regulatory affairs may be impractical, so again, utilising trade associations and consultants is often a pragmatic solution to manage the increased demands, at least in the short run before resources can be increased to manage the additional scrutiny.

FOR FIRMS WITH A DEDICATED SUPERVISOR

For the larger firms (including banks and larger investment firms) with a dedicated supervisor, it is important to understand and meet the expectations of the supervisory team. As illustrated in Figure 14.1, high-trust relationships will be characterised by meeting deadlines, open and honest

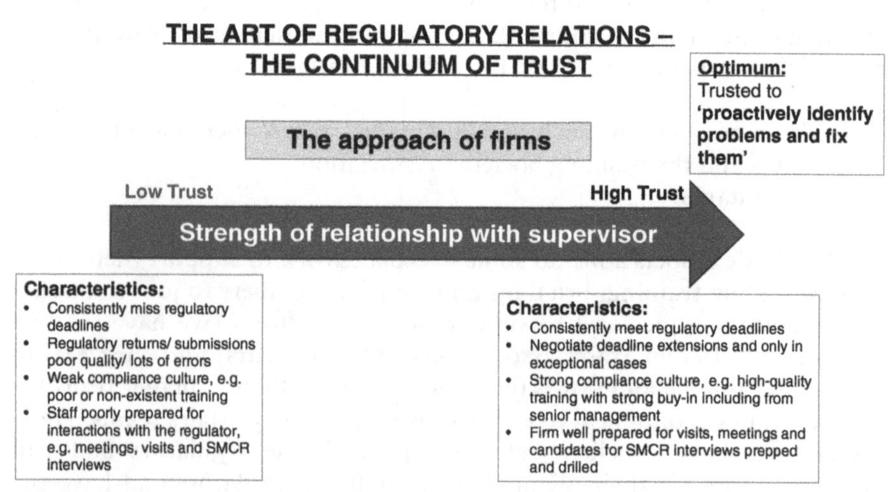

FIGURE 14.1 The Continuum of Trust – Firms

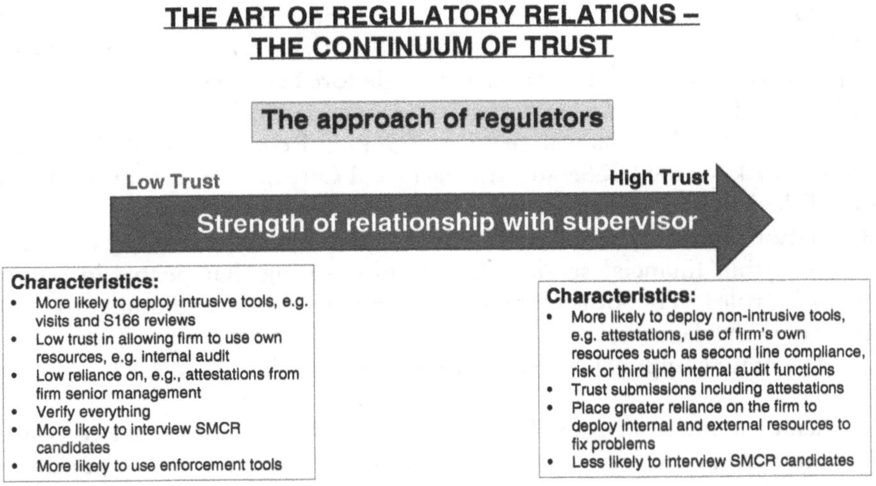

FIGURE 14.2 The Continuum of Trust – Regulators

communication, a strong compliance culture, etc. The objective should be to build a relationship of trust whereby regulators can rely on firms to identify and fix their problems.

There can be a huge dividend if a high-trust relationship is developed, and some of these are set out in Figure 14.2. The benefits can be tangible, such as a much lower likelihood that the regulator will deploy intrusive and expensive tools – including S166 reviews – for a given problem, and intangible, such as the greater willingness to apply supervisory forbearance.

HOLDING SENIOR MANAGERS TO ACCOUNT

Following the GFC, and as part of regulators' effort to improve **strategic resilience**, regulators globally sought to improve **accountability in banks**, to hold individual board members and senior managers accountable when things go wrong. One of the lessons regulators took from the GFC was that despite existing regimes like the UK FSA's **Approved Persons Regime**, clarity on accountability and senior managers' general quality/competence was insufficient. Given operational risks often arise from people either *not doing* what they are supposed to do (e.g. people failing to follow policy/procedure, failing to) or doing things they are *not supposed* to do (e.g. internal fraud, rogue trading), it is understandable that regulators would focus on this. However, the SMCR was highly prescriptive, bureaucratic and costly,[3] a bonanza for compliance consultants and HR professionals. However, as of this writing, the jury is still out on whether it achieved any of the stated objectives and whether it will even survive before being replaced or dramatically revised with changes expected to be proposed in 2025.

In the UK, The Financial Services (Banking Reform) Act 2013 laid the groundwork for the **UK Senior Managers and Certification Regime** (SMCR) established by the UK Financial Conduct Authority (FCA) and Prudential Regulation Authority (PRA), which had stated aims of increasing accountability within financial services firms and ensuring that people in senior executive roles were both competent and capable and fit and proper to hold and carry out those roles.

The main components of the SMCR are:

1. **Senior managers regime(SMR):** This applies to senior executives, with each senior manager given regulator-defined 'prescribed responsibilities'. Firms had to assign each individual a 'Statement of Responsibilities' (SoR). The SMR includes a 'duty of responsibility', requiring senior managers to take **reasonable steps** to prevent regulatory breaches in their areas. If something goes wrong (e.g. a serious compliance breach), the senior manager must demonstrate that he took reasonable steps. Otherwise, he would be held accountable and subject to various potential punishments. Firms were required to complete a voluminous application for new senior managers, which included a detailed resume and skills gap analysis. Regulators often interviewed proposed senior managers, especially in large firms, and those holding key positions (e.g. new NEDs, CEOs, CROs) in smaller firms. Senior manager interviews can be challenging and are often conducted by senior advisors at the regulator and supervisory team members. Outright failure in an interview is unusual and, more often, is a polite suggestion from the regulator that the firm might want to withdraw the application. An invitation to a second interview that would be recorded is a clear signal (as clear a signal as you will get from a regulator!) that the firm would be *better off thinking again* about the candidate!
2. **Certification regime:** For those individuals in a firm not captured by the SMR, most others were captured by the Certification Regime. This regime applies to employees in roles that could significantly impact the firm or its customers (e.g. traders, risk managers). Firms are responsible for assessing and certifying the fitness and propriety of these individuals annually, ensuring they meet conduct standards. In large firms, the number of certified staff could be very significant, and the burden of training them each year on conduct rules and issuing certificates adds another considerable compliance burden.

3. **Conduct rules:** SMCR also introduced new Conduct Rules. These are basic standards of behaviour applied to all employees. They include requirements such as acting with integrity, due skill and care and are designed to promote a strong organisational culture. In addition to the conduct rules applicable to all staff, SM&CR also introduced conduct rules specific to senior managers. Under the SMCR, senior managers in UK financial services are required to adhere to specific Conduct Rules established by the UK FCA and PRA. These rules ensure ethical behaviour, accountability and prudent management within the financial sector. The conduct rules applicable to senior managers include Acting with Integrity, Acting with Due Skill, Care and Diligence, Being Open and Cooperative with the UK FCA, PRA and Other Regulators, Paying Due Regard to the Interests of Customers and Treating Them Fairly and Observing Proper Standards of Market Conduct.

Banks and large investment firms had to implement the new regime by March 7 2016, with a second wave of all other firms implementing the regime by 2019.

The complexity, level of prescription and harsh penalties for firms and individual senior managers for non-compliance made implementation and ongoing management of SM&CR a significant challenge for firms. The challenges included:

- **Administrative complexity:** Implementing SMCR requires robust documentation, annual assessments (e.g. to support annual certification), applications for new senior managers and careful monitoring of roles and responsibilities, which can be resource intensive. Many larger organisations recruited additional staff in compliance and HR to manage the extra administrative burden of SMCR.
- **Record keeping:** Firms must maintain records for audits and compliance checks, requiring effective systems to track responsibilities and certification assessments. Many firms have implemented technology solutions to manage SMCR, primarily as a repository for evidence to support reasonable steps, e.g. committee minutes, memos, day books.
- **Training and awareness:** Ensuring that staff understand the regime and their responsibilities under it can be challenging, particularly in large organisations.
- **Cultural shift:** SMCR aims to change corporate culture, which may be difficult if there is resistance to accountability or transparency.

The risks of failing to comply with SMCR are substantial, including:

- **Fines and penalties:** Non-compliance can lead to hefty fines from the UK FCA and PRA, which may vary based on the severity and nature of the breach.
- **Increased scrutiny:** Regulatory bodies may impose closer oversight on firms that fail to comply, leading to ongoing scrutiny and additional resource burdens.
- **Reputational damage:** A failure to meet SMCR standards can severely damage a firm's reputation, affecting client trust and potentially impacting business relationships.
- **Personal liability for senior managers:** Senior managers may face individual consequences, including financial penalties and, in extreme cases, prohibition from working in the industry if found responsible for compliance failures in their areas.

Effective management of the SMCR is crucial for firms to mitigate these risks, ensure regulatory alignment and promote a culture of accountability within the firm. One of the prescribed responsibilities (known as 'Prescribed responsibility J') is compliance with the SMCR regime, which is often assigned to the Chief Compliance Officer (CCO) or, sometimes in smaller firms, to the CEO. Tone from the top on SMCR from the CEO and CCO is crucial to get the appropriate buy-in and avoid a compliance tick-box mentality to SMCR.

Anecdotal evidence suggests SMCR may have had a positive impact from an ORM perspective, including:

- ORM tools such as RCSA are being used by senior managers (including CROs) to evidence *reasonable steps* and to demonstrate they are 'in control' of their area of responsibility, which may lead to improved quality in these key tools of ORM (a demonstration of the 'use test').
- SMCR also has improved clarity on individuals' roles and responsibilities (e.g. through statements of responsibility), thereby reducing operational risks arising from potential gaps, including in relation to reporting lines and delegations, and apportionment and oversight.

MANAGING REGULATORY VISITS

An essential tool for regulators is the **supervisory visit** or, as US regulators call them, **examinations**. Calling supervisory visits 'examinations' is appropriate, as they are a significant test and challenge for firms, and the costs of flunking the exam can be extremely high. A variant of the supervisory visit is the **specialist team visit,** where specialists rather than the supervisory team (who tend to be generalists) lead the visit. Specialist team visits are usually reserved for highly technical areas such as model reviews.

Managing a successful regulatory visit in banking requires thorough preparation, clear communication and proactive follow-up. Here are five key pointers to managing supervisory visits:

1. **Preparation and documentation:** Ensure all necessary documentation is complete, accurate, readily accessible and up-to-date. Organise critical information that regulators may request, including policies, risk assessments, audit reports, compliance records and data relevant to the scope of the review. Apply project management disciplines with a clear plan and allocate roles and responsibilities. Few things are more disappointing as a regulator than when you request to see a document referred to in a meeting by a firm, only to receive it later and discover it had just been created for you!
2. **Understand regulatory focus areas:** Stay updated on current regulatory expectations, key issues and any recent regulation changes. Tailor the visit preparation to address known weaknesses and areas on which your supervision team has previously expressed concerns and issues in the regulatory priority list (e.g. in the UK FCA Business Plan and Risk Outlook).
3. **Engage and train staff:** Prepare your team through training and practice/mock interviews. Ensure everyone understands their role and responsibilities and can confidently answer questions or locate information. Run mock sessions to identify and address potential weak points. For smaller firms that do not have a dedicated regulatory relations team, consultants can be used to conduct mock interviews, review materials and provide challenges.
4. **Transparency and clear communication:** Foster open lines of communication with regulators. Answer questions directly, avoid over-explaining and be transparent about any issues or corrective actions in progress. If someone mis-speaks or inadvertently provides false information to regulators, it is important to correct this as quickly as possible – deliberately misleading regulators is a serious issue and can have dire consequences. Clear communication builds trust and demonstrates a commitment to compliance.
5. **Post-visit follow-up and remediation:** After the visit, prioritise any remediation actions, document them thoroughly and communicate your progress to regulators. Continuous follow-up demonstrates accountability and a proactive stance in addressing any compliance gaps.

Just as the above five tips can help manage visits effectively, there are some things you should not say to regulators:

- Senior business executives saying of a new business venture: 'We aim to dominate the market'
- The second line risk team saying: 'We have a great partnership with the first line'
- Business Heads saying: 'We tick the boxes for compliance, but they are a business prevention function'
- Senior executives are asking the regulator: 'What qualifications do you have to be asking these questions?'

If regulatory visits are not well managed, or if you ask regulators questions like those listed above, it can lead to significant risks that can impact the institution financially and reputationally. Key risks include:

- **Non-compliance penalties:** Poor management may expose regulatory gaps or unresolved compliance issues, leading to penalties, fines or sanctions. Regulatory bodies may impose these financial penalties for failure to meet required standards.
- **Increased regulatory scrutiny:** A poorly handled visit can lead to heightened regulatory scrutiny, resulting in more frequent and intensive follow-ups. This increased oversight can strain resources and distract from daily operations. In the worst case, the regulator may choose to commission an S166 report, which requires the firm to engage a skilled person (this is a regulator-approved list of experts in specific areas of expertise) and pay for it. S166 reports are a significant burden and punishment, and one of the measures for how well the relationship is being managed will be whether any S166 reports have been instructed.
- **Reputational damage:** Failure to effectively manage regulatory visits can tarnish the institution's reputation, decreasing customer trust and confidence. Negative perceptions may impact customer retention and deter new business.
- **Operational disruption:** Inadequate preparation may lead to inefficient responses, prolonged visit durations and interruptions in daily operations. Staff resources are often redirected from regular duties to manage regulatory inquiries, impacting productivity.
- **Legal and financial risks:** If serious non-compliance issues are uncovered, the institution may face serious consequences including enforcement, fines, claims for redress and so forth. Additionally,

addressing these issues post-visit can be costly, requiring dedicated resources, often involving senior management and investment in corrective measures.

WHAT NOT TO TELL YOUR REGULATOR – OPERATIONAL RESILIENCE

As explored in Chapter 8, operational resilience has become a significant focus for regulators. Below, we set out five things not to tell your regulator about operational resilience.

One: Vulnerabilities Due to Third (and Fourth) Parties Aren't Our Problem

In the UK, regulators published new rules and guidance on third-party risk management while issuing the new regulations on operational resilience, and they emphasised the importance of robust third-party risk management for achieving the desired resilience outcomes (see Chapter 10 for more on TPRM).

The new rules in **SS2/21** provide prescriptive regulations and guidance on the outsourcing life cycle, including procurement, materiality and risk assessments, ongoing due diligence, exit strategies and testing and the approach to fourth parties.

What has not changed is that regulators will hold the firm (and its Board of Directors) **accountable** for all activities, even those outsourced to third parties. As the mantra goes, you can outsource *the responsibility, not* the *accountability*.

It is therefore vital that vulnerabilities to resilience arising from third parties are identified promptly and action is taken to mitigate them – including identifying recovery options and 'Plan Bs'.

Two: We're Using Our Operational Risk Scenario Testing for Operational Resilience

A key activity in delivering resilience is to test Important Business Services (IBS) with severe but plausible operational disruptions to determine whether services can be recovered within established impact tolerances. For many aspects of delivering operational resilience, firms can leverage existing tools and frameworks (e.g. operational risk management). However, in the case of scenario testing, this is not likely to be sufficient as we explored in Chapter 8.

Of course, the testing done for operational risk management and business continuity management can be a useful input to resilience testing, but simply relabelling the other types of testing will not cut the mustard when meeting regulatory expectations on resilience.

Three: Our Impact Tolerances for UK Regulators PRA and FCA Are the Same

A key component of the UK regime is for firms to set **impact tolerances** related to customer harm, firm safety and soundness, market integrity and systemic firms' financial stability. All firms are required to set tolerances related to duration. Still, in a thematic letter to firms, firms have recently been encouraged to consider whether tolerances other than duration may be appropriate, e.g. related to the number of vulnerable customers impacted.

Some firms have set tolerances for consumer harm, and firm safety and soundness are the same. Regulators have provided feedback that this is inappropriate, and different tolerances should be set for both. Setting tolerances for consumer harm – which will typically be a matter of days – the same as for a risk to firm safety and soundness may also raise eyebrows at the regulator that an operational disruption could result in a threat to the firm's safety and soundness in such a short duration and might provoke a review of their ICAAP and ILAAP!

Four: The COO/SMF24 Is Dealing with Operational Resilience

UK regulators increasingly hold specific individuals accountable for key elements of regulation, and operational resilience is no exception. The COO or SMF24 (the COO function under the Senior Managers and Certified Persons Regime) should be responsible for **implementation** and **reporting** on operational resilience.

In many firms, a pragmatic approach, especially given a relatively challenging initial deadline at the end of March 2022, was for the COO/SMF24 to take the lead on the framework's design and, in many cases, ownership of the operational resilience policy. Although this was fine as an initial approach, it is not appropriate for the same first line function to own the policy and be responsible for its implementation. More appropriately, the operational resilience policy should be owned in the second line, and the first line should focus on implementation and reporting only. Many firms are adjusting, and regulators will likely scrutinise roles and responsibilities and the proper segregation of duties across the three lines.

Five: There's Plenty of Time Before the Deadline – I Don't Need to Worry About This Yet!

UK regulators are not known for providing long implementation periods for new rules, especially post-GFC. However, on operational resilience, UK regulators gave firms four years from publishing the final regulations in March 2021 to the final implementation deadline of the end of March 2025.

However, the reason for the usually long implementation period is not driven by their generosity. Regulators introduced the new rules because they were dissatisfied with the resilience of firms, who too frequently were unable to continue providing services when they suffered operational incidents – the TSB IT meltdown being the more egregious example – and as such caused harm to consumers, damaged firm safety and soundless and the integrity of the market. Regulators anticipate that firms will need to **take action** to address these vulnerabilities, which may include replacing obsolete systems or replacing critical third parties. Implementing new systems and replacing vendors takes time, and this is the reason for the extended implementation period. Telling regulators that you are waiting until the last minute to identify vulnerabilities that may not be addressed by the end of March 2025 will undoubtedly raise significant concerns and is a surefire way to an S166 or worse.

CHAPTER 15

The Rise and Fall of AMA and the Modelling Controversy

The future is unpredictable because knowledge cannot predict its own future growth[1]

—David Deutsch

This is not a book about quantitative measurement and modelling of operational risk, and readers should refer to other books and papers on this subject. In this chapter, we will tell the story of the rise and fall of the Advanced Measurement Approach (AMA) and the controversy surrounding the modelling of OR.[2]

As we discussed in Chapter 3, in 2004, the BCBS introduced what can only be described as a radical, paradigm-shifting approach to calculating operational risk capital – the AMA, launched as part of Basel 2 and the CRD. AMA was radical because, unlike previous methodologies, it did not impose a strict, top-down formulaic regulatory approach. Instead, it allowed firms to develop their models for quantifying operational risk within certain parameters defined by regulators. The goal here was not just to box everyone in and spur innovation. At the time, operational risk management was in its infancy, and the hope was to foster the growth of new, innovative methods.

The pay-off was explicit: as a firm moved further towards adopting AMA, its regulatory capital charge would decrease. A clear incentive to justify what would undeniably be a significant investment. But it was not just about the numbers or the models. To qualify for AMA, you had to prove that your risk management systems and controls were up to scratch. It was an invitation for accountability and excellence.

In his interview with *Risk.net* in October 2015, Bill Coen, Secretary General of the BCBS, caused alarm by ominously proclaiming that the 'AMA has not worked as intended' (see http://bit.ly/2eksB0I). Then, in the Basel Committee on Banking Supervision (2016), the Bank for International Settlements (BIS) said:

> A recent review of the measures related to banks' operational risk modelling practices and capital outcomes revealed that the Committee's expectations failed to materialise. Supervisory experience with the AMA has been mixed. The inherent complexity of the AMA and the lack of comparability arising from a wide range of internal modelling practices have exacerbated variability in risk-weighted asset calculations and have eroded confidence in risk-weighted capital ratios. The Committee has therefore determined that the withdrawal of internal modeling approaches for operational risk regulatory capital from the Basel framework is warranted.[3]

The Basel Committee's primary source of frustration with the AMA centred around one crucial issue: operational risk modelling techniques had failed to evolve into something 'standardised'. That is important because in any structured system, especially one dealing with something as consequential as financial risk, **predictability** matters. If you are dealing with large, comparable firms facing similar risks and seeing wildly different regulatory capital outputs, then you have a serious breakdown in coherence.

After the global financial crisis, this concept of **comparability** – assessing risk on an even playing field – was elevated in importance. It became arguably even more important than risk sensitivity itself (which had been the main driver behind the architects of Basel 2). This is because if you cannot compare things properly, you cannot regulate them properly. And that is the issue: when variability gets out of hand, it is not surprising that policymakers deem it unacceptable.

Moreover, regulators began to lose faith in internal models altogether, and who could blame them? During the crisis, we saw how these models – whether for market or credit risk – could fail spectacularly. The stories of '1-in-1000-year events' happening day after day are infamous for a reason. So, it is not a shock that internal models for **operational risk**, in particular, were eventually stripped from the Basel capital framework entirely.

The AMA was controversial since its launch, and some raised a fundamental objection to the very principle of modelling operational risk. Sceptics have argued that since most significant operational risk events ultimately boil down to human failures driven by the 'people' element of 'people, process, systems and external events' (e.g. rogue trading, misselling, benchmark abuse, cybercrime), modelling operational risk is inherently futile since it is impossible to accurately model and predict human behaviour. Some critics have, therefore, never accepted the concept of the AMA and have argued for qualitative approaches and investment in better management rather than modelling, i.e. an Advanced *Management* Approach rather than Measurement.[4]

Quantitatively, modelling OR is a challenging task due to the unique nature of OR compared to other financial risks like credit or market risk. As we have seen, operational risk refers to the potential for loss due to failed internal processes, people, systems or external events, and its modelling faces several inherent problems:

- **Limited historical data:** Operational risk events are often characterised as being infrequent but severe (e.g. fraud, rogue trading, major system failures, cyberattacks). Many organisations lack comprehensive historical data for such events, making statistical analysis difficult. Near misses, minor incidents or losses avoided by controls are often underreported or undocumented, and cultural or reputational concerns may lead to underreporting of events, especially in areas like fraud or compliance breaches. It is possible to mitigate this challenge to some extent through the use of external data, but there are then additional challenges including how to scale the data.
- **High unpredictability:** As we have seen, operational risk events often follow a 'fat-tailed' distribution, where rare, extreme losses tend to dominate. Operational risk encompasses a wide range of risks (e.g. human errors, natural disasters, cyber threats), each with distinct characteristics, making aggregation of data challenging.
- **Complexity of causation:** Operational risk is often interconnected with other risks, such as reputational or strategic risks, complicating attribution and modelling. Small operational errors can cascade into significant losses (e.g. IT system failures disrupting business operations).
- **Subjectivity in scenarios:** To overcome the lack of historical data, scenario analysis is often used to estimate potential losses from rare events, but it relies on expert judgement, which can be subjective and inconsistent.
- **Modelling challenges:** Methods like Loss Distribution Approach (LDA), Bayesian Networks or Machine Learning require large, reliable datasets, which are often unavailable for operational risk. Estimating parameters for rare events involves extrapolation, which can lead to significant inaccuracies. Operational risks often exhibit dependencies (e.g. one system failure causing multiple disruptions), requiring complex modelling techniques, which are difficult to calibrate.

- **Regulatory requirements:** Regulators require operational risk models to be transparent and explainable (i.e. to not be 'black boxes'), which can conflict with the use of complex models like Machine Learning. The cost and effort required to develop, maintain and validate sophisticated models (especially for use in regulatory capital calculations) can outweigh the benefits, even for the largest institutions where there may be significant economies of scale and pay-offs from capital reduction.
- **Emerging risks and radical uncertainties:** As the warning goes, past performance is no predictor of the future, especially when there is complexity. New operational risks, such as cyber threats and climate-related disruptions, evolve faster than models can adapt. Historical data will not reflect future risks, especially in a rapidly changing technological and regulatory environment, and where the growth of knowledge is inherently unpredictable. Many types of operational risks fit the category of risks described as 'radical uncertainties' by King and Kay (2020),[5] where the future is unpredictable, and probabilities cannot be meaningfully assigned to different outcomes. These uncertainties arise because knowledge about the future is inherently incomplete. Extreme operational losses (e.g. financial scandals, natural disasters, pandemics) dominate risk profiles but are inherently difficult to predict and model accurately. Rare, unforeseen events – black swans – are often excluded from models, leading to blind spots in risk assessments.

When the AMA was launched, there was an expectation among regulators that many firms would adopt it, not just the large so-called Basel banks but also a variety of other firms, including much simpler monoline banks and investment firms. However, despite the initial enthusiasm for the AMA, it did not prove to be popular. This was for a plethora of reasons, including the costs, complexity, lack of data, concerns and uncertainty around perceived high regulatory hurdles to get approval, as well as scepticism as to the value-add or return from using the AMA (including whether there would be a regulatory capital dividend).

In addition, when the AMA was introduced, it was believed that using it would be a valuable market signal, endorsed by regulators, that the firm had advanced ORM. It was imagined that using the AMA would bring significant value in terms of enhanced reputation through Pillar 3 disclosures. However, the reputational dividends of using the AMA never really materialised, partly because no sooner had the AMA been introduced than the significant operational risk events during and following the GFC crystallised; the AMA did not have a chance to demonstrate its predictive and preventative value. Part of the problem of proving the return on the AMA is that it is challenging to identify what operational risk events were prevented due to its use, i.e. the counterfactual if the firm had not implemented AMA.

One factor that influenced the uptake of the AMA was the calibration of OR capital, as regulators mandated that, on average, only 10% of regulatory capital should be for OR. Arguably, OR is such a significant part of credit and market risk that, plus pure operational risk, it should be 70–80% of the total risk and, therefore, of regulatory capital. However, extracting the operational risk element from credit and market risk was considered too complicated, imprecise and inconsistent. It was believed it might complicate the IRB and use of seven years of loss data (for credit risk). So, for capital purposes, we ended up with OR, not following the regulatory definition but effectively the old residual definition of 'anything other than credit, market or liquidity risk'.

The calibration was problematic because it had to work not only for large internationally active banks but also for the thousands of investment firms, which, under the EU level-playing-field principle, also had to comply with the new operational risk capital requirement. The impact studies conducted by the UK FSA demonstrated that the impact on investment firms would be catastrophic under the initial Basel calibration of the charge. The result was, therefore, a calibration of the more straightforward approaches that were much lower than regulators ideally would have liked. Because the total regulatory capital for OR was a small piece of the total pie, it undermined the business case for the significant investment needed to achieve AMA. In addition, compared with the BIA or TSA approaches, the AMA had a relatively limited scope to lead to significantly lower regulatory capital.

To try and incentivise greater uptake of the AMA and encourage the largest banks to invest in modelling ORM, the UK FSA effectively required AMA-like modelling by the backdoor, through Pillar 2. As we explored in Chapter 3, the approach taken under Basel 2 implementation in the UK to ORM capital was 'no prohibition, no compulsion'. This effectively divorced the approach for calculating regulatory capital from the broader supervisory expectations on the sophistication of risk management, such that, for example, a large complex group could adopt the simplest approach to calculating capital for operational risk. The UK FSA resolved this inconsistency for large complex groups by requiring the firm to demonstrate sophisticated AMA-like management and measurement under the Pillar 2 Supervisory Review and Evaluation Process (SREP). In time, the UK FSA hoped that firms would progress to formal AMA approval since if you are doing sophisticated modelling in Pillar 2 anyway, you might as well get AMA approval.

Again, this largely failed, and uptake of the AMA, even in the UK, where regulators were broadly supportive, was relatively low – the only banks that received approval for AMA in the UK were Barclays, Lloyds TSB, HBOS and Citigroup; the merged Lloyds – TSB and HBOS – did not retain AMA status.

Arguably, the most serious failure of the AMA was not to do with standardising modelling approaches, calibration or its uptake; instead, it was to do with something that was a key concept of Basel 2 (albeit rarely mentioned in post-crisis regulatory policy papers). That concept is the 'use test'.

The use test was arguably the most powerful new concept in Basel 2 and was based on the notion that regulatory capital models should not be isolated black boxes, understood only by highly skilled mathematicians and modellers, and never used other than to produce management information and regulatory capital numbers. Regulatory capital models (inputs and outputs) must be used in management to drive business decision-making, i.e. the use test. This alignment of regulatory capital with decision-making is fundamental. The use test was a key element of the qualitative standards for the AMA: the bank's internal operational risk measurement system must be closely integrated into the day-to-day risk management processes. Its output must be integral to monitoring and controlling the bank's operational risk profile. Unfortunately, all too often, AMA models have been criticised for their lack of integration, their irrelevance and their lack of use in risk management and decision-making. If the OR measurement system is not used to drive decision-making, it fails the use test. The failure of AMA models to pass the use test has been a critical factor in its demise.

The reasons for the failure of the AMA do not lay solely with the banks. Regulators must also take their share of the blame:

- First, a key factor in the failure of the AMA was that operational risk had far too little capital assigned to it. OR capital was new in Basel 2, and while arguments were made (by both regulators and industry) that OR should be assigned a material piece of regulatory capital, the result was a calibration that meant operational risk had only 10% of regulatory capital for a typical international active bank. OR has arguably been at the root of almost all of the biggest bank losses for a generation, from numerous rogue-trader scandals, including Barings, JPMorgan Chase, Société Générale and UBS, via a plethora of misselling scandals, such as endowment mortgages and personal pensions, to payment protection insurance (PPI) and the wholesale market conduct failures, including the LIBOR and foreign exchange benchmark abuse and market manipulation. Accordingly, OR should have a much more significant proportion of regulatory capital against it; yet, by allocating only 10%, the Basel Committee relegated OR to a second-order risk in the eyes of many, and it undermined the efforts of operational risk professionals and many national regulators to get operational risk onto the Board agenda. At only 10% of regulatory capital, the regulatory capital pay-off (i.e. the difference between regulatory capital under the BIA or TSA and what it would be under the AMA) for the significant investment needed to meet the AMA's regulatory hurdles was simply insufficient.

- Second, a more fundamental regulatory failure of the Basel 2 (and Basel 3) regulatory capital framework has been the highly uneven application globally of Pillar 2; if other regulators had embraced Pillar 2, as UK regulators have, and taken a similar approach to encouraging operational risk modelling through the SREP, perhaps the AMA would not have become an endangered species. The BCBS would do well to focus on applying Pillar 2, as what should have been the most powerful pillar in the Basel architecture is in danger of being undermined by non-compliance, not by banks, but by regulators.
- Third, the 99.9% confidence level over a one-year holding period set by regulators for AMA models was probably unreasonable and unrealistic as a soundness standard for operational risk modelling. This extremely high confidence level (simply read across from that used for IRB modelling of credit risk) led banks down a much more quantitatively complex path than would have been necessary using a simpler approach, e.g. statistical techniques such as bootstrapping or a regulatory multiple approach. It ultimately made AMA models challenging for the business and senior management to understand and 'use'.
- Fourth, one of the main reasons for the diversity in modelling approaches is that regulators could not agree on key aspects of the AMA. This is demonstrated by the US's distrust of scenarios and insistence that their banks use the loss distribution approach (LDA). It is, therefore, unreasonable for regulators to criticise the diversity in practices when the regulators could not agree on the framework in the first place. Moreover, there was an opportunity over the years following the implementation of the AMA for the BCBS to create more uniformity and standardisation, but it failed to do so.
- Fifth, despite publishing a number of best-practice papers on the AMA (Basel Committee on Banking Supervision 2011), the Basel Committee has focused almost entirely on capital standards for credit and market risk and liquidity; this is even though OR was at the root of the financial crisis. Regulators should have focused more of their attention on OR, including the development of the AMA at the largest G-SIFIs.

- Finally, the AMA, and a risk-sensitive regulatory capital regime more generally, was a bridge too far for even the best international regulators. There were many flaws in the regime's design, some of which are set out above. Still, the challenges and cost of reviewing and approving complex capital models for both credit and operational risk were enormous challenges and were never fully appreciated by regulators. The UK FSA initiated a project for Basel 2 implementation, which ran for over three years and had a large budget and significant senior management involvement. However, even at the UK FSA, which made a serious effort to implement Basel 2, the complexity and diversity of the models, serious home–host issues and key person risk within the regulator led to real practical problems that the regulators struggled to overcome.

Taking the above factors together, it is perhaps not difficult to understand why the Basel Committee decided to phase out the AMA and replace it with a single Standardised Approach. Ultimately, the AMA lost credibility and the confidence of the regulatory community, and in the horse-trading that inevitably characterises international negotiations of this sort, the advocates of the AMA always fought a losing battle.

CHAPTER 16

Selecting and Using a GRC

There has been an increasing trend for financial services firms to invest in software applications to support operational risk management.[1] These systems are commonly referred to as GRC systems.

The potential benefits of using a GRC are numerous and include:

- **Improved risk management:** GRC systems may help improve the efficiency and effectiveness of identifying, assessing and mitigating operational risks. This includes enhanced monitoring of risks and quicker and better organised responses to incidents. Organisations often derive significant benefits from using GRC systems to manage processes previously handled on spreadsheets, including RCSA and incident capture.
- **Better decision-making:** By providing more timely, potentially even real-time data, on risk, compliance and governance, GRC systems can facilitate better informed decision-making.
- **Cost savings:** Automating manual tasks related to risk management and compliance (e.g. RCSA and compliance monitoring reviews) improves efficiency, speeds up the process, reduces the risk of human error and frees risk staff to focus on managing risk rather than data.
- **Audit trail:** GRC systems provide a secure central repository of audit trails of risk and compliance activities and minutes of governance committees. Absence of evidence is evidence of absence, and a secure audit trail of activities is critical for second line oversight, internal audit reviews, external audit and regulatory inspections.
- **Clarity on accountability:** GRC tools require instantiating hierarchies, chains of escalation and approval and assignment of ownership. Encoding accountability in the GRC system for risk, compliance and governance tasks reduces the risks of gaps or tasks not being completed due to confusion on who should be doing what.
- **Integrated view of the organisation:** GRC systems integrate governance, risk and compliance into a single framework, offering a comprehensive integrated view of the organisation's risk exposure and compliance status.

- **Regulatory compliance:** GRCs can help compliance with various regulatory requirements by automating compliance reporting, testing and tracking. This reduces the risk of regulatory fines due to non-compliance and can greatly improve the efficiency of processes, e.g. many systems support processes associated with regulations like UK FSA's SMCR regime that would otherwise be resource intensive and bureaucratic.

Given the potential benefits and the relatively low cost of many GRC systems,[2] it is no surprise that many firms have implemented them. However, selecting the right one, deploying it and implementing it successfully is a significant undertaking fraught with complexity and risk. There are too many cases where firms implement a GRC and within a few years regret it and, in some cases, revert to spreadsheets. In order to get the most from GRCs, it is important to take time to select the right system and manage the implementation process effectively.

FIRST AND FOREMOST...

It is important to be realistic about what a GRC system can deliver. A GRC is not a 'solution' to existing risk management problems and challenges. A GRC is only a tool and will, if used correctly, help operate the tools and framework more efficiently. It is, therefore, essential that the ORM framework is stable and that the firm is comfortable with its maturity before instantiating it in a GRC system. A common mistake is implementing a GRC system without first addressing known weaknesses or gaps in the risk framework. It is important to review the risk framework before deciding on a system. If your ORM framework is underdeveloped, immature or has gaps, make sure you set it up appropriately to the organisation's needs; the framework leads the GRC system that supports it, not the other way around.

Before deciding on a GRC system, it can be sensible to undertake a maturity assessment of your ORM framework. This can be conducted quickly and help identify areas of the framework that need to be enhanced.

The ORM framework can be assessed against peers to determine maturity across various dimensions against the target level (which may not be 'best practice' in all dimensions). A maturity assessment can also help identify any undesirable idiosyncrasies in the framework before they are customised into the system, setting in stone a risk framework that may be flawed or over-complicated.

As with all significant projects, it is important to produce a clear business plan that addresses the following key questions:

- **What will the GRC system be used for?** Modern GRCs are extremely powerful in their functionality, but many firms only utilise a small fraction of their potential. In practice – in part to manage the scale and complexity of the implementation – firms often use the GRC in one area (often ORM) and may later expand its use to other areas.[3]
- **Who will be the users of the GRC system?** The number of users and administrators of the system influences both the price (as often GRCs are priced based on the number of user licenses – usually in bands) and the approach to implementation, including who should be involved in user acceptance testing (UAT) and training.
- **Who will own, maintain and administer the GRC?** This will probably also include managing the relationship with the GRC vendor and attending the User Group if the vendor runs one. A pragmatic approach to overcome internal organisational politics is that one function, often the ORM function, will take the lead.

SELECTING A SYSTEM

The selection process will be much smoother by having clarity on the above, and especially by being clear on how it will be used. Many GRC systems are in the market, and their functionality, design, appearance and price vary considerably. It is, therefore, essential to be clear about what you want in a system and to be disciplined about selecting it on this basis, avoiding becoming distracted by other bells and whistles. Good GRC salesmen will be experts at demonstrating the system to emphasise its strongest features. It is also important to be cognizant of future regulatory developments and consider whether you want the system to provide additional functionality (e.g. the regulatory requirements on operational resilience that are a current focus for firms as we have seen).

To organise selection, it is useful to develop a list of key criteria and use these to create an **assessment scorecard** to score each system against the required attributes. In line with robust Third-Party Risk Management (TPRM), selecting from a range of GRC systems and investigating and reviewing the systems and vendors, including the quality of their customer service.

In addition to the system functionality, there are some additional factors to consider in the assessment scorecard:

The budget for the GRC will be a key consideration, so it is important to understand the likely cost – initial and ongoing – upfront. The total cost, which will likely be an important consideration, will likely be a combination of the installation fee, the annual license (which will depend on the functionality and number of users) and most probably an annual hosting fee. GRC systems range from the modestly priced to the very expensive, so having clarity on the budget will help filter out systems that could provide the required functionality but at a price beyond the budget.

Most modern GRCs have a bewildering **capacity for customisation,** which can be extremely important, especially where the framework may have idiosyncrasies. The system's adaptability includes the capacity to address changing regulations or internal policies.

A GRC system that **integrates seamlessly with existing technology** can be highly desirable. Banks, especially larger ones, require **scalable GRC solutions** that can handle many transactions, departments and risk factors. The system should be able to grow as the bank's needs evolve.

A **user-friendly interface** and accessibility are crucial to ensuring smooth implementation and adoption. The GRC system should support both technical and non-technical users, from compliance officers to risk managers to internal auditors. A system seen as 'clunky', non-intuitive or difficult to use can become an expensive barrier rather than an accelerator.

The ability to **automate key activities,** including compliance checks, risk assessments and reporting, is crucial and an important functionality of a GRC system. Automated workflows, notifications and reports reduce manual work and improve efficiency.

The absence of evidence is evidence of absence, and a strong audit trail is essential for regulatory reviews and internal audits.

The GRC system should provide comprehensive, easily accessible and customisable **reports.** It is still relatively common to see firms buy a GRC and discover later that the system does not meet their reporting needs, so they end up using Power BI or another reporting system or, even worse, Excel! Ensuring in the selection phase that the GRC meets needs on reporting is key to avoiding this outcome.

Banking and financial services firms typically hold highly sensitive financial data (including customer data); security features such as encryption, multi-factor authentication (MFA) and data breach prevention are critical when selecting a GRC system.

It is important to ask around when reviewing systems through product demos. The financial sector is a small world, and it is important to talk to users and to ask for their recommendations and valuable tips. Vendors will usually provide references, but these are unlikely to be users with anything negative about the system.

Many firms fail to adequately research the supplier or understand the system before buying it, and there are also a number of external services and tools that can be used to help in the review and selection process:

- **Gartner's magic quadrant:** Gartner publishes a Magic Quadrant report for Integrated Risk Management (IRM) solutions covering many leading GRC systems.
- **Forrester wave:** Forrester Research provides reports that evaluate GRC platforms based on a detailed set of criteria. These reports rank systems according to their performance, ease of use, scalability and other factors critical for banks.
- **IDC MarketScape:** IDC MarketScape offers vendor assessments in the GRC space, analysing the capabilities of different platforms in terms of features, market presence and future trends.
- **Peer reviews and user communities (G2, Capterra):** Platforms like G2, Capterra and TrustRadius provide real-world reviews from users of GRC systems, which can give banks insights into the performance of a GRC system in practice, including ease of implementation and customer support.

Before making your final decision, it is advisable to see a **demo version** of the system that you can play with for a few weeks. There is no substitute for experiencing the real thing, and although it is not quite the same as using the system with your actual data, it will give you a good idea already. Some vendors are not keen on providing demo versions, and this is another red flag on a system to avoid.

Finally, before signing a contract, make sure to understand what is included fully. Too often, users accept the agreement and Statement of Work without reading it properly and then do not understand later why they are being charged for things or why the project went the way it did.

ROLLING THE SYSTEM OUT

Once a system has been selected, it is critical to dedicate enough time and resources to configure and implement it properly with **professional project management.** Implementing a GRC system should be treated as a change programme with senior sponsorship at the board level or executive level. There should be a project plan, governance committees and all the usual change management disciplines.

There have been many cases where IT change has been poorly managed – often with disastrous consequences – due to inadequate project management. It pays to invest in professional project management, either from the firm's own PMO or by usually a contractor. Some GRC vendors will insist that there is an internal project manager before they start the project because they know what happens when there isn't one.

Many firms try to implement too much too quickly, and starting with a small pilot programme with core functionality and a few departments (friendly champions) is a more sensible approach. Pilots may also provide lessons that can inform modifications to the approach for full rollout. Success from pilots and proofs of concepts can be shared with board sponsors. The successful implementations tend to be based on cautious and gradual rollouts rather than the big bangs.

Key aspects of the implementation process are around configuration and migration. The GRC vendors will rely on the firm's subject matter experts, such as risk champions, to help configure the system, so they need to be available. It is wise to avoid planning a configuration for the summer when many people may be away on holiday, causing delays in the project or poor decisions if the right person is not consulted. The configuration and implementation stages can be extremely challenging if the framework is incoherent or incomplete; hence, it is important to be confident in the framework as a prerequisite.

The main challenge will be configuring the system to align with the organisation in relation to the group structure, legal entities, functional structure, user profiles and the risk framework, including taxonomy, scoring matrix, risk and control libraries. A proper configuration makes usage far more efficient. It is also important to try to future-proof the configuration; for example, the new operational resilience regulations require a cross-functional business service lens, so it is sensible to build this into the system configuration and design.

An important decision will be migrating existing data to the new GRC system. This can be a difficult decision that depends on several factors, not least the quality of the historical data. If a decision is made to migrate existing data, completing a rigorous data cleansing exercise is essential to ensure only accurate data are moved to the new system. Many organisations choose to start afresh rather than risk introducing poor-quality historical data to the new system.

After configuring the system, **user acceptance testing** is essential to have comprehensive, proper UAT by the primary users. Vendors can usually provide check sheets to run through. Issues, glitches or design changes to the configuration can then be identified and recorded. As part of the testing and the final configuration, ensure there is a two-way dialogue between the GRC vendor, the project team and the early adopters undertaking the UAT. This is key to the successful implementation and utilisation of the new tool.

Training all users on the system is key. It should be prioritised for the primary users, who will need a good understanding of the system to add value to the configuration and the UAT. Moving from a spreadsheet to a GRC system can be all very new and different for users, so it is better to take training in small stages: learn a routine or process and then move on to the next.

UTILISATION OF THE GRC SYSTEM

Over-customisation of the system is a trap that many firms fall into. Often, users are excited about the opportunity to customise the system to replicate what they are doing in a spreadsheet. They select a customisable platform and spend time and money customising it to a great extent. Over-customisation makes upgrades difficult and sometimes impossible, as well as instantiating weird and wonderful ways of doing things into the system. The system owners – often the ORM team – need to take ownership, be disciplined and exercise careful administrative control on customisations.

It is important to have enough super-users to support and maintain the system. It is not uncommon that firms run into trouble when the only person in the risk function who understands the system leaves. It is crucial to manage and reduce key-person risk, including through succession planning and cross-training.

When the system is upgraded, for instance, with additional functionality, this will need to be understood by super-users, and users will have to be trained on any new functionality or changes to design. Most vendors run user groups (if they don't, this is a red flag), which are a great way to compare notes with other users, learn about updates and plans, provide feedback and request changes.

CHAPTER 17

GenAI – Uses and Risks

There is a palpable sense of excitement in the industry and among practitioners around potential applications of new technology in ORM and a concomitant foreboding at the possible implications of new technology for OR professionals (will technology result in their obsolescence?). New technology is often a double-edged sword; new opportunities and applications come with new risks and unforeseen consequences. Perhaps the area generating more anticipation is GenAI. This chapter will explore what this is, some potential uses and the risks and implications for the ORM discipline and professionals.

Generative Artificial Intelligence (GenAI) is an AI model capable of creating new content, insights or predictions from patterns learned during training. Although in its very early days in terms of its use in ORM, it offers enormous opportunities for ORM as a discipline and for OR professionals. By processing vast and disparate datasets at scale, GenAI can enhance decision-making, streamline operations and improve the detection and mitigation of operational risks.

As with all new technologies, GenAI has multiple dimensions: the functionality of the latest technology (both for ORM and, more generally, within the organisation) and new risks that must be identified and managed. The ORM function must ensure that novel risks associated with the use of GenAI in the business are identified and managed (providing a second line oversight functionality). It must also ensure that the risks associated with applying GenAI within the ORM framework are managed (e.g. captured in the second line risk functions RCSA and monitoring metrics). See Figure 17.1 for an illustration of the various dimensions of the ORM function's role.

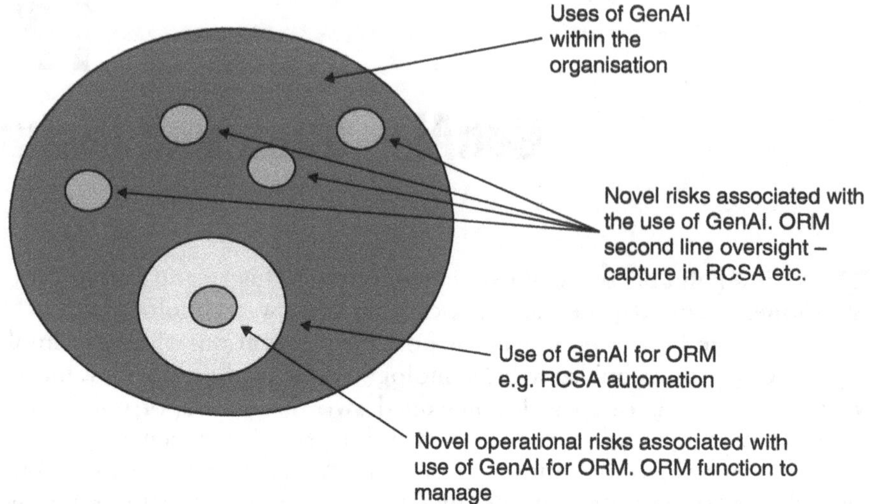

FIGURE 17.1 GenAI and Operational Risks

POTENTIAL APPLICATIONS OF GenAI IN OPERATIONAL RISK MANAGEMENT

The potential power and uses of GenAI in ORM are enormous and are only just being glimpsed. ORM functions that are not utilising GenAI profoundly limit their productivity and value, especially given the inexorable increase in the challenges of managing increasingly complex risks. This section explores numerous applications where GenAI can enhance ORM. Many modern GRCs are incorporating GenAI tools into their systems, and this can be a hugely influential enhancement to their functionality.

- **RCSA process automation:** RCSA is often criticised – especially for the users who need to complete it – for being inefficient, manual and burdensome, so the potential to use GenAI to streamline the process and reduce the resource burden of completing RCSA is enormous. GenAI can significantly enhance the efficiency, accuracy and value of this key ORM tool and ensure that those completing RCSA focus their energies on thinking creatively about risks and their mitigation rather than managing the process and administration. GenAI can help with RCSA process automation, including creating tailored RCSA templates and questionnaires for specific business units, mapping processes and identifying risks. As with all applications of GenAI, this does not absolve RCSA owners and the second line of doing their roles by providing expert input, reviewing and challenging the outputs.

- **RCSA content libraries:** GenAI can also create risk and control libraries to generate, maintain and update (as new risks emerge) a standardised library of risks and controls, which can be tailored for different organisations and business functions. GenAI can also help develop tailored risk, control and cause taxonomies based on regulatory guidance (e.g. BCBS and local regulators), industry standards and guides (e.g. trade associations, professional bodies and institutes).
- **Responding to queries:** ORM teams in the second line and Risk Champions in the business can easily find themselves devoting much of their time to responding to routine queries on completion of the RCSA process. With pressure on resources in second line functions and the reality that Risk Champions often do their role 'side of the desk', anything that can relieve pressure should be welcomed. GenAI-powered chatbots have enormous potential to ease the pressure on the second line by providing an automated response capability to routine queries. Again, the ORM team must implement appropriate oversight and controls to ensure the responses produced by the GenAI chatbots are accurate and to ensure there is still an option to speak to a team member where there is still uncertainty on the correct approach.
- **Risk identification and analysis:** GenAI can support analysis of historical data from multiple sources, including loss data (internal and external), historic RCSA data and RCSA data from other parts of the group, risk metrics (i.e. KRIs, KCIs and KPIs) and audit findings, to help predict potential risks and recommend mitigations. Even with modern GRCs, analysing and drawing linkages between disparate data sources can be challenging, especially over a long period or in large and complex groups. Hence, GenAI's power in this is potentially significant.
- **Control effectiveness assessment:** GenAI can help evaluate and suggest improvements to existing controls and devise specific action plans for risks flagged in the RCSA process. As covered in Chapter 7, it is essential to have the correct mix of controls in terms of both the mix of preventative, directive, detective and corrective controls and to ensure to the extent possible that controls are not independent so that if one control fails, the others can operate effectively (i.e. the Swiss-cheese model). GenAI can help to analyse the mix of controls and identify where there may be gaps or weaknesses far more effectively and quickly than humans. Of course, the analysis will depend on the completeness and accuracy of the data entered into the GRC – the more data entered into the GRC on controls, in terms of their type and resources required to operate them, the richer and more accurate the analysis will be.

- **Oversight and challenge:** GenAI can support the second line in its challenge and oversight function by reviewing complex risk data, MI and reports and providing analysis, including questions to ask the business. This includes the draft RCSA and can be extremely powerful for supporting the second line in its RCSA challenge function.
- **Reporting and MI:** Create dynamic, customised RCSA reports and interactive dashboards tailored to stakeholders' needs, including GenAI-generated narratives alongside visualised data for improved understanding. Instead of manually compiling risk reports, GenAI can dynamically create or update risk dashboards, executive summaries and board-level presentations. It can synthesise data from various internal and external sources, delivering concise, action-oriented findings to senior management and stakeholders.
- **Automated incident analysis and root cause identification:** GenAI can analyse past incident reports, internal audit findings and event logs to detect patterns and correlations that human analysts might miss. Root cause analysis is a fundamental tool of ORM but is often not done well. Utilising the power of GenAI to identify patterns can significantly speed up the incident investigation, improve the accuracy of identifying root causes and recurring risk drivers and enable more proactive risk mitigation strategies. Actions can be formulated more quickly and implemented to avoid recurrence.
- **Dynamic policy and regulatory compliance management:** Banking regulations and internal policies are frequently updated, voluminous and complex, and GenAI can review regulatory handbooks and legal texts, policy documents and guidelines to produce simplified summaries of changes. It can also highlight newly updated sections relevant to the bank's current operations, automatically mapping compliance requirements to existing controls.
- **Fraud detection and exception flagging:** By learning from historical data, operational losses and fraud scenarios, GenAI can flag unusual patterns that deviate from the norm. For instance, it may detect suspicious login attempts, abnormal transfer patterns or atypical employee behaviours that merit further investigation.
- **Predictive scenario generation and stress testing:** GenAI can generate plausible 'what-if' scenarios – critical for both ORM and operational resilience testing. By simulating severe but plausible hypothetical conditions, operational risk managers can identify potential vulnerabilities, test control effectiveness and refine contingency and response plans.
- **Outsourcing and third-party risk monitoring:** Organisations in financial services increasingly rely heavily on outsourcing and third-party providers for a bewildering array of services. Indeed, some of the UK's

modern 'challenger' banks outsource almost everything to third parties! GenAI can help firms enormously to continuously monitor vendor-related news/intelligence, industry reports and operational metrics. For example, if a critical supplier experiences a data breach and this is notified to the firm, GenAI can develop a mitigation plan. If the data breach is only reported in the press, GenAI can alert risk teams and recommend mitigations as soon as the news is public. It can provide early warning on supply chain vulnerabilities, strengthen vendor governance and due diligence, and support continuous improvement in third-party risk oversight.

- **Knowledge management and training:** GenAI can generate risk team training scenarios, best-practice guides and Q&A resources. It can simulate realistic operational risk events for staff to practice response protocols, thus improving their readiness and judgement in real-world incidents. It enhances staff competency through dynamic, scenario-based learning; reduces reliance on static, dated training material and ensures continuous upskilling aligned with evolving risk landscapes.
- **Regulatory mapping of risks and controls:** Managing regulatory compliance, especially as regulation has become increasingly complex and voluminous, has become a non-trivial challenge for all regulated firms of whatever size. GenAI can help regulatory compliance enormously by mapping risks and controls to relevant regulatory requirements, and it can do this dynamically as rules change.
- **Operational resilience:** As we saw in Chapter 8, operational resilience has been an increasing focus and priority for regulators. In the UK, regulators have detailed the approach firms must take to ensure they achieve higher operational resilience. GenAI can help significantly in the process, including IBS identification and monitoring, resource mapping, impact tolerance calibration and monitoring and scenario testing. An area where GenAI has great potential is in creating synthetic RCSAs. RCSA, as a key tool of ORM, should be used to identify risks and controls related to IBS. As such, RCSA must be used to help deliver the new regulatory expectations on operational resilience and identify risks to IBS. However, RCSA is usually structured around functional business units and organised by legal entities and geographies; it has a 'vertical' structure. Conversely, the critical resources required to deliver an IBS may span myriad functions, legal entities and geographies. Even with a GRC system, creating a synthetic 'horizontal' RCSA would be difficult, especially in large and complex organisations. GenAI can use IBS and resource mapping data to collate risks and controls across the entire population of RCSAs to construct

synthetic RCSAs for each IBS, which can then feed operational resilience MI. GenAI can also help collate monitoring metrics and indicators against the material risks and associated controls.

CHALLENGES AND RISK

Although the potential applications and benefits of GenAI are enormous, as we have set out above, as with all things, there are also challenges and risks associated with its use. From an ORM perspective, the potential risks from GenAI must be identified and understood well. There are numerous dimensions to the risks arising from GenAI, which will only increase as the applications multiply:

a. Risks arising from using GenAI in the business, e.g. GenAI-powered chatbots and investment advice tools. Business areas should identify the risks as part of the change governance process, and in RCSA and the second line, they should provide oversight and challenge.
b. Risks arising from the use of GenAI by the ORM team, e.g. GenAI functionality embedded in the GRC and the other applications set out above.
c. Risks arising from using GenAI by the business to manage operational risks – e.g. business areas using their own GenAI-powered tools to identify and manage operational risks. It is crucial the second line understands and oversees these risks.
d. Risks arising from the use of GenAI by vendors under outsourcing and TPRM arrangements – e.g. it is essential to identify potential risks arising from the use of GenAI in the nth-party ecosystem – including where GenAI is used to provide third-party services and to provide challenges as part of TPRM due diligence on how the risks are being managed.

Data quality and availability: The veracity and usefulness of GenAI outputs depend on the input data's quality, completeness and relevance. As the acronym GIGO goes, 'Garbage In Garbage Out' applies equally to GenAI as with any model. Inconsistent, incomplete or siloed datasets can lead to false or misleading results, leading to missed inappropriate actions or risks. Ensuring proper data governance and integration across business units is critical.

- **Model complexity and explainability:** GenAI models can function as 'black boxes', providing outputs without a clear understanding of the assumptions in the algorithm or lacking clear explanations. This lack of transparency can make it difficult for the board of directors, risk managers and regulators to fully trust or validate the outputs.

- **Integration with existing systems:** Incorporating GenAI solutions and tools into legacy risk management systems and IT infrastructures can be challenging. Organisations must invest in robust integration frameworks, APIs and change management strategies to realise the full value of GenAI, which can present challenges concerning the robustness of change management and managing the impacts of IT change on operational resilience.
- **Skills and talent gaps:** The effective use of GenAI requires specialised expertise in data science, machine learning and model governance. Many banks face a shortage of skilled professionals who can develop, fine-tune, interpret and maintain GenAI models responsibly, including understanding and managing associated risks.
- **Model bias:** GenAI models trained on historical data may perpetuate biases, as was seen recently with Google's GEMINI GenAI,[1] which produced false and sometimes comical answers to user questions because it had been trained on datasets with a critical social justice or D.E.I. 'woke' bias; this can lead to errors, unfair treatment of specific customer segments or misaligned risk assessments. Organisations must implement strict ethical guidelines, bias testing in datasets, algorithms and outputs and ensure balanced training datasets for the GenAI models.
- **Overreliance on AI:** Relying too heavily on GenAI, especially for critical decision-making without human oversight, can be extremely dangerous and will likely raise serious concerns from regulators. Automated decisions must be subject to periodic human review and the usual oversight and challenge under the three lines model, especially in sensitive areas like regulatory compliance or fraud detection.
- **Operational risk concentration:** Overuse and over-reliance on GenAI in ORM may create new operational risks, such as system outages, data privacy breaches or model misconfigurations. It is essential to consider these risks when making strategic decisions on using GenAI and to determine a clear risk appetite for its use. By explicitly considering and documenting GenAI risks in the risk taxonomy and risk register, the organisation can ensure visibility at senior management and board levels, facilitating better oversight, resource allocation and timely mitigation strategies. This proactive approach will help maintain compliance, safeguard reputation and ensure that the benefits of GenAI are realised responsibly.
- **Regulatory and compliance considerations:** The potential power and widespread use of GenAI, as well as its potential to generate operational

risks and cause harm, including to consumers, makes it a clear target for regulatory scrutiny and attention. Regulators may question the methodologies and fairness of GenAI-driven decisions. They expect board members and accountable senior managers to understand how GenAI is utilised, the risks and their mitigation. Where senior managers cannot answer the questions from regulators, and where GenAI is deployed without transparent model validation and proper documentation, firms will risk regulatory sanctions (including against accountable senior managers), fines or reputational harm.

RISK MITIGATION STRATEGIES

As we have seen above, myriad risks are associated with using and applying GenAI. Operational risks related to the application of GenAI must be carefully identified and managed using the existing ORM tools, including RCSA. Below, we set out some of the key risk mitigation strategies.

- **Capture and manage GenAI risks in RCSA:** Identifying, assessing and managing risks associated with applying GenAI in the periodic RCSA is essential. Given the rapid increase in the applications of GenAI in financial services organisations (driven in turn by the rapid evolution of GenAI as a technology), this is an area where a trigger-based RCSA review focused on only GenAI risks across the organisation may be appropriate; rather than waiting for each RCSA to be updated according to its review schedule. Incorporating GenAI-related risk types into the risk taxonomy and risk library is also essential, as well as the second line ensuring that this is high on their oversight and review radar.
- **Consideration of GenAI risks in change management:** It is essential to appropriately identify and manage the risks associated with new applications of GenAI in change management processes. The risk team has a key role in these processes to identify and manage risks within risk appetite.
- **Consideration of GenAI risks in TPRM:** Vendors in the organisation's nth-party ecosystem may be making even more extensive use of GenAI than the firm itself (especially if they are a critical ICT third-party provider). It is crucial, especially where these risks have the potential – directly or indirectly – to impact services being provided under the outsourcing or third-party arrangement, that the firm

understands these risks and has gained comfort they are being appropriately managed. GenAI-related risks must be captured in all stages of the TPRM lifecycle (see Chapter 10), including the pre-onboarding and onboarding stages, the ongoing oversight and finally, the off-boarding phase. It is vital to capture GenAI risks in the risk assessments conducted in the procurement phase and ongoing/periodic risk assessments. Relationship owners may need support from those with specialist knowledge, and the second line has a key role in review, challenge and oversight.

- **Robust model governance:** Organisations should implement formal GenAI model governance frameworks, including model validation (which includes understanding what is in the 'black box'), performance tracking, ensuring periodic audits and backtesting and maintaining robust documentation and testing models to ensure that GenAI outputs remain consistent, credible and free of the biases mentioned above.
- **Human judgement and role of SMEs:** Indiscriminately relying on GenAI model outputs without a critical human review and overlay is extremely dangerous. Humans (including SMEs) should review and interpret GenAI outputs, especially in high-consequence uses.
- **Data management and quality assurance:** As explained above, the outputs of GenAI models are only as good as the data inputs. Ensuring data are complete, accurate and free of biases is a critical challenge that must be addressed through robust data management and quality control.
- **Continuous training of GenAI models:** Regularly retraining GenAI models with updated data ensures that GenAI keeps pace with emerging risks and changing environmental landscapes. Ongoing improvement is key to maintaining and improving the accuracy of the GenAI outputs.
- **Training and awareness:** Most people have heard of AI and GenAI, and many have used GenAI tools such as ChatGPT and Google Gemini in their daily lives and at work, but their understanding of the technology and associated risks remains very low. Organisations must roll out awareness training as part of periodic ORM training to ensure employees understand the potential uses and the risks.

CHAPTER 18

ESG

In recent years, Environmental, Social and Governance (ESG) considerations have become an extremely important regulatory priority. The publication by many firms of ESG reports, coupled with the introduction of externally assessed ESG ratings, have made ESG considerations an important driver in demonstrating how firms are managed. The assessment and evaluation of ESG issues enables financial institutions to mitigate potential risks arising from a failure to incorporate ESG considerations in their businesses, activities, business plans and strategy. This should assist the firm in being more attractive to socially aware investors, increase customers and establish a positive reputation.

Before we progress it would be worth identifying some of the components of these three categories:

- **Environmental:** Reflects how firms perform in relation to the physical environment. Includes climate change and the impact of the firm on the environment;
- **Social:** Reflected in a firm's relationship and impact on its staff, customers, individual social groups and society. Includes human rights, equality, pay, employment benefits, diversity and inclusion;
- **Governance:** Refers to the way a company is managed, how its decisions are taken, how risk is managed and how conflicts of interest are avoided. Includes the firm's mission, the role and composition of its board, how the Board exercises oversight over the senior management and how the senior management is remunerated.

The Cambridge Dictionary defines ESG as a set of ideas or policies that consider the effects on the environment and on society of how business operates, for example, when choosing investments or when reporting the activities of the business. This means that ESG provides a framework to enable individual firms and their stakeholders to assess the firm's ESG practices and performance. Firms in the financial sector are increasingly looking to ensure their activities are ESG compliant in order to strengthen their reputation, improve customer retention, attract new customers and ensure they provide an acceptable profile for investors. As a result, several organisations now provide ESG ratings, using data to evaluate firms' ESG performance.

As you would expect, financial regulators are focusing on ESG, partly in response to the potential impacts climate change and ESG could have on the safety and soundness of financial systems and market integrity. While there does not appear at present to be a clear uniform line of travel for the regulatory community, climate change, ESG disclosures and greenwashing are attracting regulatory attention. For example:

- Climate change can result in physical and transition risks that could impact the safety and soundness of firms and also the financial system;
- Greenwashing reflects the concern that firms may be exaggerating their ESG credentials.

The Basel Committee on Banking Supervision published 18 Principles for the Effective Management and Supervision of Climate-Related Financial Risks in June 2022.[1] Twelve of these principles provide guidance to banks on effective management of climate-related financial risks (covering: Corporate Governance; Internal Control Framework; Risk Management Process; Management, Monitoring and Reporting; Comprehensive Management of Credit Risk; Comprehensive Management of Market, Liquidity, Operational and Other Risks and Scenario Analysis). The remaining six provide principles for the supervision of climate-related financial risks. As the focus of this book is 'Integrated Operational Risk Management', I will concentrate here on the principles with direct relevance for operational risk and will therefore focus on operational risk during the remainder of this chapter:

Principle 11: Banks should understand the impact of climate-related risk drivers on their operational risk and ensure that risk management systems and processes consider material climate-related risks. Banks should also understand the impact of climate-related risk drivers on other risks and put in place adequate measures to account for these risks, where they are material. This includes climate-related risk drivers that might lead to increasing strategic, reputational, and regulatory compliance risk, as well as liability costs associated with climate-sensitive investments and businesses. [Reference principles: BCP 25, Principles for the sound management of operational risk, Principles for operational resilience, SRP 20, SRP 30].

Paragraph 42: Banks should assess the impact of climate-related risk drivers on their operations in general and their ability to continue providing critical operations. Banks are expected to analyse how physical risk drivers can impact their business continuity and to take material climate-related risks into account when developing business continuity plans.

Paragraph 43: Banks should assess the impact of climate-related risk drivers on other risks, such as strategic, reputational, regulatory compliance and liability risk, and take such risks, where material, into account as part of their risk management and strategy-setting processes.

Principle 12: Where appropriate, banks should make use of scenario analysis to assess the resilience of their business models and strategies to a range of plausible climate-related pathways and determine the impact of climate-related risk drivers on their overall risk profile. These analyses should consider physical and transition risks as drivers of credit, market, operational and liquidity risks over a range of relevant time horizons. [Reference principles: BCP 15, Stress testing principles]

[References: These principles include a number of references that may be unfamiliar to readers:

- BCP refers to the Core Principles for Effective Banking Supervision[2] – 'These are the minimum standards for the sound prudential regulation and supervision of banks and banking systems' and have been integrated into the consolidated Basel Framework. Principle 15 deals with the Risk Management Process and Principle 25 covers Operational Risk;
- SRP refers to the Supervisory Review Process[3] – 'The Pillar 2 supervisory review process ensures that banks have adequate capital and liquidity to support all the risks in the business, especially with respect to risks not fully covered by the Pillar 1 process, and encourages good risk management'. SRP 20 contains the four key principles of supervisory review under Pillar 2 and SRP 30 contains risk management principles that reinforce how banks should manage and mitigate their risks that are identified through the Pillar 2 process;
- Stress Testing Principles[4] – These principles cover sound stress testing practices.

We have already referenced in this book:

- The Principles for the Sound Management of Operational Risk[5];
- The Principles for Operational Resilience.[6]

In February 2022, during a holiday in Australia, I witnessed first-hand the impact of climate-related risk drivers on banks' operations in general and their ability to continue providing critical operations in particular. As we arrived in Sydney, we were greeted by the smell of the bush fires that seemed to be slowly working their way towards the city. When we returned to the city a week or so later, we discovered that the fires had been extinguished by severe rainfall that was causing flooding in many places. Clearly, climate-related risk drivers were impacting the ability of banks and financial institutions to undertake some of their activities and their ability to continue providing critical operations in some locations.

As I note above, a clear line of travel for ESG in the global regulatory response has yet to emerge, for example:

- The UK FCA published policy statement 23/16 (Sustainability Disclosure Requirement (SDR) and investment labels policy statement) which introduced rules and guidance to help consumers navigate the market for sustainable investment products[7];
- The UK Bank of England published a report on climate-related risks and the regulatory capital framework[8];
- The European Council and Parliament have reached a provisional agreement on a proposal for a regulation on environmental, social and governance (ESG) rating activities which aims to bolster investor confidence in sustainable products[9];
- The US Securities and Exchange Commission issued, on 6 March 2024, rules to enhance and standardise climate-related disclosures for investors.[10]

Numerous other national regulators have issued ESG-related rules and guidance and readers are advised to undertake a detailed review of the information published by their local regulator.

The key question for those with an interest in operational risk must be what does ESG mean for my operational risk management framework, and do I need to do anything differently.

The starting point must be where does ESG fit within a firm's taxonomy. Is it a cause, risk or impact?

The EBA's consultation paper on Draft Regulatory Technical Standards on establishing a risk taxonomy on operational risk[11] introduces some attributes that are dedicated to ESG, with each of the factors (environment, social and governance) having a dedicated attribute as well as attributes on the risk attributed to greenwashing. In the consultation paper, the EBA proposes mapping environmental risk, social risk, governance risk and greenwashing risk to level 1 event types and level 2 categories. As a result, the EBA appears to be proposing that environmental risk, social risk, governance risk and greenwashing are classified as risk types.

I struggle with this interpretation, not least because a taxonomy must be MECE (mutually exclusive and collectively exhaustive). If a firm undertakes greenwashing and produces an inaccurate report and accounts as a result, is the event greenwashing or internal fraud. I am happier with an approach that captures ESG as casual factors which result in a risk, for example, applying the ORX Reference Taxonomy[12] we discussed in Chapter 5: ORM Building Blocks:

- **Environment:** Climate change may cause fires which could result in my Australian bank branch being destroyed but the level 1 risk is physical security and safety (damage to physical assets);
- **Social:** Failing to treat male and female staff equally is a cause that may result in a level 1 people risk (breach of employment regulations or regulatory requirements);
- **Governance:** A failure of governance is a cause that may result in a level 1 regulatory compliance risk (ineffective relationship with regulators).

It will be interesting to see how the taxonomy treatment of ESG within individual firms resolves over time.

As a next step, we should consider how ESG and ESG considerations could impact the Operational Risk Management Framework components described in chapters 5 (ORM Building Blocks), 6 (Risk Identification and Assessment), 7 (Controls), 9 (Incidents) and 10 (Third-Party Risk Management).

GOVERNANCE – CHAPTER 5

In Chapter 5, we noted that governance is a key component of an Operational Risk Framework and as the identification, monitoring, mitigating and reporting of ESG is an important element of the operational risk management process, the governance of ESG is equally important. As a result:

- The Board should set the ESG strategy and objectives, set the ESG risk appetite, oversee the senior management's implementation of the Board-approved ESG policy, protect stakeholders from ESG issues and set the firm's ESG culture;

- The senior management should oversee the day-to-day management of ESG, ensuring that ESG does not negatively impact the safety and soundness of the firm or its reputation and ensure compliance with ESG laws and regulations.

This raises the important question of who should own the Board-approved ESG policy. My default is always for the CRO and his team to own risk policies and for them to be implemented by the first line, in the typical interpretation of the three lines model discussed elsewhere, and I see no reason to alter my position for the ESG policy. Once again we can apply the checklist in Chapter 5 to assess the effectiveness of the ESG governance framework by ensuring that:

- The Board can demonstrate that they have given full consideration to the ESG policy;
- The Board have ensured that ESG training is part of the firm's curriculum for the Board, senior management and all other staff and that all these individuals (including the Board) are tested at least annually;
- The Senior Management can demonstrate how they have implemented the ESG policy and framework;
- The senior management established a hierarchy of ESG policies and procedures;
- The ESG Governance structure is well-defined and effective;
- ESG information flows efficiently and effectively;
- It can be demonstrated that over the last six months, key ESG issues have been escalated to senior risk committees and guidance and instructions have cascaded down;
- ESG decisions and challenges can be evidenced and are documented;
- The governance structure, delegation of ESG authorities and terms of reference all align and are supported by the ESG framework and policy hierarchy;
- ESG metrics are sophisticated and duplication and gaps in reporting and supporting processes have been removed;
- ESG is appropriately managed through a firm-wide consistent and standardised structure, which has the authority to take actions, in accordance with the governance requirements established by the overall strategy;
- ESG policies and procedures are readily available to all staff;
- Businesses and functions can demonstrate that ESG policies, procedures and guidance are read and understood by all staff;

- The ESG policy interfaces with other risk policies;
- ESG policies are fully integrated into the business or function;
- The senior management can evidence that they have promoted good ESG practices and management throughout the firm;
- The ESG policy aligns with risk appetite;
- ESG is appropriately reflected in the taxonomy.

Firms that cannot tick all these criteria have not developed and implemented robust ESG governance arrangements, or an effective policy and framework.

RISK APPETITE – CHAPTER 5

The development and approval by the Board of the firm's ESG appetite is key if ESG is to be effectively and efficiently identified, measured, monitored, mitigated and reported. The ESG risk appetite statement defines the organisation's risk appetite and tolerance for environmental, social and governance risks. The risk appetite for ESG must be clear, easily understood and consistent with the firm's appetite for other risks. For example:

- **Environmental:**
  - Has the firm established an appetite for its own carbon footprint and its impact on the environment;
  - What is the firm's appetite for funding fossil fuel extraction and its use;
- **Social:**
  - What is the firm's slavery policy;
  - What is the firm's appetite for human rights breaches and does the firm finance activities in jurisdictions or activities with poor human rights records;
  - What is the firm's appetite for equal pay and employment benefits;
  - Are male and female staff treated equally;
- **Governance:**
  - Does the firm have an appetite for differences between its mission statement and its ESG policy and framework;
  - What is the firm's appetite for differences in remuneration.

TOP-DOWN – CHAPTER 6

When considering the risks that worry the Board and Senior Management it is important to investigate whether these include ESG issues, and if so which ones. We should never forget that NEDs may have similar roles in other institutions and could provide valuable insight into top-down ESG risks elsewhere. We should certainly ask the Board and Senior Management to detail their ESG concerns.

EMERGING RISKS AND HORIZON SCANNING – CHAPTER 6

Firms should be constantly horizon scanning for emerging risks and many firms are likely to have climate change as an emerging risk, although I would argue the risk has now emerged. The horizon scanning process must include the three ESG components, in addition to those issues considered as a matter of course:

- **Environmental:** Might include whether risks are emerging that could impact how the firm performs in relation to the physical environment, including the type of fuel used to power the building and associated facilities;
- **Social:** Might include social developments in one of the firm's markets or jurisdictions. Could the firm's presence in a country with a deteriorating human rights record and growing social unrest result in reputational damage;
- **Governance:** Might include international developments that could create a conflict of interest.

RCSA – CHAPTER 6

The initial key stage of the RCSA process (see Figure 6.2) is risk identification. Once a firm has identified a risk, it should investigate whether ESG considerations could cause that risk to crystallise. For example, if the firm is concerned that they may misreport the financial position they should ask whether this could be the result of greenwashing and identify and assess the controls that would prevent greenwashing from taking place. It would be prudent to consider whether all the existing risks in the risk register could potentially be caused by ESG considerations.

INTERNAL EVENTS AND RISK INCIDENTS – CHAPTER 6

In Chapter 6, we discussed the importance of collecting internal events and included a list of loss event database contents. Firms should consider adding an additional field, enabling them to record whether the event was the result of a failure in the ESG management framework. Firms should also take account of ESG when undertaking their root cause analysis. The six causes in the Bow Tie in Figure 9.1 can already accommodate ESG issues. Environmental causes could be captured under environment, social causes could be captured under external events or people and governance failures could be captured under process. If we fail to identify ESG causes then we cannot have any confidence that the event will not recur.

EXTERNAL EVENTS – CHAPTER 6

As we have seen, analysis of external events is critical and should enable firms to answer the question, can it happen here? External events can also help a firm understand if there could be any ESG factors involved. This is important as generally customers react to ESG scandals very quickly and could, for example, withdraw deposits from a bank that has a poor record of funding fossil fuel extraction or provided funding for an activity that has caused environmental damage. When reviewing external events, firms should therefore ask could it happen here and if it does are there any ESG considerations.

SCENARIOS – CHAPTER 6

Firms undertake scenario testing for a number of reasons, in addition to scenarios for capital purposes, including risk identification and assessment and also as part of the operational resilience framework. When scenario testing is part of the risk identification and assessment process, the test should specifically consider whether there are any ESG causes, implications or impacts. Where there are weaknesses then measures should be agreed to address these issues. To ensure ESG issues are considered during the test the scenario artefacts detailed in Chapter 6 should include ESG causes, issues and considerations.

In addition, as proposed in the Basel Committee on Banking Supervision's principles for the effective management and supervision of climate-related financial risks, firms should make use of scenario analysis to assess the resilience of their business models and strategies to a range of plausible climate-related pathways and determine the impact of climate-related risk drivers on their overall risk profile.

CHANGE MANAGEMENT – CHAPTER 6

I often feel that firms place insufficient emphasis on change management, and the involvement of the operational risk function in the change assessment process is seen by many as an indicator of the maturity of the change process within a firm. My preference is for the operational risk team to be involved throughout the change management process, producing an initial assessment at the start of the process (are there any red flags or key considerations) and a final assessment as the process comes to a conclusion. The operational risk team should ensure that both assessments consider whether there are any ESG considerations and, if so, how they have been addressed. For example, if the firm is about to begin fossil fuel financing, the environmental, and therefore reputational, implications of that decision should be identified and the firm must decide whether the lending rests outside their ESG appetite.

CONTROLS – CHAPTER 7

In Chapter 7, we considered controls and the importance of the four control categories:

- **Preventative:** I have already argued that ESG is a cause of risk and firms should therefore ensure they have appropriate effective and efficient controls to prevent ESG issues from causing risk events to occur. While these preventative controls should be a significant element of the ESG focus on controls they should not be the only focus;
- **Detective:** Firms should ensure that they have controls in place to detect risks that are caused by ESG weaknesses. There should, for example, be a robust assessment of the annual report and accounts to ensure that there is no evidence of greenwashing. The 2023 annual report of a large UK bank included over 400 references to ESG, including the firm's approach to ESG, while the annual report and accounts of another contained over 200, including a section devoted to ESG. All firms must take great care to ensure that any information they produce on ESG and their ESG programmes cannot be questioned;

- **Corrective:** If ESG failures are identified, then firms must ensure that corrective action is taken to both remedy the situation and also ensure that potential reputational and regulatory repercussions are mitigated;
- **Directive:** All firms should ensure that they have in place robust and effective policies and procedures to identify, assess, manage and report ESG.

REPORTING – CHAPTER 13

While some of the larger financial institutions have mature ESG reporting frameworks, many smaller firms do not. Firms looking to develop ESC reports for the Board should base those reports on the various Board-approved ESG risk appetites in order to provide the Board with the assurance that the risk appetites are not being breached. These firms are also advised to review the annual reports and ESG-related publications of the larger financial institutions to gain insight into items that could be covered in the regular Board ESG report. The Board may, for example, wish to know:

- **Environment:**
  - Progress to any emissions risk appetite;
  - Progress to any targets for reducing fossil fuel financing;
- **Social:**
  - How many senior management roles are held by women and what is the target percentage and date;
  - How do employees feel about working for the firm, how many are planning to leave in the next year;
- **Governance:**
  - How is the firm's governance perceived externally;
  - Is the firm's ESG assessed by any independent parties and what is the rating.

As we have seen, the annual report and accounts of larger firms can also provide a fertile source of inspiration for those firms who are only just beginning their ESG journey. These firms should also take the time to review the reports and accounts of their peers.

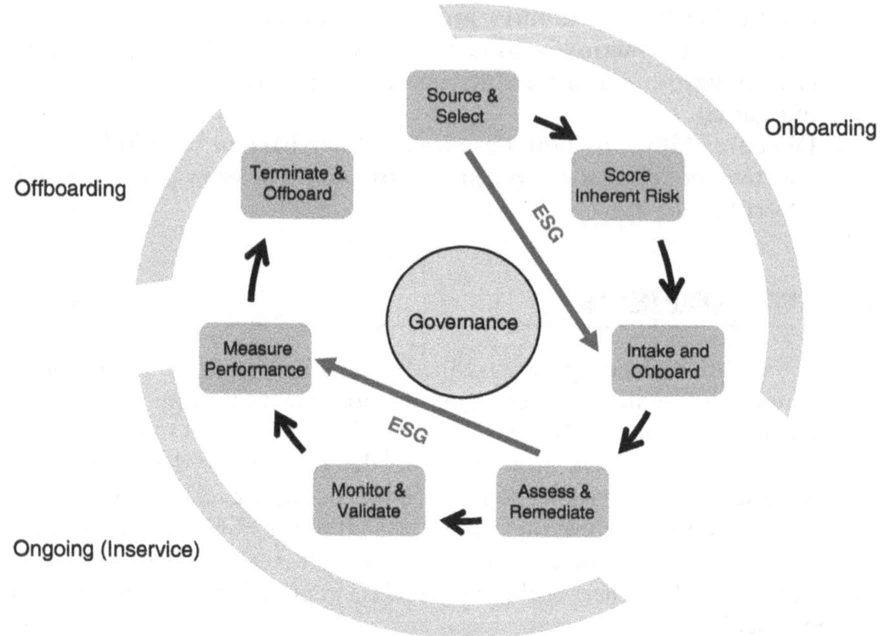

FIGURE 18.1 TPRM Life cycle and ESG

THIRD-PARTY RISK MANAGEMENT – CHAPTER 10

Firms must ensure that their third-party arrangements, including outsourcing, do not impact their exposure to ESG issues and concerns. Consideration of ESG must take place throughout the third-party life cycle especially at onboarding and during ongoing oversight. In Figure 18.1, I have adapted the diagram first shown in Figure 10.2, to show where ESG considerations should impact the third-party process.

As part of the third-party and outsourcing process firms should understand and take account of a number of factors, including:

- **Onboarding:**
  - Is the third party rated by an independent third party and what do those ratings tell us;
  - Have there been any ESG incidents involving the third party;
  - Are there any negative press reports or social media coverage;
  - Is there any likelihood of greenwashing;
  - Have there been any ESG incidents or concerns as a result of the geographic location of the third party;

    - Are ESG factors considered as part of the inherent risk assessment;
    - Can the third party meet your ESG policy and minimum standards;
    - Does the third party pose a threat to the reputation of your firm;
    - Does the third party have an ESG policy and has it been reviewed;
    - Does the third party meet its ESG disclosure requirements;
    - Is ESG incorporated into SLAs and contracts;
    - Do any nth parties meet the firm's requirements as detailed above;
- **Ongoing:**
    - Have the third party's ESG ratings changed and what does that mean;
    - Have there been any ESG incidents involving the third party since onboarding;
    - Are there any negative press reports or social media coverage;
    - Is there any likelihood of greenwashing;
    - Have there been any ESG incidents or concerns as a result of the geographic location of the third party;
    - Can the third party still meet your ESG policy and minimum standards;
    - Does the third party pose a threat to the reputation of your firm;
    - Have there been any changes to the third party's ESG policy and what do the changes mean;
    - Does the third party continue to meet its ESG disclosure requirements;
    - Are the ESG requirements incorporated into SLAs and contracts being met;
    - Do any nth parties continue to meet the firm's requirements as detailed above.

In many firms, the operational risk framework is a static document that changes little over time. However, the risks facing firms are constantly changing, and nowhere is the need for the operational risk framework to evolve and develop better illustrated than with regard to ESG. As part of this evolution, firms must adopt an ESG mindset and constantly question whether activities and processes have a potential impact on the firm's ESG exposure.

CHAPTER 19

The Future Challenges and Opportunities

Nothing is certain except death and taxes

—Benjamin Franklin, 1789

In his 2013 speech titled 'Turning the Red Tape Tide', Andrew Haldane, then Executive Director for Financial Stability at the Bank of England, discussed the significant growth in financial regulation over recent decades. He cited numerous examples from the UK and US, citing the dramatic growth in banking regulation, in the tax code, in the number of regulators and in the costs of compliance (including the armies of compliance officers directly employed to deal with the regulation and the indirect costs including regulatory consulting). While the past is not a predictor of the future, the growth in regulation will likely continue. Not least, the constellation of private interests that invariably initiate new regulations and the interests of regulators to expand their remit, role and budget will sustain.

As such, it is also likely that ORM and operational risk managers will continue to be a focus of regulators, and managing regulations and regulators will continue to be an essential component of ORM. Indeed, the current focus of regulators on operational resilience has increased the profile of ORM very significantly. We expect increased regulatory scrutiny on ORM frameworks and tools and the different components of ORM, especially TPRM (see Chapter 10), in the coming years.

Operational risk is one of the few areas where it has been relatively common to hear practitioners say they would like to see more regulation and guidance (with the PRA's handbook longer than War and Peace, it might be surprising for anyone to want more rules!). It is a source of frustration for many practitioners that after a decade, there is still enormous variability in approach between firms – even concerning the essential tools such as RCSA and core concepts such as appetite and tolerance – and this highlights a lack of standardisation and maturity. The regulator's focus on operational resilience may deliver what is needed. What is more, this is a global regulatory focus under the Basel Operational Resilience Working Group, so we can expect a significant degree of global consistency in approach (countering the worrying trend of fragmentation in regulatory approach whereby regulators have all too often ploughed their furrow, creating an enormous challenge for global firms trying to establish a consistent international standard).

THE FUTURE OF OPERATIONAL RISK MANAGEMENT AND MANAGERS

The importance of ORM, and of taking an integrated approach to its management, has never been more important, especially with regulators focusing on using ORM to achieve operational resilience **outcomes** (see Chapter 8). The challenges from the heightened demands from regulators on operational resilience are also an excellent opportunity for operational risk managers to adapt and add enormous value. Cometh the hour cometh the practitioner! It is time for operational risk managers to grasp this opportunity to demonstrate the value of their frameworks and tools and to ensure that the regulatory-driven renaissance in operational risk management is not wasted again! If operational risk managers fail to step up, their prospects face several threats:

- **Automation and GenAI:** Advances in AI and machine learning are automating risk identification, monitoring and reporting processes through the new GRC systems. The potential for GenAI-powered systems to provide oversight and challenge could reduce the need for human operational risk managers, especially in routine tasks. ORMs may find their roles diminishing in areas traditionally reliant on manual analysis and reporting. With GenAI-driven chatbots also being developed to answer queries, operational risk managers may become increasingly marginal within firms.
- **Integration into enterprise risk management (ERM):** Many banks are moving towards an integrated risk management (IRM) approach, which consolidates operational, credit, market and other risks into a single integrated framework. Operational risk management may be absorbed into broader risk functions, leading to a reduced emphasis on dedicated operational risk roles. New technology and tools, in

addition to the regulatory focus on outcomes and removing risk silos, may exacerbate this trend.

- **Regulatory simplification:** We saw in Chapter 3 how regulatory requirements in response to scandals were a key driver for the origins and evolution of ORM. Simplifications or shifts in regulations could decrease the focus on operational risk. Changes in Basel regulations have greatly simplified the regime for operational risk capital requirements to a single simple methodology (the Standardised Approach). Regulators are also increasingly focusing on the resilience outcomes of effective ORM rather than the minutiae of the framework and tools. A lower regulatory burden could lead to decreased demand for dedicated ORM professionals.
- **Cost pressures and outsourcing:** Banks face significant cost pressures, leading to outsourcing or offshoring of operational risk functions. The role of in-house operational risk managers could shrink as banks outsource risk functions to third-party providers or centralised hubs.
- **Lack of value-add:** Because operational risk management evolved in response to new regulations, it is sometimes viewed as a compliance or support function rather than a strategic value driver. Activities like RCSA have become risk *compliance* activities in many organisations where completing the annual exercise is considered more important than the outcomes. If operational risk managers cannot demonstrate their value in improving business outcomes, their role could be marginalised.
- **Evolving risk types:** Emerging risks, such as cybersecurity, climate risk and ESG (see Chapter 18), as well as ever-greater demands on more traditional risks like TPRM, are reshaping priorities in risk management. Focusing on these highly specialised risks may require expertise beyond traditional ORM skillsets, potentially sidelining operational risk managers. Specialists in these new risk types must support the generalist operational risk manager.
- **Increased use of GRC systems:** GRC platforms are increasingly centralising and automating operational risk activities. GRCs can produce risk dashboards offering real-time insights, automated incident reporting and response and streamline key tools such as RCSA. GRC tools could further reduce the need for traditional ORM roles, particularly those focused on data aggregation, analysis and production of MI.
- **Cultural resistance:** Cultural challenges within organisations, such as resistance to embedding operational risk management into business processes, can limit the perceived effectiveness of ORM functions,

which may lead to reduced investment in ORM or its integration into other risk functions or a fully integrated ERM function.

- **Skillset obsolescence:** Traditional operational risk management skillsets, such as manual risk assessments and static reporting – the bread-and-butter of ORM for more than a decade – may become outdated due to new technology and the evolving risk landscape. Operational risk managers who fail to adapt to new challenges – especially new technology – and demands may find themselves obsolete.
- **Emerging competitors for risk oversight:** Specialised risk functions, such as cybersecurity, data privacy and ESG teams, may take over areas traditionally managed under operational risk. This could result in a narrower scope of responsibilities for operational risk managers, which is further narrowed by GRCs and GenAI tools.

To meet the challenges, remain relevant and avoid extinction, operational risk managers must adapt and here are 10 ways in which they must do this:

(i) They must possess a **holistic understanding of the business.** Banks increasingly operate in silos, with each area focusing only on its narrow function. However, due to the broad nature of operational risk, the operational risk manager must know and understand the whole business.

(ii) They must have an **expert understanding of risk** (including emerging risks) **and control.** They must have both a theoretical understanding and a practical approach, including the ability to identify causations, identify risk clusters and linked events and understand what controls are likely to be most effective, taking account of the firm's risk culture and observations from psychology and behavioural economics. They must also understand other categories of risk – some estimate that as much as 70% of what is generally considered to be credit and market risk *is* operational risk, and it is vital to be cognisant of this.

(iii) They must bring a strong **sense of judgement** and the ability to respond proportionately to issues, events and problems. They should be the ones to counter Corporal Jones' frantic cries of 'Don't Panic' with a measured and calm response and a focus on resolution and action rather than crying over spilt milk or pointing fingers/blame culture.

(iv) They must have a **mastery of the operational risk toolkit and know how technology, including GenAI, can be implemented.** Even in a post-AMA world, the business need for sophisticated analytics will continue. The modelling of operational risk is in its infancy, and huge advances are just waiting to be made, including those from behavioural economics. In particular, modelling qualitative data, e.g. from BEICFs, is potentially far more valuable for business management than modelling historical loss data. Regulators are also likely to continue to demand sophisticated approaches to measuring operational risk through Pillar 2, especially for larger and more complex firms. They must strive to push the boundaries on analytics, demonstrating the business value and the 'use test' in modelling for Pillar 2, and win the business case for continued investment.

(v) They must have a **challenging mindset** and the confidence not to be fazed by the most belligerent business heads. The operational risk manager should also be prepared to tackle and break down the silos and expose the cliques and disruptive organisational politics that can poison an organisation's culture.

(vi) They must **desire to engage** with all areas of the business and support functions and provide support, challenge and oversight. Too often, operational risk functions (as with other control functions) have been too remote from the business. More than anyone in the firm, the operational risk manager must be highly visible and be out talking with business areas, observing, understanding and challenging. What is written in a policy or procedure is one thing, but 'what actually happens' is key to understanding risk and control effectiveness. They must also be able to engage with technical and non-technical people and must be able to engage people of all levels and in all areas of the business.

(vii) They must have **highly developed forensic skills of investigation** analysis and the ability to manipulate and assess data and sift evidence, getting to the root of the problem, understanding complex causal chains and recognising patterns.

(viii) They must be a **great communicator and deliverer of training,** with the ability to demonstrate the business value of operational risk management and to educate and inform all staff.

(ix) They must drive **risk culture change** by continuously demonstrating and promoting the value of strong risk culture and strong risk management. The 'demonstrating' bit is crucial – 'tone from the top' is essential, but the example senior managers set to the rest of the organisation by their behaviour is far more critical.

(x) They must bring a **strategic outlook** to issues, problems and risks and the ability to see the big picture to avoid getting lost in the details. They should be front and centre on hot topics like geopolitics, leading scenario analysis, assessing the plausibility and impact of different outcomes and helping to generate mitigation strategies.

We should not be unrealistic; even operational risk managers are only human. However, the operational risk manager is almost unique within the firm in having the breadth of knowledge and understanding – necessitated by the pervasive nature of operational risk – to address the significant emerging challenges requiring an integrated enterprise-wide perspective. The recent demise of the AMA in the post-GFC Basel 3 reforms is regrettable, but amid the pessimism from the demise of the AMA, there is a reason for optimism. The demise of the AMA was a watershed for operational risk management, but it may mark the beginning of a renaissance in the discipline and profession – the opportunity is there for the taking.

Notes

Chapter 2

1. The COSO Enterprise Risk Management – Integrating with Strategy and Performance Executive Summary can be found at https://www.coso.org/_files/ugd/3059fc_61ea5985b03c4293960642fdce408eaa.pdf.
2. The BCBS Revisions to the Principles for the Sound Management of Operational Risk are available free of charge and can be found at https://www.bis.org/bcbs/publ/d515.pdf.
3. The June 2011 BCBS Principles for the Sound Management of Operational Risk are available free of charge and can be found at https://www.bis.org/publ/bcbs195.pdf.
4. The BCBS website is located at https://www.bis.org/bcbs/index.htm.
5. The July Financial Reporting Council's UK Corporate Governance Code, July 2018, can be found at https://www.frc.org.uk/library/standards-codes-policy/corporate-governance/uk-corporate-governance-code/.

Chapter 3

1. https://www.cnbc.com/2020/02/26/barings-collapse-25-years-on-what-the-industry-learned-after-one-man-broke-a-bank.html, 'The Barings collapse 25 years on: What the industry learned after one man broke a bank', https://www.cnbc.com/elliot-smith/.
2. Leeson and Whitley (1996) *Rogue Trader*. Little Brown & Co, p. 62.
3. Ibid., p. 62.
4. Report of the Board of Banking Supervision Inquiry into the Circumstances of the Collapse of Barings, Bank of England (1995): https://assets.publishing.service.gov.uk/media/5a7ca783ed915d6969f46688/0673.pdf.
5. In the most infamous of the misselling scandals, that of Personal Protection Insurance (PPI), while much of the sales took place in the 1990s, this scandal didn't crystallise until much later so didn't influence the policymakers developing Basel 2.
6. https://researchbriefings.files.parliament.uk/documents/SN00429/SN00429.pdf, pp. 1 and 9.
7. See "Paternalism Fails Again", Hinchliffe and Dowd, reprinted in Dowd (2001) *Money and the Market Essays on Free Banking*. Routledge.

8. We will explore the demise of the AMA in Chapter 15.
9. In the UK, supervision of Barings was split between the Bank of England and the Securities and Futures Authority (SFA).
10. ARROW or 'Advanced Risk Reactive Operating frameWork' was developed by UK FSA to replace the risk-based operating models of the predecessor regulators including the Bank of England and SFA.
11. https://www.theirm.org/news/irm-brings-the-institute-of-operational-risk-ior-into-its-growing-global-risk-management-community/.

Chapter 4

1. Insight into the BCBS is available free of charge at https://www.bis.org/bcbs/index.htm.
2. The institutions represented on the BCBS comprise Argentina (the Central Bank of Argentina), Australia (the Reserve Bank of Australia and the Australian Prudential Regulation Authority), Belgium (the National Bank of Belgium), Brazil (the Central Bank of Brazil), Canada (the Bank of Canada and the Office of the Superintendent of Supervision), China (the People's Bank of China and the National Financial Regulatory Administration), European Union (the European Central Bank and the European Central Bank Single Supervisory Mechanism), France (the Bank of France and the Prudential Supervision and Resolution Authority), Germany (Deutsche Bank and the Federal Financial Supervisory Authority (BaFin)), Hong Kong SAR (the Hong Kong Monetary Authority), India (the Reserve Bank of India), Indonesia (Bank Indonesia and the Indonesia Financial Services Authority), Italy (the Bank of Italy), Japan (the Bank of Japan and the Financial Services Agency), Korea (the Bank of Korea and the Financial Supervisory Service), Luxembourg (the Surveillance Commission for the Financial Sector), Mexico (the Bank of Mexico and the Comision Nacional Bancaria y de Valores), Netherlands (Netherlands Bank), Russia (Central Bank of the Russian Federation), Saudi Arabia (the Saudi Central Bank), Singapore (the Monetary Authority of Singapore), South Africa (the South African Reserve Bank), Spain (the Bank of Spain), Sweden (Sveriges Riskbank and Finansinspection), Switzerland (the Swiss National Bank and the Swiss Financial Market Supervisory Authority (FINMA)), Turkiye (the Central Bank of the Republic of Turkey and the Banking and Regulation and Supervisory Agency), United Kingdom (the Bank of England and the Prudential Regulation Authority) and the United States (the Board of Governors of the Federal Reserve System, the Federal Reserve Bank of New York, the Office of the Comptroller of the Currency and the Federal Deposit Insurance Corporation). In addition, there are currently eight observers: Chile (the Banking and Financial Institutions Supervisory Agency), Malaysia (the Central Bank of Malaysia), the United Arab Emirates (the Central Bank of the United Arab Emirates), the Bank for International Settlements, the Basel Consultative Group, the European Banking Authority, the European Commission and the International Monetary Fund.

3. The Revisions to the Principles for the Sound Management of Operational Risk are available free of charge and are located at https://www.bis.org/bcbs/publ/d515.pdf.
4. The Principles for Operational Resilience are available free of charge at https://www.bis.org/bcbs/publ/d516.pdf.
5. The European Central Bank's website can be found at https://www.ecb.europa.eu/home/html/index.en.html.
6. The European Banking Authorities website can be found at https://www.eba.europa.eu/homepage.
7. The Prudential Regulation Authorities website can be found at https://www.bankofengland.co.uk/prudential-regulation.
8. The Financial Conduct Authorities website can be found at https://www.fca.org.uk/.
9. The PRA's Operational Resilience requirements can be found in the authorities Supervisory Statement SS1/21 which can be located at https://www.bankofengland.co.uk/-/media/boe/files/prudential-regulation/supervisory-statement/2021/ss121-march-22.pdf and the UK FCA's PS21/3 while the UK FCA's Operational Resilience requirements can be found at https://www.fca.org.uk/publication/policy/ps21-3-operational-resilience.pdf.
10. Details of the UK FCAs New Consumer Duty, including links to the Policy Statement and Final Guidance, can be found at https://www.fca.org.uk/publications/policy-statements/ps22-9-new-consumer-duty.
11. The Federal Reserve Board of Governors website is located at https://www.federalreserve.gov/.
12. The Federal Reserve Bank of New York's website is located at https://www.newyorkfed.org.
13. The Office of the Comptroller of the Currency's website is located at https://www.occ.gov/.
14. The Federal Deposit Insurance Corporation's website is located at https://www.fdic.gov/.
15. The Japanese Financial Service Authorities website is located at https://www.fsa.go.jp/en/.
16. The Bank of Japan's website is located at https://www.boj.or.jp/en/.
17. The Australian Prudential Regulation Authorities website is located at https://www.boj.or.jp/en/.
18. The list of institutions represented on the Basel Committee on Banking Supervision, together with the observers, is available free of charge at https://www.bis.org/bcbs/membership.htm.

Chapter 5

1. The original diagram is contained in the ORX Operational Risk Reference Framework and can be found at https://orx.org/resource/operational-risk-framework-practice-benchmark.

2. The ORX website is located at https://orx.org/.
3. The BCBS Revisions to the Sound Management of Operational Risk are available free of charge at https://www.bis.org/bcbs/publ/d515.pdf.
4. See the South African Reserve Bank's note D9/2021 which can be found at https://www.resbank.co.za/content/dam/sarb/publications/prudential-authority/pa-deposit-takers/banks-directives/2021/D9-2021%20-%20Principles%20for%20the%20Sound%20Management%20of%20Operational%20Risk.pdf.
5. The UK FCA's Senior Managers and Certification Regime: Guide for UK FCA solo-regulated firms' can be located at https://www.fca.org.uk/publication/policy/guide-for-fca-solo-regulated-firms.pdf.
6. Non ORX members can locate the link to download summaries of the ORX reference taxonomies free of charge using their work emails at https://orx.org/operational-risk-reference-taxonomy.
7. At the time of writing, the EBA consultation paper on Regulatory Technical Standards on operational risk loss could be downloaded from the following page https://www.eba.europa.eu/publications-and-media/events/consultation-regulatory-technical-standards-operational-risk-loss.
8. The BCBS Principles for Operational Resilience are available free of charge and can be found at https://www.bis.org/bcbs/publ/d516.pdf.

Chapter 6

1. The BCBS Revisions to the Principles for the Sound Management of Operational Risk are available free of charge and can be found at https://www.bis.org/bcbs/publ/d515.pdf.
2. Details of the BCBS paper 'The Basel Framework' are available free of charge and can be found at https://www.bis.org/baselframework/BaselFramework.pdf.
3. Details of the ORX scenario library can be found at https://orx.org/scenarios.
4. Details of the RiskBusiness scenario library can be found at https://riskbusiness.com/wp-content/uploads/2021/06/content-scenario-library.pdf.
5. Details of the ORIC Scenarios can be found at https://www.oricinternational.com.
6. Details of the RiskSpotlight Portal can be found at https://www.riskspotlight.com/.
7. Details of ORX News can be found at https://orx.org/news.
8. Details of the ORIC Risk Events and Emerging Risk offerings can be found at https://www.oricinternational.com.

Chapter 7

1. The Executive Summary of the COSO publication ' Internal Control – Integrated Framework' can be found at https://www.coso.org/_files/ugd/3059fc_1df7d5dd38074006bce8fdf621a942cf.pdf.
2. The BCBS Revisions to the Principles for the Sound Management of Operational Risk can be found free of charge at https://www.bis.org/bcbs/publ/d515.pdf.

Chapter 8

1. Operational resilience – a progress report, Nick Strange, Director, Supervisory Risk Specialists, 21st Annual Operational Risk Europe Conference, London, 14 May 2019.
2. https://www.bankofengland.co.uk/-/media/boe/files/speech/2018/resilience-and-continuity-in-an-interconnected-and-changing-world-speech-by-lyndon-nelson.pdf.
3. In psychology, there is a theory called transactional analysis developed by Eric Berne – the SMCR demonstrated a definite shift in approach to a parent–child relationship!
4. The disruption at Ulster Bank impacted nurses working in the Northern Irish health service.
5. Megan Butler, UK FCA Annual Public Meeting, 17 July 2019.
6. Including 'Internet Organised Crime Threat Assessment (IOCTA)', Europol, 2019; and 'Report on Cybercrime during COVID-19', Interpol, 2020.
7. McCafree report reference https://partners.trellix.com/enterprise/en-us/assets/reports/rp-quarterly-threats-nov-2020.pdf.
8. FBI Internet Crime Report (2020) https://www.ic3.gov/AnnualReport/Reports/2020_IC3Report.pdf.
9. BCBS, Principles for Operational Resilience, March 2021: https://www.bis.org/bcbs/publ/d516.pdf.
10. https://www.bis.org/bcbs/publ/d516.pdf.
11. https://www.bankofengland.co.uk/prudential-regulation/letter/2025/artis-2025-priorities.

Chapter 9

1. The BCBS Revisions to the Principles for the Sound Management of Operational Risk can be found free of charge at https://www.bis.org/bcbs/publ/d515.pdf.

Chapter 10

1. The UK FCA's Consumer Duty Policy Statement PS22/9 is located at https://www.fca.org.uk/publication/policy/ps22-9.pdf.
2. See paragraph 2.1 of the UK's Prudential Regulation Supervisory Statement SS2/21 'Outsourcing and third-party risk management' which is available at https://www.bankofengland.co.uk/-/media/boe/files/prudential-regulation/supervisory-statement/2021/ss221-march-21.pdf.
3. The UK FCA's CP24/28, Operational Incident and Third Party Reporting is located at https://www.fca.org.uk/publication/consultation/cp24-28.pdf.
4. The BCBS Consultative Document is available free of charge at https://www.bis.org/bcbs/publ/d577.pdf.
5. The PRA's Supervisory Statement SS2/21 Outsourcing and third-party risk management can be found at https://www.bankofengland.co.uk/-/media/boe/files/prudential-regulation/supervisory-statement/2021/ss221-march-21.pdf.

6. The European Authorities revised Guidelines on outsourcing arrangements can be accessed from the following location https://www.eba.europa.eu/activities/single-rulebook/regulatory-activities/internal-governance/guidelines-outsourcing.
7. The Financial Stability Board's paper Enhancing Third-Party Risk Management and Oversight, a toolkit for financial institutions and financial authorities is located at https://www.fsb.org/wp-content/uploads/P041223-1.pdf.
8. IOSCO Principles on Outsourcing Final report is located at https://www.iosco.org/library/pubdocs/pdf/IOSCOPD687.pdf.
9. The Office of the Superintendent of Financial Institutions Third Party Risk Management Guideline is located at https://www.osfi-bsif.gc.ca/en/guidance/guidance-library/third-party-risk-management-guideline.
10. The UK FCA's proposed third-party reporting data table is currently located at https://www.fca.org.uk/publication/forms/mtpreporting-template.xlsx.

Chapter 11

1. The BCBS Revisions to the Principles for the Sound Management of Operational Risk are available free of charge at https://www.bis.org/bcbs/publ/d515.pdf.

Chapter 12

1. Santomauro, D.F., Herrera, A.M.M., Shadid, J. et al. (2021). Global prevalence and burden of depressive and anxiety disorders in 204 countries and territories in 2020 due to the COVID-19 pandemic. *The Lancet* 398 (10312): 1700–1712.
2. WHO (2022). World Health Statistics. https://cdn.who.int/media/docs/default-source/gho-documents/world-health-statistic-reports/worldhealthstatistics_2022.pdf.

Chapter 13

1. BCBS Principles for the Sound Management of Operational Risk (2021): https://www.bis.org/bcbs/publ/d515.pdf.
2. Be careful the response to a maximum page limit on risk reports is not a reformatted report, with the same content squeezed into the new page limit in a font so small it is impossible to read! We've all heard anecdotes of this kind, and although some are inevitably apocryphal, many are not.

Chapter 14

1. Mr Andrew G Haldane, Executive Director, Financial Stability, Bank of England, at the International Financial Law Review Dinner, London, 10 April 2013. https://www.bis.org/review/r130411d.pdf.
2. The staff of the Financial Services Authority which in turn was a merger of staff from predecessor regulators SIB, PIA, SFA, the Bank of England and DTI.

3. The estimated compliance costs for implementing the SMCR varied significantly across firms and were impacted by factors such as size, complexity and the scope of necessary changes. According to the UK FCA, estimates provided during consultations for banks and large firms (Initial 2016 Implementation), the UK FCA estimated initial compliance costs for large banks could range from £20 million to £50 million per firm. This included costs for setting up governance frameworks, developing and documenting new policies, training staff and implementing monitoring systems. For smaller firms and firms in the 2019 Extension, the 2019 extension to all UK FCA-regulated firms included an estimated compliance cost of £160,000 to £310,000 for medium-sized firms, while smaller firms faced lower costs, averaging £50,000 to £100,000. These costs were primarily related to training, certification processes and implementing conduct rules. Firms also incur ongoing compliance costs related to annual certifications, training and monitoring, which can be substantial, particularly for larger institutions. The UK FCA estimated these costs would vary but would generally be lower than initial implementation costs, as much of the framework would already be in place. If the SMCR is substantially revised (as is being muted), this will again impose costs of compliance, which impact disproportionately on smaller firms and can act as a serious barrier to entry, therefore damaging competition.

Chapter 15

1. David Deutsch, *The Beginning of Infinity: Explanations That Transform the World,* 2011.
2. This chapter draws on an earlier paper: Hinchliffe, J. M. (2016). The death of one thousand flowers or the AMA reborn?. *Journal of Operational Risk* 11 (4).
3. BCBS (2016). Standardised Measurement Approach for operational risk. https://www.bis.org/bcbs/publ/d355.pdf.
4. The ORM practitioner community has long been divided on this issue, which was the subject of a notable IOR debate event in 2017, where practitioners debated whether modelling of OR had added value for its management. Professor Tony Blunden Chaired the event, with practitioners Philip Umande, Dr Rodney Coleman and John Thirlwell debating it, with questions from the audience.
5. Radical Uncertainty: Decision-Making Beyond the Numbers, by John Kay and Mervyn King, 2020.

Chapter 16

1. This chapter draws on an earlier White Paper published on Chapelle Consulting's website, called 'Selecting and Implementing a GRC', Chapelle and Hinchliffe: https://www.chapelleconsulting.com/featured-content?hsCtaTracking=ceadede0-e7d0-4f88-a21a-ec2b3933edf0%7C9b50b381-06a8-47ab-b500-5d6ba921a4da.

2. The market for GRCs is highly competitive, with a large number of vendors and great diversity of systems, functionality and price.
3. Ideally, it is best to avoid the scenario where different GRC systems are bought by different functions (i.e. one GRC in ORM, another in compliance, another in Internal Audit and yet another for managing governance).

Chapter 17

1. See 'Why Google's "woke" AI problem won't be an easy fix', https://www.bbc.com/news/technology-68412620.

Chapter 18

1. The BCBS Principles for the effective management and supervision of climate-related financial risks are available free of charge from the BCBS website and are located at https://www.bis.org/bcbs/publ/d532.pdf.
2. The Core Principles for Effective Banking Supervision are available free of charge from the BCBS website and are located at https://www.bis.org/publ/bcbs230.pdf.
3. The Supervisory Review Process is available free of charge from the BCBS website and is located at https://www.bis.org/basel_framework/standard/SRP.
4. The Stress Testing Principles are available free of charge from the BCBS website and are located at https://www.bis.org/bcbs/publ/d450.pdf.
5. The Revisions to the Principles for the Sound Management of Operational Risk are available free of charge from the BCBS website and are located at https://www.bis.org/bcbs/publ/d515.pdf.
6. The BCBS Principles for Operational Resilience are available free of charge from the BCBS website and are located at https://www.bis.org/bcbs/publ/d516.pdf.
7. The UK FCA's PS23/16 Sustainability Disclosure Requirement (SDR) and investment labels policy statement can be found at https://www.fca.org.uk/publication/policy/ps23-16.pdf.
8. The Bank of England report on climate-related risks and the regulatory capital frameworks can be found at https://www.bankofengland.co.uk/prudential-regulation/publication/2023/report-on-climate-related-risks-and-the-regulatory-capital-frameworks.
9. The press release 'Environmental, social and governance (ESG) ratings: Council and Parliament reach agreement' can be found at https://www.consilium.europa.eu/en/press/press-releases/2024/02/05/environmental-social-and-governance-esg-ratings-council-and-parliament-reach-agreement/.
10. The press release covering the SEC's adopted rules to enhance and standardise climate-related disclosures by public companies and in private offerings can be found at https://www.sec.gov/newsroom/press-releases/2024-31.

11. The EBA's Consultation Paper on Draft Regulatory Technical Standards on establishing a risk taxonomy on operational risk that complies with international standards and a methodology to classify the loss events included in the loss data set based on that risk taxonomy on operational risk under Article 317(9) of Regulation (EU) 575/2013 can be found at https://www.eba.europa.eu/publications-and-media/press-releases/eba-consults-new-framework-operational-risk-loss-part-implementation-eu-banking-package.
12. Non-ORX members can locate the link to download summaries of the ORX reference taxonomies free of charge using their work emails at https://orx.org/operational-risk-reference-taxonomy.

Index

Please note that page numbers referring to Figures are followed by the letter '*f*', while references to Tables are followed by the letter '*t*'.